Police Integrity
and
Ethics

Matthew Hickman

Alex R. Piquero

Jack R. Greene

WADSWORTH

™

THOMSON LEARNING

Wadsworth/Thomson Learning
10 Davis Drive
Belmont, CA 94002-3098
USA

For information about our products, contact us:
Thomson Learning Academic Resource Center
1-800-423-0563
http://www.wadsworth.com

International Headquarters
Thomson Learning
International Division
290 Harbor Drive, 2nd Floor
Stamford, CT 06902-7477
USA

UK/Europe/Middle East/South Africa
Thomson Learning
Berkshire House
168-173 High Holborn
London WCIV 7AA

Asia
Thomson Learning
60 Albert Street, #15-01
Albert Complex
Singapore 189969

Canada
Nelson Thomson Learning
1120 Birchmount Road
Toronto, Ontario MIK 5G4
Canada
United Kingdom

ISBN 0-534-19802-3

The Adaptable Courseware Program consists of products and additions to existing Wadsworth Group products that are produced from camera-ready copy. Peer review, class testing, and accuracy are primarily the responsibility of the author(s).

Table of Contents

Forward

Samuel Walker, Series Editor

Police Integrity is an outstanding addition to the Wadsworth Professionalism in Policing Series and to the literature on policing. The issue of police integrity is extremely important and has received an increasing amount of public attention among policy makers and the general public. Unfortunately, the academic literature has not adequately addressed this very important subject. We are very proud, therefore, to publish a volume that fills a major void in the literature and will be of interest to scholars, teachers, and policy makers alike.

This volume brings together many of the leading experts on the subject of police integrity who address a number of key issues. The list of authors is a virtual Who's Who of the best minds on the issues of integrity, police use of force, accountability mechanisms, and public perceptions of the police. Some of the topics addressed here have not previously been presented in published form. The chapters in this book offer readers an informed guide to the most current thinking about each subject.

This book is an important contribution to the field of police professionalism and to public understanding of police integrity.

Introduction

Misconduct & Integrity: An Introduction
Jack R. Greene Northeastern University

Who shall guard the guardians? This single question has dominated much public debate about the role and accountability of the police in a democratic society. This question focuses on issues of public trust in democratic institutions. At its core is a concern with regulating governmental power; in the case of the police this power manifests itself in concerns about abuse of authority, or rather how the police perform their duties while maintaining fidelity to the rule of law. More pointedly, such concerns ask whether the police display integrity in the performance of their duties—as individuals and as organizations. A focus on police integrity reminds us that for the police to be accepted as legitimate they must enforce the law impartially and within the confines of the law. In its broadest sense to do less is to be corrupt.

Police integrity is a central element in due process, the cornerstone of democratic jurisprudence. For our system of law to function properly—and with the consent of the governed—it must be administered fairly and impartially. Of course the impartial administration of justice begins with the police, who on a day-to-day basis define, shape and apply a myriad of local customs, conventions and ordinances, as well as state and federal laws. In many respects the police give life to the law as they apply it to everyday problems. Such application of the law necessitates police discretion—fitting the application of the law to circumstances where public order has been violated or the law broken. While we acknowledge that the police need discretion to effectively apply the law, it is in its use that we fear problems with police integrity.

It is in the shaping of our criminal codes, by their application, where concern for "watching the police" is most prominent. This has been true since the formation of the first modern-day policing systems. We as a society acknowledge the need for formal social control, while at the same time being wary of government intrusion into matters of private life.

It is the fear of a corrupt police service—a service that uses values other than the fair and equitable treatment of those brought before the criminal law— that gives rise to public concern. Whether that discretion is applied through values that support law abidingness or whether discretion is used to further the personal aims of individual police officers, or the cultural codes of the police, is the central issue surrounding police integrity.

The essays in this volume address police integrity from a variety of vantage points. First, the various meanings of and processes for identifying and measuring police integrity are brought into greater focus. This is in no way a small matter; rather the measurement of integrity focuses our attention on the underlying values and cultures of the police, how they identify "good" and "bad" police practice, how they would sanction negative police behavior, and how they would expect their leaders to sanction such behavior.

Collectively, such analyses help to define the nature and level of "ethics" in any police agency, as well as the factors shaping those ethics. From this perspective and contrary to past foci on police corruption, police ethics is seen as one of several independent variables shaping the ultimate level of police misbehavior and corruption.

Second, essays in this collection examine the efficacy of the "early warning" approach—internal police systems that seek to identify officers "at risk" of integrity lapses. Such systems focus on the selection, workplace monitoring and retention of police officers with the view of creating a systemic process to acquire, regulate and adjudicate problems of police integrity on an ongoing basis. Moreover, such systems seek to reinforce positive police behavior as well as rooting out unethical behavior. Historically, police agencies have treated police corruption as an effect rather than a cause. That is to say, all too often we have focused on police failures (the effect), rather than the antecedent processes that led to such failures (the causes). Knowing the path to failure creates the opportunity for early intervention. Such early warning systems also provide some public assurance that those leading police agencies are also monitoring the police in their interactions with the wider community. To many individuals, such monitoring systems are necessary for the police to be accountable, both individually and organizationally.

Third, as police corruption (lack of integrity) often plays out in response to situational conditions, the role of contextual and individual factors are seen as important to diagnosing how and under what circumstances the police become engaged in negative behaviors. Here, two larger issues are ascendant—situational context, and extra-legal factors shaping police decision-making. In the former, concern with police enforcement of vice laws, especially those dealing with drugs that may invoke the use of force are considered, while in the latter the focus is on individual factors—those of the police officer or the citizen—that lead to police misbehavior and corruption. Knowing the types of situations in which the police are likely to be corrupted provides those monitoring them with a better understanding of the dynamics of corruption. Knowing the range of decisions that police make, as well as the degree to which factors outside of the law creep into police decisions, provides opportunities to review decisions with an eye for integrity lapses. Together, the study of situational context and police decision making provides researchers and police leaders with better on-the-street "predictors" of integrity failures.

Perhaps the most important focus in the assessment of police integrity lies external to police agencies; that is, how the police are received by their communities, and the level of trust that is attached to police acceptance by the community.

And, when the community is concerned about its police, the mechanisms for police oversight and accountability become a central administrative and political issue. Here the focus is on "righting" the police service to assure the larger community that policing will once again be "on the level". Absent such public belief, the police will be in a perpetual "crisis of legitimacy" the dimensions of which have been revealed in recent police scandals.

Police integrity is thus best conceived of as the product of both police behavior and the public perception of that behavior. Police accountability, then, depends in large part on police acceptance of public opinion. Specifically, accountability depends on whether the behavior that the public views as a violation of trust is acknowledged by the police and other governing bodies as such, and whether steps are taken to both correct the behavior and to restore faith among the public. It becomes clear that the police must then monitor not only police behavior, but also public opinion.

Collectively the essays compiled here point to the complex set of factors that shape police integrity and which ultimately predict successful police careers or their failure. These essays also consider the impact of police integrity issues on the larger community. Finally, these essays focus on the empirical assessment of police integrity and/or corruption, not on the underlying morality associated with such actions. Historically, police corruption (the lack of integrity) has been dealt with in a moralistic and individualized fashion. Today, empirical research has demonstrated patterns of thought and action from which police integrity (or the lack thereof) can be inferred. Such assessments set the stage for predicting police failures, thereby creating opportunities to help individual police officers confront the ethical challenges of their occupation. Such analyses can also help assess the "ethics" of police agencies and shed light on the level of public acceptance of policing in neighborhood settings.

Police integrity then affects individual police officers, is shaped by community and police culture, internal police administrative practice, and ultimately impacts the ability of the police to work with the community. Ethical government—especially in policing—has become a growing public concern. Ultimately hanging in this balance is public respect for the law and for those who are charged to enforce it. Such issues are the focus of this volume.

Mapping Integrity Issues in Policing

This volume seeks to map the complexity in defining and measuring police integrity, while at the same time identifying situations and decisional frameworks that diminish the integrity of the police. To that end, this volume includes work organized around four broad themes: (1) defining and measuring integrity; (2) early warning and intervention, (3) situational contexts and their impact on integrity; and (4) community issues in the maintenance of police integrity. The chapters in this volume generally conform to these broad themes, although each chapter invariably addresses the other themes in less direct ways. The chapters are briefly reviewed below, and additional discussion is provided in the introductions to each section of the book.

In the first chapter, Klockars and Ivkovich outline a framework for measuring police integrity more directly; that is through the assessment of the values and norms the police express in reaction to several scenarios that surface integrity issues. These authors then describe issues of integrity and police organizational responses across a large sample of agencies stratified by size. They identify patterns common to police across sites and consider the policy and administrative issues attendant to such patterns. In this light, Klockars and Ivkovich provide a macro-level view of the ethical contours of policing and police culture, as well as policy and administrative constraints to such decision making.

In Chapter 2, Walker and Alpert outline in a broad fashion what is meant by "early warning" or "early intervention" systems. These authors describe the historical development of these personnel and ethical monitoring systems, the general components of current and proposed systems, and provide an illustration of system development in the City of Miami, Florida. This brief case study demonstrates many of the issues affecting the adoption of early warning or intervention systems, including definitional problems, administrative, community and rank-in-file interpretations of the utility and focus of such systems, and problems related to integrating these systems into ongoing supervisory and administrative processes within police agencies.

In Chapter 3, Timm considers both the methods and data sources used in the assessment of federal security clearances, and a range of measures that might be used by local police to better assess officer ethical problems. Building on federal initiatives to investigate security clearance violations and then adjudicate these cases, Timm provides insight into the predictive validity of a host of measures previously thought to identify those likely to breach their security clearance. This information contributes to our understanding of how early warning and/or intervention may work, and the complexity of assembling such data to "predict" police failures.

In Chapter 4, Hickman, Piquero and Greene provide a glimpse of data analyzed as part of the development of early warning processes in Philadelphia, Pennsylvania. Here the authors report on an assessment of police integrity focused on officer pre-employment characteristics and linked to police academy and field performance. In this regard, this chapter is perhaps one of the more complete assessments of the issues shaping police ethical decision making, excepting the immediate situations confronting police officers that call for such decisions. Hickman and his colleagues, employing a risk factor model, examine those factors that pose risk of ethical problems in this sample of police officers. In addition, these authors consider the variation in risk factors over a range of negative police behaviors including physical abuse complaints, verbal abuse complaints, police shootings, and departmental discipline. The authors tentatively conclude that preemployment background characteristics and police academy performance can be associated with later performance on the street, most particularly being the subject of complaints, increased shooting events and increased discipline.

In Chapter 5, Lersch and Mieczkowski focus attention on police drug related corruption and police use of drugs. They begin by reviewing several drug-related police scandals and point to the use of drugs by the police as one of many of the drug corruptions that the police face. They review related drug related corruption documented in several other studies, and consider various explanations for officer involvement in drugs or drug corruption, and then assess attempts to monitor the police workforce for drug use. Lersch and Mieczkowski provide data from "Eastern City" where both trainees and sworn officers were tested for drug use. They conclude that, while the vast majority of police officers do not show up in police agency drug monitoring programs, a smaller number of officers are identified as drug users. The implications of both drug assessment methods and the implications of community support for the police are briefly considered.

In Chapter 6, Garner, Maxwell and Heraux. examine the provision of equitable services as a measure of police integrity, focusing on the extent to which variations in police use of force may be useful in characterizing departmental integrity. Garner and his colleagues examine extant research on police use of force with particular concern for variation in suspect race and sex. They find that use of force across racial categories to effect arrest is about equal, while there is variation in the use of force when comparing racial groupings of women and men.

In Chapter 7, Smith examines questions of citizen behavior and the use of force by the police. Using data from a supplement to the National Crime Victimization Survey (NCVS), called the Police Public Contact Survey (PPCS), Smith assesses citizen-reported contact with the police and police use of force. Smith reports that while over 400,000 persons reported police threat or use of force for the time period under study, about 14% actually reported such force issues to authorities. With respect to the range of citizen behaviors that were reported as accompanying police use of force, most reported that they had done nothing at all, or were in some way disobeying the officer prior to the officer's actions against them. And, while many reported being subjected to police force, only about 42% reported that they were actually arrested, suggesting that the police may indeed use force as a means of "street justice" independent of arrest decision making. Finally, Smith suggests that much work needs to be done to adequately capture the temporal order of police-citizen contacts and that surveys need to be supplemented with more qualitative assessments of police use of force.

In Chapter 8, Terrill and Mastrofski extend our consideration of police use of force to those situations where non- lethal force is used. While it is generally acknowledged that lethal force is used infrequently, the coercive nature of police nonlethal force often falls below the radar of public inspection. Terrill and Mastrofski review several studies regarding police use of non-lethal force, concluding that verbal police coercion far exceeds physical coercion. Furthermore, these authors suggest that the "causes" of police use of force are indeed many and review several studies of the antecedents to police use of force. The authors conclude their assessment by identifying several issues that challenge the reliable assessment of police use of non-lethal force. Here, Terrill and Mastrofski argue that the using the "force continuum", where police response to resistance is proportional, is an important beginning in adequately assessing police use of all forms of coercive power.

In Chapter 9, Mazerolle and Prenzler consider the shift toward "third party policing": police initiated efforts to influence or coerce "non-offending" persons (third parties), typically property or business owners, to take responsibility for crime prevention and control. Here the shift toward third party policing can be to partner with businesses or other government agencies to address persistent crime problems. Training and other forms of socialization are often associated with this approach. But on the "crime control" side of the fence the police may actually coerce participation through threats to confiscate property or to take other civil and criminal actions to gain compliance of the third party, even though the third party is not the intended criminal target of police action. The authors review both legal and moral issues that arise from police use of coercive tactics to gain compliance from third parties. Their analysis identifies several ethical challenges posed by such third party interventions, and concludes by identifying some guiding principles that might be used to more ethically structure police relations with third parties.

In Chapter 10, Weitzer focuses on public perceptions of police misconduct and attempts to reform the police. He specifically reviews research on predictors of citizen attitudes toward the police: race, social class, personal experience with the police, controversial incidents appearing in the media and in the reports of special commissions, and geographic locale. Weitzer suggests that: (1) Blacks more consistently believe that the police act in a racially biased manner; (2) social class affects people's experiences with the police and hence their opinions; (3) personal experiences with the police are more often negative—or at least the negative experiences outweigh the positive ones; (4) controversial incidents can dramatically shape negative public images of the police, particularly in minority communities; and (5) little is actually known about city and neighborhood influences on community perceptions of the police.

With respect to reforms to insure police integrity, Weitzer suggests that minorities are not confident about the police ability to oversee and control police abuse of authority, that civilian review boards and police commissions are not always seen as capable of ameliorating community problems with the police, and that consent decrees coupled with external monitors are often seen as necessary to control agencies that appear to be beyond the control of internal measures. Regarding racial diversification as a means of making the police socially accountable, there is agreement that this approach is fruitful—despite any empirical evidence supporting such a contention - while there is some evidence that community attitudes toward the police can improve using community policing as an accountability strategy.

Finally, Weitzer concludes that sometimes leadership change is necessary to assure community acceptance that the agency will be more responsive and accountable, although this typically occurs after some extra-ordinary event (e.g., the Rodney King incident in Los Angeles). He also suggests that training that improves police-citizen encounters goes a long way in improving public assessments of the police.

In Chapter 11, Davis, Ortiz, Henderson and Miller outline the implementation of a federal consent decree in the City of Pittsburgh. Pittsburgh had experienced several complaints outlining problems with police use of excessive force, abuse of citizens, false arrest and imprisonment, and a departmental failure to adequately supervise and/or discipline officers. The City came under a consent decree that mandated the police department make considerable changes in the way it trained, supervised and disciplined officers. Moreover, the decree mandated the creation of an early warning system to track officer behavior, and improvements to the complaint processing system. This was all to be overseen by a monitor. The authors provide an interesting and detailed "case study" outlining the policy and program changes implemented and their effects. The authors concluded by outlining the "lessons learned" in this process and highlight some of the improvements that have actually taken place as part of the decree and its monitoring process.

Collectively, the chapters presented in this volume explore the nuances of police integrity issues along with attempts to hold the police more publicly accountable. The material presented makes it clear that the assurance of police integrity is a complex, multi-level enterprise. It requires attention to how and why people become police officers, what happens to them once entering the police department, how they deport themselves in community settings, and the degree to which the public accepts and thereby legitimates police action. The readings provide a foundation for further research and program intervention to assure the integrity of individual police officers and their police agencies. They are not the end to this process; rather, they collectively suggest the need for continued clarity in what is an emergent and quite complex set of policy, information and interpretation requirements.

Part I
Definitions and Measurement

Police corruption can and does have many definitions. At its broadest level, police corruption refers to misuse of authority in all of its potential forms (e.g., graft, excessive use of force, mistreatment of the community, and the like). Often corruption of the police is defined as police use of formal authority to benefit their own personal ends. At its lowest level, we often think of the proverbial "cup of coffee," and at its most grievous end police shaking down drug dealers for money in return for protection of illegal businesses.

By contrast, police integrity refers to the underlying values and ethical attachments of the police and how those values and ethics affect police behavior. All too often we infer integrity from its demonstrated absence. That is to say, research that focuses on corruption infers ideas about integrity absent its measurement. And, like some public policy questions—such as pornography—we may find it (integrity) difficult to define, but know it when we see it, or fail to see it as the case may be.

Several "virtues" are often associated with integrity (Vicchio, 1997: 14-15) including prudence, trust, effacement of self-interests, courage, intellectual honesty, justice and responsibility. These are difficult psychological and social- psychological states to measure, and it is simply not clear that they "add up" in some way to produce a measure of police integrity. Police integrity is a complex composite variable involving many things: individual officer values and ethics, situational contexts, police decision making, organizational and work group cultures and community tolerances and expectations of the police. Such forces cumulatively shape police decisions—those that are lawful and those that are not.

Police misbehavior, not integrity, has been studied from several perspectives. At the individual officer level, officers brought forward on complaints or departmental charges have been the dominant measures of police corruption. The "rotten apple" metaphor has often been used to describe and explain individual police failures. Where police officers fail they are said to be among a small number of "rotten apples" in an other-wise good police service.

Measuring police officer failures as a function of individual attributes is only part of the measurement issue. Today, police corruption—the absence of integrity—is associated with a metaphor emphasizing "rotten barrels" or failures in the internal cultural or administrative oversight systems of the police. The shift is from individual to system flaws. Still, such measurement does not fully account for community, situational and other extra-legal factors that shape police decisions and actions—good or bad.

In many ways police integrity is both an independent and dependent variable. It is a dependent variable as it is affected by a host of individual, organizational and community variables that help shape police decision making and ethics. It is also an independent variable as it shapes police actions in the community leading to community support or condemnation. The search for integrity in policing then is a search for the causal networks that produce police ethics (good or bad), as well as their application in community settings.

Notwithstanding the difficulty in measuring police integrity, researchers and police leaders have fashioned approaches to better tap what might be called dimensions of police integrity. The readings in this section illustrate both agency- and individual- level approaches, from the theoretical to the more operational, and employ a broad range of data sources and methods. The readings also span the range of direct and indirect attempts to measure integrity.

In *Measuring Police Integrity*, Klockars and lvkovich present an organizational/occupational culture approach to the measurement and study of police integrity. Using scenario methodology, they focus on officer knowledge of rules concerning police behavior, estimations of the seriousness of behaviors, level of discipline warranted, and willingness to report fellow officers engaged in the behaviors portrayed. These data are used to characterize an agency's occupational culture of integrity, relative to other agencies.

In *Early Intervention Systems*, Walker and Alpert describe the historical development and structure of early warning/intervention systems, including a case study of the Miami, Florida Police Department's early warning system. Definitional problems, as well as administrative, community and officer interpretations of such systems are discussed. Importantly, Walker and Alpert argue that early warning/intervention systems are shifting in focus from the identification of a few "problem" officers to being used as a tool for assessing personnel performance and integrity in a broad sense.

In the final reading in this section, *The Search for Integrity*, Timm describes the methods and data behind the Federal security clearance process, with an eye for measures indicative of integrity lapses that might be used by police agencies for selection and retention decisions. Timm concludes with several suggestions for improving the efficiency, effectiveness, and fairness of law enforcement selection and monitoring processes.

1

Measuring
Police Integrity

Carl B. Klockars, University of Delaware
Sanja Kutnjak Ivkovich, Harvard University

This project has been funded by the National Institute of Justice Grant # 95-IJ-CX-0058. The opinions expressed in this report are those of the authors and do not necessarily reflect the policies or positions of the National Institute of Justice or of the United States Department of Justice.

The recent scandal in the Rampart Division in the Los Angeles Police Department,[1] the scandal in the 75th Precinct in the New York Police Department in the 1990s,[2] and the River Cops scandal in Miami in the 1980s[3] are among the more recent illustrations of how readily police officers can succumb to illegal temptations associated with their occupation. Such incidents should not be surprising, considering that police officers routinely engage in a highly discretionary, coercive activity that frequently takes place in private settings, out of the sight of supervisors, and before witnesses who are often regarded as unreliable. Due to the very nature of their occupation, police officers are highly susceptible to various types of temptations to abuse the rights and privileges of their occupation.

Measuring Police Corruption

Police corruption—the abuse of police authority *for personal gain*—has been particularly difficult to control. Because corruption benefits the typical parties involved in the corrupt transaction, police officers and citizens alike, neither normally has the motive to report corrupt activities. Furthermore, other potential eyewitnesses to the corrupt transaction may be reluctant to report it either as friends and allies of the citizen or police colleagues of the officer, respectful of what has come to be called "The Code of Silence" or "The Blue Curtain."

Adding to the difficulties of controlling corruption is the reluctance of police administrators to admit the existence of corruption. Until recently, police administrators viewed corruption through the lenses of the "rotten-apple theory." The basic premises of this theory, according to the Knapp Commission,[4] are that, "[f]irst, the morale of the Department requires that there be no official recognition of corruption, even though practically all members of the Department know it is in truth extensive; second, the Department's public image and effectiveness require official denial of this truth." According to this theory, corruption is seen as largely reflective of the moral defects of individual police officers. Police administrators fought corruption by carefully screening applicants for police positions and aggressively pursuing morally defective officers.

Organizational Approaches to Police Corruption

An alternative understanding of police corruption, pioneered by Goldstein,[5] stresses the importance of four dimensions of corruption that go beyond the understanding of it as a problem of the moral defects of individual "bad-apple" police officers. They open horizons to a substantially different understanding of the problem, suggest alternative control mechanisms, and allow the development of a novel methodological approach to the study of police corruption. Unlike the individualistic approach to police corruption, each of these four dimensions is profoundly *social* and *organizational* in nature.

Organizational Rules—The first organizational dimension concerns how the organization's rules that govern corruption are established, communicated, and understood by the police. In nations in which police agencies are highly decentralized (e.g., the United States), police organizations differ markedly in the types of activities they officially prohibit as corrupt behavior. This is particularly true of marginally or *mala prohibita* corrupt behavior, such as off-duty employment and acceptance of favors, gratuities, small gifts, free meals, and discounts. The problem is further complicated by the fact that in many agencies, while an agency's official policy formally prohibits such activities, the *agency's* unofficial policy, supported firmly but silently by supervisors and administrators, is to permit and ignore such behavior as long as it is limited in scope and conducted discreetly.

Corruption Control Techniques—The second organizational dimension emphasized in contemporary approaches to police corruption includes the whole range of mechanisms police agencies employ to prevent and control it. Examples include education in ethics, proactive and reactive investigation of corruption, integrity testing, and corruption deterrence through the discipline and punishment of offenders. The extent to which police agencies employ these and other organizational anti-corruption techniques varies greatly.

"The Code of Silence"—The third organizational dimension of corruption, inherent in the occupational culture of policing, is The Code of Silence or The Blue Curtain. It is the informal prohibition against reporting the misconduct of fellow police officers. The contours of The Code—precisely what behavior it covers and to whom its benefits are extended—vary *enormously* among police agencies. While The Code may cover only low-level corruption in some agencies, it may cover corruption of even the most serious degree in others. Furthermore, whom and what The Code covers can vary substantially not only among police agencies, but also within police agencies. Particularly in large police agencies, the occupational culture of integrity may differ substantially among precincts, service areas, task forces, and work groups.

While most police administrators probably understand that circumscribing both whom and what the Code covers should be an administrative priority,[6] the

Code develops in virtually every police agency as a response to the punitive orientation of the quasi-military police administrative system. Put too simplistically, quasi-military police administration works, to the extent it works, by creating hundreds and sometimes thousands of rules and punishing deviations from those rules severely. On the other hand, the very nature of police work requires officers to protect their colleagues and shield fellow officers from harm. It is a sociological inevitability that under such administrative and organizational conditions some 7 form of the Code will evolve.[7]

The Influence of Public Expectations on Police Integrity—The fourth organizational dimension that contemporary police theory emphasizes is the influence of the social, economic, and political environments in which police institutions, systems, and agencies operate. For example, some jurisdictions in the United States have long, virtually uninterrupted traditions of police corruption (e.g., Chicago, New Orleans, Key West). Other jurisdictions have equally long traditions of minimal corruption (e.g., Milwaukee, Kansas City), while still others have experienced repeated cycles of scandal and reform (e.g., New York, Philadelphia). Such histories indicate that public expectations about police integrity exert vastly different pressures on police agencies in different jurisdictions. These experiences also suggest that public pressures to confront and combat corruption may be successfully resisted.

Methodological Challenges to the Study of Police Corruption

In order to overcome the difficulties inherent in attempts to measure corruption, we chose to invert the problem and measure corruption's conceptual opposite: integrity. We define integrity as *the normative inclination to resist temptations to abuse the rights and privileges of their occupation.*[8] In contrast to the tremendous limitations on the direct study of corrupt behavior, the major propositions of an organization al/occupational culture approach to the study of police integrity involve questions of *fact* and *opinion* that can be explored directly, without arousing the resistance that direct inquiries about corrupt *behavior* are likely to provoke. Using this approach, it is possible to ask non-threatening questions about officers' *knowledge* of agency rules and their *opinions* about the seriousness of particular violations, the punishment such violations would deserve or actually receive, and their estimates of how willing officers would be to report such misconduct without asking them directly about their own or others' corrupt *behavior*.

Furthermore, the two approaches to understanding of corruption are characterized by sharply different goals and visions of police integrity. The individual theory of corruption envisions the police agency of integrity as one from which all morally defective individual officers have been removed and in which vigilance is maintained to prevent their entry or emergence. By contrast, the organizational/occupational culture theory envisions the police agency of integrity as one whose culture is highly intolerant of corruption.

Methodologically, the consequences of these different visions are critical.

Although it may be possible to measure the level of corrupt behavior, the number of morally defective police officers, and an agency's vigilance in discovering corruption, the obstacles to doing so are enormous. Using the organizational/occupational culture approach, by contrast, modern social science can much more readily measure the ability of police officers to recognize misconduct, how seriously police officers regard misconduct, how amenable they are to supporting its punishment, and how willing they are to tolerate misconduct in silence. In an effort to measure the occupational culture of police integrity, a systematic, standardized, and quantitative questionnaire was designed. The survey sought Information in key areas that constitute the foundation of an organizational/occupational culture theory of police integrity. At the same time, survey responses could be used to satisfy certain basic informational needs of practical police administrators. The questionnaire attempted to provide answers in a systematic, standardized, quantitative manner to the following five questions crucial to an organizational/occupational culture theory of police integrity:

1. Do officers in this agency know the rules governing police misconduct?
2. How strongly do they support these rules?
3. Do officers know what disciplinary threat they face if they violate those rules?
4. Do they think the discipline is fair?
5. How willing are they to report misconduct?

The questionnaire presented police officers with 11 hypothetical case scenarios. Displayed in Exhibit 1, the scenarios cover a range of activities, from those which merely give an appearance of conflict of interest (Case 1) to incidents of bribery (Case 3) and theft (Cases 5 and 11). A single scenario (Case 10) described the use of excessive force.

Respondents were asked to evaluate each scenario by answering seven questions (see Exhibit 2). Six of those questions were designed to assess the normative inclination among police to resist temptations to abuse the rights and privileges of their occupation (i.e., the level of integrity). To measure this dimension, the six questions were paired as follows:

• Two questions pertained to the perceptions of the *seriousness* of each case one addressed the respondent's own view and the other concerned the respondent's perception of the views of other officers.

• Two related to the severity of *discipline*-one addressed the discipline the respondent thought the behavior *should* receive and the other addressed the discipline the officer estimated it *would* receive.

• Two concerned *willingness to report* the misconduct-one addressed the respondent's own willingness to report it, and the other concerned the respondent's perception of other officers' willingness to report it.

The seventh question asked of each scenario required respondents to determine whether or not the behavior described in the scenario was a violation of the agency's official policy.

Incidents described in the scenarios were not only plausible and common forms of police misconduct, but ones that were uncomplicated by details that might introduce ambiguity into either the interpretation of the behavior or the motive of the officer depicted in the scenario. Some scenarios were based on published studies that had employed a case scenario approach.[9] Others drew on our own experience. Respondents were asked to assume that the officer depicted in each scenario had been a police officer for five years and had a satisfactory work record with no history of disciplinary problems.

The Sample of U.S. Police Officers

The overall sample consisted of 3,235 officers from 30 U.S. police agencies. Some characteristics of the samples from each of the thirty agencies are summarized in Table 1. In order to prevent identification of specific agencies we have identified each agency by assigning it random number from 1-30 and reported only an approximate number of sworn employees. It is for this reason that we provide only approximate individual agency response rates.

Although these agencies were drawn from across the nation and the sample is quite large, it was nonetheless a convenience sample resulting in the overrepresentation of particular types of police agencies and particular regions of the country. Since the sample includes no state police agencies, only one sheriff's agency, and only one county police agency, it, thus over represents municipal police agencies. Our sample also over represents police agencies from the Northeast. Although the sample does include agencies from the South, Southeast, and Southwest, it does not include agencies from the West, Northwest, or Midwest.

A second systematic bias probably exists in the police officer sample. Not all agencies we asked to participate in the study accepted the invitation. While one of the reasons why we opted to study integrity instead of studying police corruption was precisely to weaken the reluctance of the police agencies to participate in the study and to curtail the potential resistance by the police officers to fill out the questionnaires, police agencies were careful about opening their doors to us. Our assumption is that many if not all of these agencies refused to participate because they believed they had something to hide. Agencies declined to participate despite assurances that their participation in the survey would be kept confidential; that all individual responses would remain anonymous; and that respondents would be asked only about their opinions and not about actual misconduct.

Nevertheless, the sample includes some seriously troubled police agencies. Key contacts in a number of such agencies, including senior officers and high-ranking union officials, exercised sufficient influence to arrange the participation of these agencies in the survey.

In each agency we relied upon the efforts of a liaison officer to distribute the questionnaires and collect those that had been completed. In some agencies this was done by distributing the questionnaires to all agency personnel through the agency's internal mail system and having officers return the completed questionnaires by mail directly to the liaison officer. In other agencies the questionnaires were distributed to unit or division supervisors and they assumed responsibility for distributing and collecting them within their respective units or divisions. In still others, an officer assumed direct responsibility for distributing and collecting the surveys and did so personally, visiting shifts, and standing by while officers completed the surveys.

Although we guaranteed anonymity to the respondents and asked a very limited number of questions about their demographic characteristics in order to reduce of their fear that they might be identified, we ultimately relied on the police officers' willingness to participate in the study-participation in the study was voluntary. In addition, some of the police officers could not be included in the study (i.e., they could not even be given the opportunity to participate) because they were either on vacation, sick leave, or appearing in the court on the day when the questionnaires were distributed.

In the end, the response rates vary from 16% to 93% (Table 1).10 However, in over one half of the agencies in the sample (57%), the *majority* of police officers employed by the agency participated in the study. Furthermore, in additional one-quarter of the agencies (23.3%) between 40% and 50% of the police officers participated, and in only 20% of the agencies was a response rate lower than 40%. Analyses indicate that the variation in response rates had no significant effect on the ranking of the agencies on our integrity scale. The representation of supervisors among the respondents from each agency is not systematically related to the response rates.

As **Table 1** illustrates, the majority of the surveyed police officers were employed in patrol or traffic units (63.1%). The overwhelming majority of our respondents were line officers; only one out of five police officers was a supervisor. The mean length of service for the entire sample was 10.3 years, and it varied from 9.18 years for the very large agencies to 12.29 years for the medium-size agencies.

Table 1: Characteristics of the Police Agency Sample

Agency Type	% of National Sample	Sample Size	%Supervisory	%Patrol/Traffic	Mean Length of Service
All Agencies	100%	3235	19.8%	63.1%	10.30 yrs.
Very Large (500+ Sworn)	59.9%	1937	14.8%	64.2%	9.18 yrs
Large (201-500 Sworn)	19.7%	638	23.2%	60.3%	12.05 yrs.
Medium (76-200 Sworn)	9.0%	292	29.9%	59.0%	12.29 yrs.
Small (25-75 Sworn)	8.5%	275	30.8%	66.1%	11.70 yrs.
Very Small(<25 Sworn)	2.9%	93	35.9%	64.8%	11.29 yrs.

Survey Results

We will first report the summary findings for our overall sample of police officers from 30 different police agencies, and then examine the differences in the integrity levels across the agencies. While the first analysis examines the answers provided by *all* police officers *regardless of a particular police agency* they are employed in, the second analysis primarily focuses on the *agency-driven* comparisons.

Summary Findings

Offense Seriousness—We calculated the mean for each case based of the individual respondents' estimates of seriousness and compared these means across different cases. The results indicate that, in terms of perceived seriousness, the 11 cases fall into three general categories (**Table 2**). Four cases were not considered very serious by the police respondents: Case 1, off-duty operation of security system business; Case 2, receipt of free meals; Case 4, holiday gifts; and Case 8, cover-up of a police DUI Such a result should not be surprising, since the acceptance of free meals and holiday gifts is sometimes perceived by police officers as the unofficial perk of the job. In addition, one case—operating an off-duty security system business—describes behavior that was not regarded even as a violation of agency policy by the majority of police respondents.

Table 2: Police Officer Perceptions of Offense Seriousness, Punishment, and Willingness to Report

CASE NUMBER & DESCRIPTION	SERIOUSNESS				DISCIPLINE				
	Own View		Other officers		Should Receive			Would Receive	
	0	(rank)	0	(rank)	0	(rank)	(Mode)	0	(rank)	(Mod
Case 1 Off-Duty Security System Business	1.46	1	1.48	1	1.34	1	None	1.51	1
Case 2 Free Meals, Discounts on Beat	2.60	2	2.31	2	2.13	2	Verbal Reprimand	2.37	2
Case 3 Bribe from Speeding Motorist	4.92	10	4.81	10	4.92	9	Dismissal	4.86	9
Case 4 Holiday Gifts from Merchants	2.84	3	2.64	3	2.53	3	Verbal Reprimand	2.82	3
Case 5 Crime Scene Theft of Watch	4.95	11	4.88	11	5.66	11	Dismissal	5.57	11
Case 6 Auto Repair Shop 5%Kickback	4.50	7	4.26	7	4.40	8	Suspend w/o pay	4.46	8
Case 7 Supervisor: holiday for tune-up	4.18	6	3.96	6	3.59	5	Written Reprimand	3.43	5
Case 8 Cover-Up of Police DUI Accident	3.03	4	2.86	4	2.81	4	Suspend w/o pay	3.21	4
Case 9 Drinks to Ignore Late Bar Close	4.54	8	4.28	8	4.02	7	Suspend w/o pay	4.08	7
Case 10 Excessive Force on Car Thief	4.05	5	3.70	5	3.76	6	Suspend w//o pay	4.00	6
Case 11 Theft from Found Wallet	4.85	9	4.69	9	5.09	10	Dismissal	5.03	10

Respondents considered four other cases to be at an intermediate-level of seriousness: Case 10, the use of a modest amount of excessive force on a car thief following a foot pursuit; Case 7, a supervisor who offers a subordinate time off during holidays in exchange for tuning up his personal car; Case 9, acceptance of free drinks in exchange for ignoring a late bar closing; and Case 6, receipt of a kickback.

The third category includes the most serious cases (Case 3-Bribe from Speeding Motorist; Case 5-Crime Scene Theft of Watch; and Case 11-Theft from Found Wallet). These cases have one common characteristic: they describe *serious criminal* activities—hard-core police corruption or opportunistic theft committed by the police—in which police officers clearly abused their power in order to obtain described material gain (e.g., money, watch).

Discipline—Since the disciplinary scales are of the ordinal nature, we used medians instead of means to compare the severity of discipline across the cases. With the exception of Case 4 (Holiday Gifts from Merchants), for which the police officers most frequently said that the discipline that would happen in reality would be more serious than it believed it should be, the modal answers for the discipline that officers believed would happen and should happen were the same.

In general, police officers thought that the four cases they regarded as being of a low level of seriousness warranted no discipline (Case 1-Off-Duty Security System Business) or relatively mild discipline, such as verbal or written reprimand (Case 2-Free Meals, Discounts on Beat; Case 4-Holiday Gifts from Merchants). The only exception from that rule is Case 8 (Cover-Up of Police DUI Accident) for which respondents most frequently reported that suspension should and would be in order.

For the three cases from the category of intermediate seriousness (Case 6-Auto Repair Shop 5%]Kickback; Case 9- Drinks to Ignore Late Bar Close; and Case 10-Excessive Force on Car Thief), the respondents most frequently selected suspension as both the appropriate and expected discipline. For Case 7, describing misconduct by a supervisor, police officers most frequently said that the less serious disciplinary option-written reprimand-should and would be used.

Finally, the most frequently selected disciplinary option for the three cases from the most serious category was dismissal. It is the most frequent choice as both the appropriate and expected discipline.

The Contours of The Code—Finally, we examined the contours of the Code of Silence among the police officers in the sample by analyzing their answers to the questions about willingness to report. One approach to this issue is to compare the means across various cases. For the least serious four cases, the means are all below the mid-point (3.0) and are closer to the nonreporting end of the scale. On the other hand, for the cases of intermediate seriousness, and especially for the cases evaluated as the most serious ones, the means are all above the mid-point.

Another way of examining the same issue is to compare the percentage of the police officers who said that they would not report [11] the case, that is, the extent of the Code of Silence. The majority of the police officers in our national sample said that they would not report a fellow police officer who engaged in the behavior described in any of the four cases classified as the least serious. By contrast, the majority said that they would report a fellow police officer who engaged in behavior described in any of the cases classified as either cases of intermediate or high levels of seriousness.

Measuring Integrity—The results of this survey show that the more serious police officers regarded a behavior, the more severely they thought it should and would be punished, and the more willing they were to report it. Extraordinarily high rank-order correlation among the responses to the survey questions (all were .973 or higher) suggest that all of the six questions (the two on seriousness, the two on discipline, and the two on willingness to report) successfully measure the same phenomenon-the degree of police intolerance for corrupt behavior, i.e., the level of integrity with respect to for-gain misconduct.

Examining Differences in Environments of Integrity

While measuring the inclination of a nation's police to resist temptations to abuse the rights and privileges of their occupation may prove useful for academic, historical, or cross- cultural studies of police, national averages nevertheless may mask great differences in the contours of integrity among the individual agencies that compose them. However, the ability to measure the culture of integrity of an individual police agencies is more relevant to police administrators who are responsible for them and citizens who are policed by them.

To unmask these differences and to allow comparisons to be made, we devised a system that permitted us to compare and rank the responses of officers in a particular agency with those of officers from the other agencies in the national sample. To determine an agency's overall ranking on how its officers perceived the seriousness of a particular offense, the mean score of all responses by officers in that agency to each of the 11 cases was compared to the mean scores of the remaining 29 agencies. The agency was then awarded 3 points if its mean score placed it among the top 10 agencies on any question, 2 points if it scored in the middle 10, and 1 point if it scored by the lowest 10. These scores were then totaled for all 11 cases. Using this scaling system, an agency's score on its officers' perceptions of the seriousness of the offenses could range from 11 (if it ranked in the lowest third of agencies on all 11 cases) to 33 (if it ranked among the highest third of agencies on all 11 questions). [12]

The summary scores formed the basis for placing agencies in rank order from 1 to 30 (with 1 being the highest integrity rating), making it possible to say that an agency ranked "n out of 30" in its officers' perceptions of offense seriousness. This procedure was used to calculate a summary score and an integrity ranking for each agency's responses to each of the six questions about the case seriousness, discipline that should and would be received, and willingness to report the offense. **Table 3** summarizes those rankings.

Table 3: Composite Seriousness, Discipline, and Willingness to Report Scores, Rank Ordered by Agency

AGENCY	OWN OPINION OF SERIOUSNESS	OTHERS? OPINION OF SERIOUSNESS	DISCIPLINE SHOULD RECEIVE	DISCIPLINE WOULD RECEIVE	OWN WILLINGNESS TO REPORT	OTHERS? WILLINGNESS TO REPORT	INTEGRITY PROFILE RANK SCORE	
1	3	3	3	3	3	3	1	18
3	3	3	3	3	3	3	1	18
4	3	3	3	3	3	3	1	18
6	3	3	3	3	3	3	1	18
10	3	3	3	3	3	3	1	18
17	3	3	3	3	3	3	1	18
30	3	3	3	3	3	3	1	18
2	3	2	3	3	3	3	8	17
18	2	2	3	3	3	3	9	16
7	3	2	2	2	3	3	10	15
11	3	3	2	2	2	2	11	14
12	3	3	3	1	2	2	11	14
5	2	2	2	3	2	2	13	13
19	3	2	2	2	2	2	13	13
20	3	2	2	2	2	2	13	13
29	2	3	2	1	2	2	16	12
26	3	2	2	2	1	1	17	11
27	2	2	2	1	2	2	17	11
24	2	2	1	1	2	2	19	10
21	1	1	2	3	1	1	20	9
22	1	1	2	2	1	2	20	9
9	2	1	2	1	1	1	22	8
16	1	1	1	1	2	2	22	8
13	1	2	1	1	1	1	24	7
14	1	1	1	2	1	1	24	7
15	1	1	1	1	2	1	24	7
23	1	1	1	2	1	1	24	7
25	1	1	1	2	1	1	24	7
8	1	1	1	1	1	1	29	6
28	1	1	1	1	1	1	29	6

Contrasts in the Environment of Integrity in Two Agencies

To illustrate how environments of integrity differ among U.S. police agencies, it is useful to contrast the responses from two of the agencies in the sample. Agency 2, which ranked 8th in the integrity of the 30 agencies surveyed, and Agency 23, which ranked in a 5-way tie for 24th place. Both are both large municipal police agencies (**Tables 4 and 5**). Agency 2 has a national reputation for integrity, is extremely receptive to research, and is often promoted as a model of innovation. Agency 23 has a long history of scandal, and its reputation as an agency with persistent corruption problems persists, despite numerous reform efforts. Although a local newspaper once dubbed it as "the most corrupt police department in the country," half-a- other departments in the sample appear to have an integrity environment that are as poor or poorer.

In both agencies, the correlation of the scores' rank ordering seriousness,

Table 4: U.S. Police Agency 2 and 23 Reports of OWN Seriousness, Discipline SHOULD, and OWN Willingness to Report*

	Agency2 (O_1) vs. Agency 23(O_2) OWN Seriousness				Agency2 (O_1) vs. Agency 23(O_2) Discipline SHOULD				Agency2 (O OWN Wi	
	O_1	O_2	O_1-O_2	t-test	O_1	O_2	O_1-O_2	t-test	O_1	O_2
Case 1- Off Duty Security System Business	1.57	1.36	0.21	-2.82 p<.05	1.47	1.24	0.23	-3.60 p<.001	1.57	1.2
Case 2- Free Meals, Discounts, on beat	3.04	2.85	0.19	-1.80 p<.01	2.50	2.31	0.19	-2.48 p<.01	2.42	1.7
Case 3- Bribe from speeding Motorist	4.94	4.78	0.16	-3.72 p<.001	5.02	4.44	0.58	-6.28 p<.001	4.67	3.0
Case 4- Holiday Gifts from Merchants	3.07	2.79	0.28	-2.47 p<.01	2.73	2.59	0.14	-1.35	2.74	2.0
Case 5- Crime Scene Theft of Watch	4.97	4.79	0.18	-4.21 p<.001	5.85	4.90	0.95	-12.64 p<.001	4.92	3.3
Case 6- Auto Repair Shop 5% Kickback	4.58	4.02	0.56	-6.74 p<.001	4.41	3.74	0.67	-6.47 p<.001	4.38	2.7
Case 7- Supervisor: Holiday for Tune-Up	4.16	4.05	0.11	-1.24	3.58	3.51	0.07	-0.72	3.68	2.6
Case 8- Cover-Up of Pol. DUI and Accident	3.16	2.68	0.48	-4.32 p<.001	2.85	2.57	0.28	-2.69 p<.05	2.67	2.0
Case 9- Drinks to Ignore Late Bar Closing	4.68	3.77	0.91	- 9.96p<.001	4.10	3.17	0.93	- 10.45p <.001	4.21	2.4
Case 10- Excessive Force on Car Thief	4.45	3.49	0.96	-10.12 p<.001	3.15	3.97	-0.82	-8.30 p<.001	4.02	2.5
Case 11- Theft from Found Wallet	4.94	4.55	0.39	-6.85 p<.001	5.42	4.13	1.29	-14.17 p<.001	4.74	2.9

discipline, and willingness to report was very high, as it was for most agencies in the sample. However. while differences in the rank ordering of the scenarios were minimal, both within and between the two agencies, discrepancies in the agencies' absolute scores were substantial. Estimates of seriousness were consistently higher for Agency 2 than for Agency 23. These differences were especially large (between 0.5 and 1.0 on a 5-point scale) for three scenarios: Case 6 (Auto Repair Shop 5% Kickback), Case 9 (Drinks to Ignore Late Bar Closing), and Case 10 (Excessive

Table 5: Police Agency 2 and Police Agency 23 Reports of MOST POLICE Seriousness, Discipline WOULD, and MOST POLICE Willingness to Report

	Agency2 (O_1) vs. Agency 23(O_2) MOST POLICE Seriousness				Agency2 (O_1) vs. Agency 23(O_2) Discipline WOULD				Agency2 (O POLICE	
	O_1	O_2	O_1-O_2	t-test	O_1	O_2	O_1-O_2	t-test	O_1	$O.$
Case 1- Off Duty Security System Business	1.52	1.31	0.21	-1.61	1.70	1.33	0.37	-5.08 p<.001	1.52	1.
Case 2- Free Meals, Discounts, on beat	2.53	2.57	-0.04	0.41	2.77	2.51	0.26	-3.27 p<.05	2.07	1.
Case 3- Bribe from speeding Motorist	4.82	4.60	0.22	-4.25 p<.001	4.90	4.45	0.45	-5.06 p<.001	4.23	2.
Case 4- Holiday Gifts from Merchants	2.73	2.61	0.12	-1.10	3.07	2.88	0.19	-1.94 p<.01	2.49	2.
Case 5- Crime Scene Theft of Watch	4.93	4.62	0.31	-6.16 p<.001	5.73	4.93	0.80	-10.33 p<.001	4.63	3.
Case 6- Auto Repair Shop 5% Kickback	4.31	3.75	0.56	-6.28 p<.001	4.45	3.91	0.54	-5.35 p<.001	3.92	2.
Case 7- Supervisor: Holiday for Tune-Up	3.85	3.85	0	0.04	3.24	3.52	-0.28	2.78 p<.05	3.34	2.
Case 8- Cover-Up of Pol. DUI and Accident	2.80	2.54	0.26	- 2.61p<.05	3.33	3.83	-0.50	- 4.92P<.001	2.40	1.
Case 9- Drinks to Ignore Late Bar Closing	4.32	3.44	0.88	-9.13 p<.001	4.11	3.29	0.82	-8.92 p<.001	3.79	2.
Case 10- Excessive Force on Car Thief	4.01	3.22	0.79	-8.00 p<.001	4.11	3.46	0.65	-6.86 p<.001	3.44	2.
Case 11- Theft from Found Wallet	4.83	4.24	0.59	-8.53 p<.001	5.24	4.25	0.99	-10.79 p<.001	4.38	2.

Force on Car Thief). Police officers from Agency 2 evaluated each of these cases as substantially more serious than did police officers from Agency 23.

The mean scores for discipline indicate that, in almost every case, police officers in Agency 2 not only expected more severe discipline than did officers in Agency 23, but they also thought that more severe discipline was appropriate. The differences in perceptions of discipline were especially great for the most serious types of corruption, such as the scenarios described in Case 3 (Bribe from Speeding Motorist), Case 5 (Crime Scene Theft of Watch), and Case 11 (Theft from Found Wallet), as well as for Case 10 (Excessive Force). While officers in Agency 2 thought that dismissal would result from the four most serious cases, officers in Agency 23 expected that the dismissal would follow only one scenario, Case 5 (Theft from a Crime Scene).

The most systematic and dramatic difference between Agencies 2 and 23, however, is evident in their attitudes toward The Code of Silence. In both agencies, few officers said that they or their police colleagues would report any of the least serious types of corrupt behavior (Cases 1, 2, 4, and 8). Officers from Agency 2 reported that they and their colleagues would report the behavior described in the seven other cases. In Agency 23, however, there was no case that the majority of officers indicated that they would report. Moreover, in all cases except Cases 3 and 5, the *majority* of officers said that they would *not* report the behavior described. In sum, while The Code is under control in Agency 2, it remains a powerful influence in Agency 23, providing an environment in which corrupt behavior can flourish.

Conclusions and Implications

Shifting the focus of our study from police corruption (i.e., the abuse of police authority for gain) to police integrity (i.e., the normative inclination among police to resist temptations to abuse their authority) overcomes the typical challenges associated with the empirical study of police corruption and enables direct measurement of the major propositions of organizational/occupational theory of police integrity. Thus, we were able to ask nonthreatening questions of fact and opinion that provide answers crucial for practitioners and scholars alike.

The instrument employed in the study asks six questions—two about seriousness, two about discipline, and two about willingness to report—all of which measure the same organizational phenomenon: police integrity. The survey and the measures created to describe its results do not measure the amount or extent of corruption in any police agency or institution. The measures and the survey do not identify either corrupt or honest individual officers, nor do they provide any evidence whatsoever of any type of abusive or dishonest practice, past, present, or future. They do describe, in a fairly precise and specific way, the levels and the areas in which the culture of a police agency makes it likely to resist or tolerate certain types of misconduct on the part of its employees.

The research shows that police attitudes toward the seriousness of misconduct, the discipline it should and would receive, and the willingness of officers to tolerate it in silence can be measured in a systematic and quantitative manner. Moreover, the measurements reported in the national sample are not only relatively easy to collect but demonstrate substantial, measurable differences in the environments of integrity in U.S. police agencies.

The ability to measure environments of integrity in police agencies holds great potential for both academic studies of police and practical police administration. Academically, quantitative cross-cultural, historical, and national comparisons that were previously unthinkable become readily feasible.

More importantly, such measurements have direct implications for practical police administration because each of the propositions of the organizational theory of integrity implies a specific administrative response. If officers do not know what a violation of agency policy is or if they do not know the disciplinary threats the agency makes, there is a clear administrative responsibility to teach them. If they do not regard a certain type of misconduct as sufficiently serious, if they regard discipline as too severe or too lenient, or if they are willing to tolerate the misconduct of their police peers in silence, there is an obvious administrative obligation to find out why. There are specific actions a police administrator can take to deal with each of these different types of problems.

Finally, the survey instrument used in this study was designed to assess only one aspect of police integrity. In all cases but the one involving the use of excessive force, the misconduct described was motivated by personal gain. In discussing environments of integrity, therefore, this survey says nothing about abuses of discretion in arrest, order maintenance, discourtesy to citizens, or other police misconduct not usually motivated by temptations of gain. A second generation of the survey will explore those problems.

Exhibit 1: Case Scenarios

Case 1: A police officer runs his own private business in which he sells and installs security devices, such as alarms, special locks, etc. He does this work during his off-duty hours.

Case 2: A police officer routinely accepts free meals, cigarettes, and other items of small value from merchants on his beat. He does not solicit these gifts and is careful not to abuse the generosity of those who give gifts to him.

Case 3: A police officer stops a motorist for speeding. The officer agrees to accept a personal gift of half of the amount of the fine in exchange for not issuing a citation.

Case 4: A police officer is widely liked in the community, and on holidays local merchants and restaurant and bar owners show their appreciation for his attention by giving him gifts of food and liquor.

Case 5: A police officer discovers a burglary of a jewelry shop. The display cases are smashed and it is obvious that many items have been taken. While searching the shop, he takes a watch, worth about two days pay for that officer. He reports that the watch had been stolen during the burglary.

Case 6: A police officer has a private arrangement with a local auto body shop to refer the owners of the cars damaged in the accidents to the shop. In exchange for each referral, he receives a payment of 5% of the repair bill from the shop owner.

Case 7: A police officer, who happens to be a very good auto mechanic, is scheduled to work during coming holidays. A supervisor offers to give him these days off, if he agrees to tune-up his supervisor's personal car. Evaluate the SUPERVISOR'S behavior.

Case 8: At 2 A.M. a police officer, who is on duty, is driving his patrol car on a deserted road. He sees a vehicle that has been driven off the road and is stuck in a ditch. He approaches the vehicle and observes that the driver is not hurt but is obviously intoxicated. He also finds that the driver is a police officer. Instead of reporting this accident and offense he transports the driver to his home.

Case 9: A police officer finds a bar on his beat which is still serving drinks a half hour past its legal closing time. Instead of reporting this violation, the police officer agrees to accept a couple of free drinks from the owner.

Case 10: Two police officers on foot patrol surprise a man who is attempting to break into an automobile. The man flees. They chase him for about two blocks before apprehending him by tackling him and wrestling him to the ground. After he is under control both officers punch him a couple of times in the stomach as punishment for fleeing and resisting.

Case 11: A police officer finds a wallet in a parking lot. It contains the amount of money equivalent to a full-day's pay for that officer. He reports the wallet as lost property, but keeps the money for himself.

Exhibit 2: Case Scenario Assessment Options

1. How serious do **you** consider this behavior to be?

Not at all serious				Very serious
1	2	3	4	5

2. How serious do **most police officers in your agency** consider this behavior to be?

Not at all serious				Very serious
1	2	3	4	5

3. Would this behavior be regarded as a violation of official policy in your agency?

Definitely not				Definitely yes
1	2	3	4	5

4. If an officer in your agency engaged in this behavior and was discovered doing so, what if any discipline do **you** think **should** follow?

1. None
2. Verbal reprimand
3. Written reprimand
4. Period of suspension without pay
5. Demotion in rank
6. Dismissal

5. If an officer in your agency engaged in this behavior and was discovered doing so, what if any discipline do **you** think **would** follow?

1. None
2. Verbal reprimand
3. Written reprimand
4. Period of suspension without pay
5. Demotion in rank
6. Dismissal

6. Do you think **you** would report a fellow police officer who engaged in this behavior?

Definitely not				Definitely yes
1	2	3	4	5

7. Do you think **most police officers in your agency** would report a fellow police officer who engaged in this behavior?

Definitely not				Definitely yes
1	2	3	4	5

Endnotes

[1] Los Angeles Police Department, Board of Inquiry, *Rampart Area Corruption Incident* (2000).

[2] *New Your City Commission to Investigate Allegations of Police Corruption and the Anti-Corruption Procedures of the Police Department, Commission Report,* (July 7,1994)(Milton Mollen, Chair).

[3] Dale K. Sechrest and Pamela Burns, Police Corruption: The Miami Case, 19 Crim. Just. & Behav. 305 (1992).

[4] Knapp Commission, *Report on Police Corruption* 6 (Dec. 1972)(Whiteman Knapp, Chair).

[5] See Herman Goldstein, *Police Corruption: Perspective on Its Nature and Control* (1975) and Herman Goldstein, *Policing a Free Society* (1977). See also Lawrence Sherman, *Scandal and Reform* (1978); G. Marx, *Surveillance* (1991); Maurice Punch, *Conduct Unbecoming: The Social Construction of Police Deviance and Control* (1986); and and Peter K. Manning & L. L Redlinger, *The Invitational Edges of Police Corruption,* in Thinking About

[6] Tom Barker and Robert 0. Wells, *Police Administrators' Attitudes Toward the Definition and Control of Police Deviance,* 51 FBI L. Enforcement Bull. 8-16 (1982).

[7] On this and other unfortunate consequences of the quasi-military organization of police see Egon Bittner, *The Functions of Police in Modern Society* (1970) and *Aspects of Police Work* (1990). See also Carl B. Klockars, *The Idea of Police* (1985); T. Jefferson, *The Case Against Paramilitary Policing* (1990); D. Guyot, *Policing as Though People Matter* (1991).

[8] For a detailed discussion of the definition of integrity, see Carl B. Klockars, Sanja Kutnjak Ivkovich, Maria R. Haberfeld, & Aaron Uydess, *Enhancing Police Integrity (A Report to the National Institute of Justice,* 2001).

[9] There have been a number of studies of police corruption that have employed a research strategy that asked police officers to evaluate hypothetical corruption scenarios. They include Janet E. Fishman, *Measuring Police Corruption* (1978); Christine Martin, *Illinois Municipal Officers' Perceptions of Police Ethics* (1994); Gail F. Huon, Beryl L. Hesketh, Mark G. Frank, Kevin M. McConkey, & G. M. McGrath, *Perceptions of Ethical Dilemmas* (1995); and Larry S. Miller & Michael C. Brasswell, *Police Perceptions of Ethical Decision-Making: The Ideal vs. The Real,* 27 AM. J. of Police (1992).

[10] If our sample were a probabilistic sample, we could try to determine the sampling error. However, the chances of error cannot be calculated for a convenience sample such as ours (See Herbert F. Weisberg, Jon A. Krosnick, & Bruce D. Bower, *An Introduction to Survey Research, Polling, and Data Analysis* 68 (1996).

[11] We analyzed the frequency distribution of the answers on the question about their own willingness to report. The five-point scale of offered answers ranged from I="definitely not" to 5="definitely yes." If the cumulative frequency for 1 and 2 was above 50%, we concluded that the police officers indicated that they would NOT report. If, on the other hand, the cumulative frequency for 4 and 5 was above 50%, we concluded that the police officers indicated that they WOULD report.

[12] An alternative summary ranking system could, of course, be based upon the full range of 30 point rankings for each of the 11 scenarios. This would create a scale that could range from 330 for an agency that scored the lowest of all thirty agencies on all six questions for all eleven scenarios to 1980 for an agency that scored the highest of all thirty agencies on all six questions for all eleven scenarios. Such a scoring system would, however, magnify small and largely meaningless differences in mean scores, creating a false sense of precision. The ranking system we developed intentionally seeks to blunt any false sense of precision by allowing agencies to score, in a sense, only "high," "middle,"or "low" on any given question.

2

Early Intervention Systems: The New Paradigm

Samuel Walker • *University of Nebraska*
Geoffrey P. Alpert • *University of South Carolina*

Introduction

Early Intervention (EI) systems are increasingly recognized as an effective mechanism for enhancing accountability. Many businesses and organizations are developing systems that can alert managers to employees whose actions fit a predetermined pattern of behavior.[1] The business of law enforcement is no different. In fact, The Commission on Accreditation for Law Enforcement Agencies CALEA), now requires a Personnel Early Warning System for all large agencies (CALEA, 2001: Standard 35.1.15). EI systems are one of the recommended "best practices" in a 2001 report on *Principles for Promoting Police Integrity* issued by the Civil Rights Division of the U.S. Department of Justice (2001). Variations of EI systems are also included in virtually all of the consent decrees and memoranda of understandings negotiated by the Civil Rights Division of the U.S. Justice Department (U.S. Department of Justice, 2002).

The term Early Intervention is being used for programs that have been traditionally known as "early warning" (EWA systems. The change in terminology is part of a paradigm shift that is the central argument of this chapter (Walker, 2002). Since their initial development a little more than twenty years ago, EI systems have grown, and developed to the point where law enforcement agencies have considerable experience developing and managing them. The literature on EI systems, however, has not kept pace with developments in the field. At present there is only one study of EI systems and the published articles on the topic are based on that study alone (Walker, Alpert, and Kenney, 2001).

The purpose of this chapter is to explain the general components of EI and to synthesize the most important developments in the field. The basic argument is that *EI systems have entered a new era and that a new paradigm has emerged regarding their role with respect to police accountability*. In brief, a proper EI system does not focus narrowly on identifying "problem" or potentially problem officers, but instead is an instrument for conducting comprehensive assessment of personnel performance. As a 1989 report by the International Association of Chiefs of Police (IACP) explains, EI system is "a proactive management tool useful for identifying a wide range of problems [and] not just a system to focus on problem officers" [italics in original] (IACP, 1989:80) The old paradigm might be called a "catch and counsel" approach which focuses narrowly on so-called "problem officers" identified on the basis of a relatively narrow range of indicators. The new paradigm characterizes EI systems as a "personnel assessment" approach.

A second aspect of the new paradigm is that an ideal EI system is integrated into the routine supervision within an agency, in which first-line supervisors actively utilize the system on a regular basis. In the old paradigm, an EI system tended to be regarded by officers in the field as something "over there" (i.e., internal affairs) that watches us. In the new paradigm, the EI system is "in here" and is something we use. In this respect, an EI system has the potential for altering the organizational culture of a police department, not only establishing high standards of professionalism but also giving first-line supervisors a data-driven tool to enforce those standards.

The History and Development of EI Systems

EI systems developed 20 to 25 years ago as a crisis management response to public concern over police use of force. The concept was discussed in the 1970s as part of an emerging concern with police use of deadly force. While there are reports of some EI systems in those years none appear to have survived and little is known about them (Milton, et. al., 1977; Walker, Alpert, and Kenney, 2001).

The concept received its first important endorsement from the U.S. Civil Rights Commission (1981:91-86) in its 1981 report, no is *Guarding the Guardians?* The first EI systems that have maintained continuous operation through the present are believed to be in the Miami-Dade and City of Miami police departments. The PPI system in the Los Angeles County Sheriffs Department was launched in 1991 and became fully operational by 1993 (Bobb, 1999). Many other departments have adopted EI systems in the past ten years.

The initial evidence in support of the EI concept was largely anecdotal, with police managers commenting that "50% of our problems are caused by 5% of our officers." The U.S. Civil Rights Commission (1981:166-168) made the first formal recommendation of EI systems in 198 1, based on data from the Houston police department indicating that a small percentage of officers were responsible for a disproportionate number of all citizen complaints. The Report explained that

> The careful maintenance of records based on written complaints is essential to indicate officers who are frequently the subject of complaints or who demonstrate identifiable patterns of inappropriate behavior. Some jurisdictions have 'early warning' information systems for monitoring officers' involvement in violent confrontations. The police departments studied routinely ignore early warning signs" (United States Commission on Civil Rights 1981:159).

The concept received a major boost in 1991 when the Christopher Commission (1991) identified 44 problem officers in the Los Angeles Police Department who had particularly serious performance records. The Commission recommended the development of an EI system for the LAPD.[2] Meanwhile, several stories by investigative journalists in Kansas City, Boston and other cities reported similar findings about the existence of a small number of officers with high rates of citizen complaints (Walker, Alpert, and Kenney, 2001).

The first EW systems that survived to the present day developed independently in several departments in the late 1970s. These systems were created on an ad hoe basis, without the guidance of model programs or any literature describing the structure and process of such a system. Several departments began using indicators of activities to monitor officers' involvement in citizen contacts that involved specified activities, such as the use of force (Milton et al. 1977). Some of these programs incorporated the review of arrest reports to identify officers who had citizen complaints filed against them.

The Components of an EI System

EI systems consist of three basic components. The first involves the identification and selection of officers in need of formal intervention. Identification is based on an analysis of performance indicators that are entered into a computerized data base. These indicators include use of force reports, deadly force incidents, citizen complaints, resisting arrest charges, officer involvement in civil litigation, sick leave use, and any other indicators that a department deems appropriate. There is a broad consensus that the use of a single indicator, such as citizen complaints as was the case in some early EI systems is inappropriate. Any single indicator fails to capture the full scope of officer performance.

There is no consensus, however, regarding the formula or thresholds to be used in analyzing the performance data. Some early systems used crude mechanistic formulas (e.g., three complaints in a 12 month period), but this approach is now generally regarded as inappropriate. There may be legitimate reasons why an officer would receive a certain number of complaints or use force within any given time period. This extremely complex issue is discussed in detail at the end of this chapter.

Officers who are selected by the system are subject to formal intervention. Generally, this involves a confidential counseling session conducted by that officer's immediate supervisor. The session may result in an officer being referred for retraining or professional counseling for personal problems. Some departments have the sessions conducted by a panel of two or three officers. A few departments require groups of officers to attend a class that includes other offices selected by the system.

The third component involves post-intervention follow-up. In some departments follow up consists of informal monitoring by the immediate supervisor. Others monitor performance indicators to ensure that an officer's performance improves. Finally, some departments require supervisors to observe and evaluate officers' performance and file signed reports.

At present, there is no consensus regarding the best overall structure of an EI system. The CALEA Standard, for example, does not address the details of an EI system (CALEA, 2001). The consent decrees that include EI systems generally specify what performance indicators are to be used but are silent on other aspects of system administration (U.S. Department of Justice, 2002).

A Case Study: The City of Miami, Florida

One of the first EI systems to survive to the present was developed in Miami, Florida. In 1979, The City of Miami, Florida Police Department command staff became concerned with their officers' behavior that generated citizen complaints. In a May 29, 1979 memorandum to the Chief, the Commander of the Internal Security Unit suggested an early warning system based on organizational development. His suggestion was for a "cyclical model where the problem is diagnosed, external professional are consulted, strategies are developed, programs are implemented and evaluated, and results are fed back to begin the cycle again" (Ross 1979: 1). Commander Ross demonstrated his ideas by identifying a list of officers, by assignment, who had two or more citizen complaints during a 2-year period (1976-1978). He also compiled a list of officers who had received 5 or more complaints during that period. Commander Ross found that the average number of complaints filed against a Miami police officer was .65 per year and 1. 3 complaints for two years. He found that 5% of the officers accounted for 25% of all complaints. He noted, "That is, if this group were suddenly removed from our department, our complaint picture could be reduced by as much as one-fourth. Obviously, this group should warrant some special attention, if we are to reduce our complaint incidence" (Ross 1979: 2-3). At the middle of the study, the average Miami police officer was 32 years old and had been with the department for 8 years. The officers with five or more complaints were 27½ years old with 4.2 years of service. These officers with the most complaints were disproportionately assigned to midnight shift. The specific complaint of excessive force made up 9% of all complaints against all officers, but for those with 2-4 complaints, it increased to 13% of the complaints and for those with five or more complaints it was 16% of their complaints. A similar relationship was found with complaints for Harassment.

Commander Ross suggested that supervisors should be systematically provided with information "that can be used to identify problem officers" (Ross 1979:7). He also noted that off-duty employment, including rock concerts, wrestling matches and football games generate a high number of citizen complaints. He reasoned that fatigue may "heighten an officer's opportunity to react in an aggressive manner" (Ross 1979: 10). He suggested that the department should respond to these officers before they become involved in self-destructive activities or develop a trend of violating departmental orders. His proposal included more intensive supervision, counseling by outside professionals and training in tactics and strategies. He concluded that (1977:12) :

The problem will not vanish, but it can be reduced through constant attention. The solutions will not be cheap, they will be time consuming, and may be difficult to implement. However, the potential is there to make a significant impact on the citizen complaint's (sic) against police officers.

The Miami early warning system evolved into one of the most comprehensive approaches to monitoring police officers in the United States at the time.[3] As officers are included, their supervisors are informed. It is the supervisor's responsibility to meet with the officer and to determine if he or she needs any assistance, counseling, training or other intervention. The Miami system uses four categories of behavior to identify officers (Departmental Order 2, Chapter 8):

1. *Complaints:* A list of all officers with 5 or more complaints, with a finding of sustained or inconclusive, for the previous two years.
2. *Control of Persons (Use of Force):* A list of all officers involved as principals in 5 or more control of persons incidents for the previous two years.
3. *Reprimands:* A list of all employees with 5 or more reprimands for the past 2 years.
4. *Discharge of Firearms:* A list of all officers with 3 or more Discharge of Firearms within the past 5 years.

Officers who are placed on the system are informed by their supervisor who must investigate the incidents, officer's assignment(s) reasons and write a memorandum to the Commander of Internal Affairs with a recommendation. Internal Affairs provides the supervisor with a report of each incident, which must be evaluated. The supervisor must make a recommendation which may include one or more of the following:

1. Reassignment;
2. Retraining;
3. Transfer;
4. Referral to an Employee Assistance Program;
5. Fitness for Duty Evaluation; or
6. Dismissal pursuant to Civil Rules and Regulations.

Once a plan is agreed upon by the supervisors in the chain-of-command to the Commander of Internal Affairs, it is managed and monitored by the officer's first-line supervisor.

During the development of the early warning system in Miami, the Dade County (Florida) Sheriff s Department (now Miami-Dade Police Department) was also developing a system for tracking officers' performance and potential problems. An Employee Profile System was adopted to track all complaints, use of force incidents, commendations, discipline and disposition of all internal investigations. As an off-shoot of the Employee Profile System, the department implemented its Early Identification System (EIS) under the supervision of the Internal Review Bureau (Internal Affairs).

In 1981, Quarterly and Annual reporting systems were started. The

Quarterly reports listed officers who had received two or more complaints that had been investigated and closed, or involved in three or more use of force incidents during a three-month reporting period. The Annual system listed employees who had been identified in two or more Quarterly reports. The requirement that complaints had to be investigated and closed before they would qualify to be included in the Quarterly report created a timing problem as many complaints would take months or a year before they were investigated and closed. As a response to the timing concern, monthly reports were begun in 1992, which listed employees who had received two or more complaints during the past 60 days (regardless of disposition). Major Dan Flynn[4] (nd:2) has reported that:

> ...patterns of certain kinds of officer behavior, such as serious disputes with citizens and/or coworkers, or an above- average rate of using force, can be very predictive of more serious stress-related episodes to follow. Even though not all complaints and disputes are the fault of the involved officer, a process that enables a review of those events is invaluable. It makes it possible to reach officers who may be experiencing an escalating level of stress, before it gets out of hand and results in serious misconduct.

The reports are disseminated to the supervisors of the listed officers and serve as a resource to evaluate and guide an employee's job performance and conduct (Charette, nd: 5). The EIS data are used in conjunction with other information to provide a comprehensive understanding of an officer's performance.

The Lessons of Experience with EI Systems

Early Intervention systems have spread throughout the law enforcement profession in the last 10 to 15 years, there is now a substantial body of practical experience with them. This section synthesizes that experience. It is based on three principal sources of information. First, it draws upon the authors' previous study of EI systems in three major city police departments (Walker, Alpert, and Kenney, 2001). Second, it draws upon a series of consultations with local police departments regarding the development or refinement their EI system. Third it draws upon a survey of police managers regarding their perceptions and experiences with EI systems. The findings of this survey are reported in the following section.

The PERF Survey

A survey of police managers who are members of the Police Executive Research Forum (PERF) was conducted by the University of Nebraska at Omaha in collaboration with PERF and DiscoverWhy, a survey research firm that has developed a technology for on-line surveys and focus groups (www.discoverwhy.org) . PERF provided a list of email addresses for its members. Each member then received an email invitation to participate in the survey. Those individuals indicating they wished to participate then received a password allowing them access to the survey instrument. Participants could then log on and participate at their convenience.

The DiscoverWhy technology permits an electronic survey, with both closed-ended and open-ended questions that may be accessed and completed at the participant's convenience. The open-ended questions are particularly valuable for tapping qualitative assessments of EW systems and eliciting valuable data embedded in mixed and ambiguous responses. The Police Executive Research Forum submitted a mailing list of 831 names. Email invitations were sent to 521 members with currently active email addresses. A total of 135 members participated in the survey, for a response rate of 26% percent. About 40% of the respondents work in departments with EI systems, while 60% are in departments without systems (Walker, 2002). This distribution of agencies with systems is consistent with the findings of an earlier survey(Walker, Alpert, and Kenney, 2001).

The principal findings of the survey are as follows.

1. Impact on Policing and Supervision—Police managers experienced with EI systems report that they have a positive impact on officer performance and that they strengthen supervision. These managers report very positive experiences with their EI systems: 64 % reported a positive general assessment and 32 % reported a mixed general assessment. Managers overwhelmingly reported that the EI system had at least some positive impact on the quality of on-the-street police service. Almost half (49%) reported a positive impact, while 28% reported a mixed impact. Observations by managers included such comments as:

> "As command staff members, we are constantly looking for ways to pick up on officers in need of assistance. The EWS has picked upon several officers in the department who were headed down the wrong path. "

A large number of managers explained how the EI system had proven to be a useful tool for strengthening supervision.

> [It is] "A useful tool to involve supervisors and lieutenants in non-traditional model of problem solving. It has served to enhance their management skills and help round out their people interaction skills."

> "Supervisors pay more attention to what is going on, document all activities more thoroughly, and talk with officers when things might look like a problem"

An important part of the new paradigm of EI systems is that the role of supervisors, particularly sergeants and lieutenants is transformed. As a comprehensive data base of officer performance, the EI system provides timely data that allows them to monitor officer behavior on a close and continuous basis.

EI systems also address a problem that exists in large departments where there is steady reassignment of personnel and, because of the size of the department, supervisors are assigned officers about whom they know little or nothing. As one manager explained,

"There is a lot of movement of personnel, so supervisors often do not know the histories of their officers. The EWS report brings them up to speed in a much more timely fashion."

   2. *Response of Rank and File Officers and Police Unions*—One of the most significant findings is that police managers experienced with EI systems report little opposition from rank and file or from police unions. Eighty-four percent of the manager with EI systems report having had no problems with their union regarding the system. This finding is particularly surprising since police managers in departments without EI systems anticipate significant opposition from the rank and file and police unions.

   Early Intervention systems do not have a significantly negative impact on officer morale. Among the managers with EI experience, twice as many (12%) reported that the EI system had a positive impact on morale among rank-and-file officers as reported a negative impact (6%). Slightly more than half (52 %) reported that the EI system had a mixed impact on officer morale. Finally, 30% reported that the EI system had no impact on rank and file morale. One of the more notable comments was that EI systems improve morale because good officers see the department taking action against officers guilty of poor performance "Nothing hurts morale like no action being taken against problem officers. It shows supervision that problem people can be dealt with. Officer attitudes toward the EI system seemed to improve once they became familiar with the EI system." One manager commented that "The system was met with much cynicism and distrust when first introduced. Experience and education has reduced those attitudes."

   3. *Major Problems with EI Systems*—The major problems with EI systems reported by experienced managers are essentially management problems of planning, implementation and follow-through. These include primarily the failure of departments to communicate the purpose of the system to all personnel, to involve officers from all ranks in the planning process, and the failure of officials to follow through on their responsibilities once the system is established. In short, the problems encountered by experienced managers are not related to the concept or basic nature of EI systems.

   With respect to communicating the purpose of the EI system, managers offered such comments as:

   "[The department' Did not explain the purpose of the program well"
   "[Needed better] Training and introduction to the first line supervisors."

   "Could have done a better job of pre selling and training on the benefits of an EWS"

   Regarding the follow-up by administrators once the system was operating, one manager commented that

"The program does not hold a prominent place in the organization. As a result, no results are provided to commanders as to its effectiveness or benefits."

Another observed that

"Our program lacks real involvement from the commanders. Typically the officer's actions are justified or rationalized by the commanders and rarely is there a consequence for the officer."

The major policy implication of the results of the PERE survey is the importance of careful planning in the development of an EI system. Major issues include communicating the nature to the system to personnel and involving officers from all ranks in the planning process. A closely related problem involves follow-up once an EI system has been developed to ensure that the key officials effectively carry out their responsibilities. As the NIJ study of EI systems concluded, EI systems are high maintenance programs that require a substantial amount of close and on-going administrative attention to ensure their full implementation. The comments from police managers in the PERF survey confirm this earlier conclusion.

4. The Perceptions of Mangers Without EI Systems—The responses from police managers without EI systems in their departments help to place the responses from experienced managers in context. Two findings stand out as particularly important. First, as already noted, managers in departments without EI systems overestimate the opposition they will face from rank and file officers and from police unions. As reported above, experienced managers found very little opposition from unions and fairly positive responses from rank and file officers.

Second, managers in departments without EI systems underestimate potential administrative problems they will face in planning, implementing, and managing an EI system. There were almost no comments from managers that reflected an understanding of the administrative complexity they would face in managing an EI system.

Unresolved Issues Regarding EI Systems

While increasingly recognized as an important instrument for enhancing police accountability, EI systems are still a "work in progress." Many unresolved questions remain, however, regarding the design, administration and impact of EI systems. The most important questions are discussed below.

1. The Optimum "Thresholds" for Identifying Officers for Intervention—The most difficult issue that EI system managers are currently wrestling with involves that proper thresholds for identifying officers for intervention. There is a general consensus that an EI system should use a comprehensive set of performance indicators. Some of the early EI systems used only citizen complaints and/or officer use of force reports. The performance indicators should include citizen complaints, use of force reports, involvement in civil litigation, arrests, resisting arrest charges, use of deadly force, use of sick leave, tardiness, commendations, traffic stops, field stops and interrogations, among others (Walker et al., 2001).

There is, however, no consensus regarding the formula to be used in analyzing the performance data to identify officers in need of intervention. Some early systems used a rigid and mandatory formula, such as three citizen complaints within the last twelve months. It is increasingly recognized that such an approach may inappropriately identify hard working officers assigned to high crime areas who are more likely to receive complaints and/or use force more often than other officers simply by virtue of their work habits and assignment. Some departments have attempted to resolve this problem by identifying those officers who are above average with respect to problem indicators (e.g., complaints). This approach is only a partial solution, however, since an active, hard-working officer in a high crime area is very likely to be "above average" in this regard. A better resolution to this problem involves analyzing the ratio between problem indicators and desired activity levels. In a site visit to one major department that was still developing its EI system, for example, the performance data indicated one officer who had five use of force reports during the reporting period but had made only eight arrests in that period. Another officer who had three times as many use of force reports had a force/arrest ratio of I to 30. Clearly, the first officer is the potential "problem" officer, and for two reasons: not just the alarmingly high force/arrest ratio but the suspiciously low level of arrest activity. Most EI systems, however, would have identified the second officer.

Using a set of ratios to identify problem officers is more easily said than done. The use of ratios imposes enormous demands of the EI system in several respects. The system must have the technical capacity to incorporate and analyze a comprehensive set of performance indicators. Most systems at present do not include arrest activity. Even if the system software incorporates arrest data, collecting and entering them is an enormous administrative burden. Finally, supervisors who manage the EI system must be sophisticated enough to interpret performance ratios properly.

2. Ensuring Consistency in the Delivery of Interventions—By design, the formal intervention phase of EI systems are confidential. No record regarding the substance of an intervention is placed in an officer's file. This approach ensures that the intervention remains separate from a department's disciplinary process and can be both early and informal, allowing for a wide-ranging discussion of an officer's performance and possible personal problems.

Confidentiality, however, creates problems with respect to accountability. Generally, the fact that an intervention occurred is documented in a memorandum, but the substance is not. Given this fact, it is difficult for higher level supervisors to ensure that the intervener (usually a field sergeant) acted in accord with the purposes of the EI system: discussing the officer's performance problems, conveying the message that misconduct is not tolerated by the department, exploring for possible underlying problems (e.g., family or substance abuse problems), and suggesting corrective action. There is no way of ensuring, however, that the intervener does not convey an inappropriate message: "don't worry about it;" "this is all bull shit;" this system will be forgotten in a year;" "I'll take care of you," etc.

Several steps can be taken to guard against such inappropriate action. Most important, sergeants and others delivering intervention must be appropriately trained before an EI system begins operation. Follow-up, in-service training is also advisable. Based on information available on EI systems throughout the country, it is not clear that the appropriate training has been provided in many agencies. A number of comments from managers in the PERF study suggest that pre-implementation training only was inadequate.

At the same time, in order to enhance their effectiveness in intervention sessions, sergeants and other potential interveners should be given a specific menu of possible alternative actions: family counseling, retraining, reassignment, etc. Discussion of the appropriate application of particular actions, along with role playing, should be part of the preimplementation training. Nonetheless, even with appropriate pre- implementation training, there remains the problem of ensuring the appropriate and consistent delivery of interventions in a context where confidentiality guarantees prohibit the traditional forms of documentation. This is an unresolved issue that needs further attention.

3. Building the EI System into Routine Supervision—Under the new paradigm, the EI system becomes an integral part of routine supervision. Sergeants and other supervisors should actively use the system on a regular basis: accessing the data base, reviewing the performance of officers under their command, looking for and identifying potential problems, and taking appropriate remedial steps. In this scenario, the EI system becomes something that is "in-here" rather than "over-there;" it becomes something "we do" rather than something "done to us."

This model of an EI system imposes some new demands on a department. The first demand is purely technical. A department's computer system must permit sergeants and other supervisors to access the system at their work place. (Given this, a password system permitting access to officers and only those officers under a supervisors command is not a problem under current computer systems.).

Not all police departments have computer systems that will permit this, however. A recent evaluation of one department found that the system was accessible from only one computer, in internal affairs (Jerome, 2002). The authors are familiar with other departments where the computer technology is simply inadequate. Thus, a commitment to create an effective EI system may impose substantial dollar costs on an already financially pressed department. A different challenge is posed by the goal of getting sergeants and other supervisors to use the system on a regular and proactive basis. On this point, the PERF survey is far more hopeful. It seems clear that many experienced managers understand the new possibilities created by an EI system but embrace it as an opportunity to improve the quality of police service in the department.

Some EI systems have the technical capacity to facilitate the transformation of the role of sergeants and other supervisors. Some have the capacity to record the number of times a supervisor accesses the system. This access record can then serve as data for the performance review of each supervisor. Assuming that supervisors are clearly instructed that their responsibilities include regularly accessing the system and taking appropriate action, failure to access the system regularly can be interpreted as evidence of unsatisfactory performance.

Some departments are experimenting with using the EI system as a tool for evaluating sergeants; some others recognize the potential and are discussing adopting this approach. Responses in the PERF survey suggest that a certain number of sergeants understand the potential of an EI system and are using it on an on-going basis to evaluate officers' performance. This is an important emerging aspect of EI systems that requires detailed case study investigation in the near future. If it can be demonstrated that in a given department sergeants regularly access the system, intervene with officers even before they trip the system's formal thresholds, are evaluated on the basis of this activity, and that overall officer performance improves in measurable ways, then the new paradigm of EI systems will have been achieved. For the moment, however, the new paradigm is a concept that can guide the development of EI systems.

Research and Policy Needs

There is a critical need for additional research and policy development related to EI systems. The law enforcement community should sponsor continuing policy development that includes a regular series of meetings involving experienced managers who will develop a recommended set of "best practices" regarding the design and administration of EI system. Special attention should be given to the unanswered questions discussed above for the different needs of large, medium-sized and small departments. In addition, additional research on the impact and effectiveness of EI systems needs to be conducted. The one existing study, conducted by the authors of this chapter, found EI systems to be effective, but suffered from a number of limitations. Most importantly, the available data sets did not include activity levels for desired performance (e.g., arrests), was not able to investigate potential adverse impact of the EI system, and was not able to investigate ratios between "problem" indicators and desired indicators. Future studies should be prospective wherein investigators can determine in advance the data to be collected and monitor data reporting.

Conclusion

Early Intervention systems have emerged as an important instrument for enhancing police accountability. Managers experienced with EI systems report very positive results with respect to the quality of on- the-street policing and supervision. Most importantly, they do not report significant opposition from rank and file officers and police unions. They also report significant problems regarding the planning, implementation, and administration of EI systems.

Early Identification systems are an evolving management tool. A paradigm shift is occurring in their organization and role and in the larger context of police management and accountability efforts. Under the old paradigm EI systems were seen in narrow terms focusing on "problem" behavior by a few "problem" officers. The new paradigm views EI systems as part of a comprehensive performance assessment review, with supervisors using the system on a routine basis to review the performance of all officers.

Many unresolved questions remain about aspects of EI systems. The law enforcement profession and the federal government should sponsor a continuing program of research, evaluation, and policy development that would help to realize the full potential of EI systems in improving the quality of police service.

References

Bobb, Merrick. 1999. *An Overview of the Personnel Performance Index.* Unpublished memorandum.

Charette, Bernard. Nd. *Early Identification of Police Brutality and Misconduct.* Miami: MetroDade Police Department.

Christopher Commission. 1991. *Report of the Independent Commission on the Los Angeles Police Department.* Los Angeles: City of Los Angeles.

Commission on Accreditation For Law Enforcement Agencies. 2001. Standard 35.1.15.

Flynn, Dan. nd. *Reducing Incidents of Office Misconduct: An Early Warning System.* Miami: Metro-Dade Police Department.

International Association of Chiefs of Police. 1989. *Building Integrity and Reducing Drug Corruption in Police Departments.* Washington: Government Printing Office.

Jerome, Richard. 2002. *Police Oversight Project: City of Albuquerque.* Los Angeles: Police Assessment Resource Center.

Milton, Catherine, Jeanne Halleck, James Lardner and Gary Albrecht. 1977. *Police Use of Deadly Force.* Washington, DC: The Police Foundation.

Ross, John S. 1979. Memorandum from Commander John Ross to Chief Kennith 1. Harms. *"Citizen Complaints Against Police Officers."* (May 29).

U. S. Commission on Civil Rights. 1981. *Who is Guarding the Guardians.* Washington DC: The United States Commission on Civil Rights.

U.S. Department of Justice. 2002. Civil Rights Division. Special Litigation Section. web site. www.usdoj.gov/split.

2001. *Principles for Promoting Police Integrity.* Washington, DC: Government Printing Office.

Walker, Samuel. 2002. *Early Intervention Systems for Law Enforcement Agencies: A Planning and Management Guide.* Report submitted to the Office of Community Oriented Policing Services.

Walker, Samuel and Geoffrey P. Alpert and Dennis Kenney. 2001. *Early Warning Systems: Responding to the Problem Police Officer.* Washington, DC: Government Printing Office.

Endnotes

[1] A web search for "early warning systems" reveals that the concept is extensive used in weather forecasting, with a special emphasis on the impact on agricultural production, international conflict, and health issues. The term probably first appeared in the 1950s with a system for detecting nuclear attacks on the United States (DEW = Distant Early Warning).

[2] The fate of the EI system in the LAPD (referred to there as the TEAMS program) is itself a tangled and cautionary tale about organizational reform. When the Rampart scandal erupted in 2000 it was revealed that the TEAMS program had never been implemented, and that the LAPD had not even spent a $175,000 grant from the U.S. Justice Department awarded for that specific purpose. Implementation of TEAMS is now mandated by the consent decree between the Justice Department and the LAPD..

[3] The Miami EI system represents another cautionary tale: this one regarding the implementation and impact of a system over time. As this chapter is being written (*summer 2002) the Miami police department is under investigation by the U.S. Justice Department for a "pattern or practice" of abuse of citizens's rights and a number of officers have been indicted for excessive use of force, planting weapons on suspects, and other abuses. Evidently, the original EI system failed to curb these abuses.

[4] Now Chief, Savannah, Georgia Police Department.

3

The Search for Integrity:
Findings and Tools for Investigating and Adjudicating Federal Security Clearance Cases Applicable to Law Enforcement Selection and Retention

Howard William Timm[1] Defense Personnel Security Research Center Monterey, CA

The year 1985 is sometimes referred to as the year of the spy (Webster, 1985). During that year several Americans were arrested for committing espionage against the United States. Among them were John, James and Arthur Walker; Jerry Whitworth; Sharon Scrange; Michael Tobis; Edward Lee Howard; Larry Wu-Tai Chin; Jonathan and Anne Pollard; Randy Jeffries; Ronald Pelton; and Edward Buchanan (Security Research Center, 1999). During that same year the Secretary of Defense established a commission, chaired by General Richard Stilwell (Ret.), to identify systematic problems contributing to the espionage problem and to make recommendations for fixing them. One of the Commission's recommendations was to substantially increase funding for security research (U. S. Department of Defense, 1985, pp. 86-88). In response to that recommendation the Defense Personnel Security Research Center (PERSEREC) was established in 1986. Its mission is to make the Department of Defense personnel security system more efficient, effective and fair. Since its inception PERSEREC has worked with government and nongovernment researchers to help stimulate personnel security research and reduce unwanted duplication of effort.

In our society it is normal for people to be granted special authority, which enables them to take actions or have access to people, objects, and/or information not granted to the general public. Teachers and babysitters are granted access to children and are permitted to direct the actions of those children. People working in financial institutions are granted access to funds and financial information belonging to the firm's clients. People granted Federal security clearances are eligible for access to classified/restricted information, facilities, and/or materials. In some cases the restricted information, facilities, or materials involved pertains to weapons of mass destruction or to other highly sensitive matters that could greatly affect our nation's security. Police officers are also granted special authority that enables them to take actions and have access to things not granted to the general public. Frequently police are granted a) access to restricted information, facilities, weapons, and contraband and b) the authority to pursue and apprehend people they believe to be criminals and to use force—even deadly force in certain circumstances. Granting the wrong person any of these forms of special authority could have devastating consequences.

After a brief description of how national security vetting is performed, selected findings and tools drawn from that sphere are presented that appear particularly relevant to the integrity issues found within law enforcement.

Current National Security Vetting Process

The two primary Federal security clearance levels are: SECRET and TOP SECRET. The levels are differentiated by the amount of damage that might result if classified information at that respective level was compromised. Unauthorized release of SECRET level classified information could reasonably be expected to cause serious damage to national security; whereas, unauthorized release of TOP SECRET information could reasonably be expected to cause exceptionally grave damage to national security. People granted access to TOP SECRET level information are authorized to see and hear both SECRET and TOP SECRET level information, but only if they have a "need to know" that information in order to perform their official duties.

Federal personnel security requirements are specified in Executive Order 12968. Eligibility for access to TOP SECRET level classified information requires a favorably adjudicated full-field background investigation. Among the components of that investigation are: a review of the subject's personnel security questionnaire, an FBI criminal history check; a check of DoD and OPM investigation index files; a credit check; verification of the subject's place of birth, citizenship, and education; a local law enforcement agency check; subject interview; former spouse interview (if applicable), employment interviews; reference interviews and neighborhood interviews. Among the components of the investigation required for a SECRET level security clearance are: a review of the subject's personnel security questionnaire, an FBI criminal history check, a check of DoD and OPM investigation index files; a credit check; verification of the subject's place and date of birth; and a local law enforcement agency check.

Federal regulations and policies state that people holding TOP SECRET level security clearances must be reinvestigated not later than five years from the date of their previous investigation. The reinvestigation is similar in scope to the subject's initial investigation, with the exception that it includes a search of Treasury databases associated with large cash transactions and money laundering. Reinvestigations required for SECRET level clearances must be completed every 10 years and are similar in nature to the ones performed initially for that clearance level.

Adjudicators review all the information collected during the course of personnel security investigations and make determinations whether or not the people under consideration should be granted new or continued eligibility for access to classified information. Those determinations are based upon common sense and whether doing so would be clearly consistent with the interests of national security. They take into consideration the following 13 adjudication criteria (Director of Central Intelligence, 1998):

1. Allegiance to the United States
2. Foreign Influence
3. Foreign Preference
4. Sexual Behavior
5. Personal Conduct
6. Financial Considerations
7. Alcohol Consumption
8. Drug Involvement
9. Emotional, Mental and Personality Disorders
10. Criminal Conduct
11. Security Violations
12. Outside Activity
13. Misuse of Information Technology

Adjudication criteria 4-13 appear highly relevant to making law enforcement hiring, retention, and assignment decisions. Federal criminal investigators are required to undergo a full-field background investigation, and many hold security clearances so they can have access to classified information pertaining to criminal acts their organization is charged with investigating. For example, Customs Service and DEA Special Agents may benefit from classified information pertaining to drug smuggling operations obtained through intelligence sources. Secret Service and FBI Special Agents might benefit from access to classified information pertaining to terrorist activities. In addition, Special Agents working for the Army Criminal Investigation Division, Air Force Office of Special Investigations, Naval Criminal Investigative Service, and the FBI may be assigned to counterintelligence duties.

Personality Studies Funded by PERSEREC

Personality can be defined as the traits or patterns of behavior that characterize how people respond to situations in their environment compared to how others behave. For example, some people are shy in new social situations, while others are more extroverted. It was hoped that the dimensions measured on standardized personality tests could be used to differentiate between people predisposed to engage in acts of public trust betrayal compared to those predisposed to act in a responsible and trustworthy manner when serving in positions of trust.

The first large-scale personality study PERSEREC funded in this area was a doctoral dissertation conducted by Judith Collins at Iowa State University (Collins, 1991). Collins developed a personality-based function for predicting white-collar criminality. Three hundred sixty-rive (365) inmates convicted of white-collar crimes and 344 white collar employees holding positions of trust completed five self-report psychological tests. Those tests were the California Personality Inventory, the Irritability Scale, the Biographical Questionnaire, the PDI Employment Inventory, and the Probscor Questionnaire. Fifteen scales drawn

from those instruments were used in a discriminate function that correctly catego-
rized 89% of the non-offenders and 90% of the offenders in the developmental
sample and an astonishing 84% of the non-offenders and 78% of the offenders in
the holdout sample that was used for validation. The fifteen scales used in her discriminate function were:
1. Performance (non-offenders scoring higher)
2. Extra-curricular (non-offenders scoring lower)
3. Probscor (non-offenders scoring lower)
4. Sibling rivalry (non-offenders scoring higher)
5. Socialization (non-offenders scoring higher)
6. Academic Interest (non-offenders scoring lower)
7. Responsibility (non-offenders scoring higher)
8. Tolerance (non-offenders scoring higher)
9. Anxiety (non-offenders scoring lower)
10. Social Extraversion (non-offenders scoring lower)
11. Frankness (non-offenders scoring higher)
12. Work Orientation (non-offenders scoring higher)
13. Well-being (non-offenders scoring higher)
14. Self-control (non-offenders scoring higher)
15. Narcissism (non-offenders scoring lower)
As can be seen from the traits above, non-offenders tended to be more conscientious, tolerant, humble, and comfortable with who they are. The offenders
had opposite traits and appeared to seek and enjoy venues where they would try
to attain the admiration of people they did not know well.

A second personality study (O'Connor-Boes, Chandler, & Timm; 1997) was
initiated with the hopes of achieving similar levels of success in being able to differentiate between offenders and non-offenders. This time the actual pre- employment personality tests of 439 police officers who betrayed the public trust were
compared to those obtained for an equal number of police officers presumed not
to have engaged in those type of behaviors. Sixty-nine local and state police
departments that administered psychological screening tests and were able to identify one or more offenders participated in the study. The participating departments represented all regions of the country. Violators were a) identified by their
department as having engaged in at least one act of corruption, b) had their
involvement in that act corroborated, and c) were formally punished for committing that violation. Matched non-violators were chosen for the control group by
attempting to select police officers from the same department, recruit class, age,
and gender as the violator with whom each non-violator was respectively paired.

Two-thirds of the cases were placed in a developmental sample, which was
used to try to identify scales that predicted corruption. The other third was used
as a "hold-out" sample to cross-validate those scales.

Overall, the predictive scales did very poorly during the attempted cross-
validation. This indicates that at best only modest improvements in combating
corruption can be made through better utilization of the personality data that

many police departments are already collecting. The few personality measures that had any success in the cross- validation attempts, tended to indicate that:

Corrupt police officers tended to have *more*
difficulty getting along with others, delinquent histories, and indications of maladjustment, immaturity, irresponsibility, and/or unreliability.

They also tended to be *less*
tolerant of others,
willing and able to maintain long-term positive relationships with others,
willing to accept responsibility and blame,
controlled by guilt and remorse, and/or
willing to respond on the test in a manner that might reflect negatively upon them.

The lower than anticipated relationship between the personality measures and later acts of corruption was probably due to several factors. Environmental factors undoubtedly played a key role in affecting the outcome, such as whether the officer a) was assigned to work with a supervisor, partner or training officer who was corrupt; b) worked in a precinct, department or community where offering and accepting bribes is commonplace; c) was assigned to work in high corruption-prone duties; and/or d) had suffered personal set-backs that might make the officer more vulnerable to temptation. However, those factors should have also affected the outcome of other corruption and trust betrayal studies. The magnitude of the personality effect would have been reduced to some extent by some of the police applicants with certain personality-related problems being screened out either by the psychological testing or by issues of concern being identified during the background investigation. Potential police applicants with troubled pasts may also have chosen to eliminate themselves from consideration because they knew one of the selection requirements was having the ability to pass a thorough background investigation. However, the primary differences between this study and others that have found much higher correlations with personality measures appear to be:

1. This study was based on the actual pre-employment screening tests completed by subjects who were applying for positions of trust,

2. The subjects were probably motivated to hide past problems and issues during the psychological testing phase as opposed to prisoner-based studies where violators may be motivated to reveal their past problems, and

3. The findings reflect the extent to which police pre-employment personality test information predicts subsequent acts of corruption as opposed to those in prisoner- based studies that reflect the extent to which personality test information differentiates convicted inmates from a selected group of non-inmates who have been asked to take part in a study.

The single best predictor of corruption found in the second personality study was not a personality measure. It was post-hire misconduct excluding accidents.

Officers who got into trouble with their supervisors for volitional acts of misconduct were significantly more likely to be punished for later engaging in acts of corruption. One of the recommendations of the study was to expand the length of the probationary period. Another was to clearly articulate integrity standards and ensure they are being consistently administered at all levels of the organization.

Taken together, the two personality-based studies suggest that personality may provide a useful means for conceptualizing the differences between people prone to betray trust and those who are not. However, instead of relying on self-report measures to assess people on those dimensions for actual screening purposes, it may be necessary to select "harder measures" that are not as prone to self-distortion and manipulation. Perhaps the best indications of whether people tend to behave in a trustworthy and responsible manner are the results obtained during thorough background investigations. For example, conscientious, trustworthy, and reliable people should be less likely than people who do not have those attributes to be fired from prior positions. By looking for employment gaps on resumes, then if necessary seeking information that would identify prior employers from secondary sources (e.g., creditors who opened accounts during that period or from the Social Security Administration's wage and employment records), it is possible to identify most prior employers even if subjects intentionally omit unfavorable references from their employment applications. Credit, criminal history, high school records, and other sources that are not very susceptible to reporting manipulation can also provide good assessments of how reliable, trustworthy, and conscientious people were at different points during their lives.

Studies Addressing the Concept of Background Investigation Source Expansion

In the last decade, two national commissions have criticized the procedures used by the Federal government to assess the continued reliability and trustworthiness of people who have been granted eligibility for access to TOP SECRET level classified information and Special Compartmented Information (Commission on Protecting and Reducing Government Secrecy, 1997; Joint Security Commission; 1994). The Joint Security Commission (1994) recommended that current reinvestigation policies be refined to increase efficiency. It noted that an a-periodic reinvestigation interval would offer a greater deterrent effect and would provide agencies with more flexibility to focus their resources on priority investigations (p. 46).

The Commission on Protecting and Reducing Government Secrecy (1997) stated:

> Greater attention needs to be directed toward making continuing evaluation programs more effective. For example, using existing public and private data bases—with the express advance permission of the individual under review—to periodically scan for criminal history, as well as credit, travel, and business history, normally would provide more accurate information at less cost than standard field reinvestigations.

Personnel security professionals could monitor the behavior of cleared personnel on a continuing basis in a more effective, cost-efficient, and nonintrusive manner. Given the evidence that there is little likelihood of catching spies through the current standard investigative or reinvestigative process, better continuing assessment programs could enhance the probability of deterring or identifying espionage activities. Most of the information needed is already available in existing databases; private industry experiences suggest that efforts to utilize automation to access such data can be very cost-effective as well as productive. Nevertheless, because some automated tools can be expensive, a cost- benefit assessment should be completed prior to utilizing them.

Resources should be focused on those individuals in the most sensitive positions or where there is some evidence of suspect behavior; in an era of diminishing resources and frequent budget cuts, more effective continuing assessment can be accomplished only by concentrating on the areas of greatest vulnerability. In addition, those holding what are identified as the most sensitive positions could be subjected to more frequent, "in house" reviews similar to the personnel reliability programs used by the Defense and Energy Departments, as described above. These measures provide a cost-effective way to monitor and assess employees with greater regularity and frequency, but without necessarily having to direct additional resources toward the traditional field investigation. (pp. 86-87)

Automated Continuing Evaluation System

An Automated Continuing Evaluation System (ACES) is presently under development by the Department of Defense (Timm, 2000). That system embodies the aforementioned Commission recommendations. Instead of waiting five years to elapse before evaluating whether cleared personnel have been engaging in behaviors of serious security concern, ACES will check relevant databases far more frequently. It also incorporates a rationally based a-periodic follow-up investigation strategy. Follow-up investigations will be triggered based on such factors as evidence of behaviors of security concern, individuals' access to particularly sensitive information or materials, length of time since the last full-scale investigation, and random chance.

PERSEREC conducted a retrospective study to estimate the number of full-scale reinvestigations that would have been triggered based upon ACES determinants alone. The population distribution included in that study consisted of 11,065 Office of Personnel Management (OPM) periodic reinvestigation cases for people holding high-level Federal security clearances. An assessment was also made of the number of serious issue cases identified under the present system that would have been missed by ACES. Under the present continuing evaluation system, full-scale reinvestigations are required to be conducted on all personnel holding high-level clearances who have not been investigated for five years. Under

ACES, computerized security-related information (e.g., criminal history, foreign travel, and credit database files) will be regularly checked. Either full-scale or limited issue reinvestigations in individual cases could be triggered any time. Under the most radical version of ACES being considered, full-scale reinvestigations might never be initiated in certain cases. The decision to trigger an investigation would be based upon the results of the electronic checks, as well as consideration of other risk-management factors.

A majority of the security clearance holders in the OPM reinvestigation sample would not have needed full-scale reinvestigations based solely upon the ACES criteria. In addition, no serious issue and very few moderately serious issue cases detected by the present system would have been missed had the ACES procedures that were evaluated been in effect for those cases. ACES is likely to detect some serious issue cases currently being missed because the offenders quit before their periodic reinvestigations were initiated. Consequently, even the most radical version of ACES is likely to detect more serious issue cases than the present system. It should also detect those serious issue cases sooner and at less cost than the current periodic reinvestigation approach. These findings should be considered preliminary in nature due to methodological limitations inherent in the assessment described. They are, however, supportive of the continued development of ACES and other personnel security continuing evaluation procedures that are based upon similar strategies.

The ACES concept appears just as applicable to conducting post-hire integrity assessments within law enforcement as it is for conducting personnel security continuing evaluation assessments for national security positions. While the idea of designing automated "early warning mechanisms" for surfacing law enforcement integrity problems is not new, most of those systems rely almost exclusively on internal data (disciplinary actions, citizen complaints, absenteeism, performance ratings, etc.). ACES draws more heavily upon external commercial and government databases, such as credit, criminal history, real estate holdings, and large currency transactions.

Joint Phased Reinvestigation Productivity of Sources Study

A second study addressing personnel security reinvestigation source expansion strategies was conducted jointly by PERSEREC and the Intelligence Community's Personnel Security Managers' Research Group (Heuer, Crawford, Kramer & Hagan, 2001). This project also assessed whether information obtained early in the reinvestigation could be used to effectively trigger when additional investigative follow-up measures are needed. This way more intensive investigative resources would be applied to the cases where they were needed the most as opposed to being expended evenly across all cases. Unlike the prior study, data from four different Federal agencies were utilized and experts coded individual case files from 4,721 periodic reinvestigations instead of relying exclusively on electronic data that was already available from just one agency.

The authors reported:

There was an inverse relationship between investigative cost and value of the information. Some of the least expensive sources of information were the most productive, and some of the most expensive sources, such as the character reference interviews (employment, listed and developed reference, and residence interviews), were among the least productive. For example, residence interviews were estimated to account for almost 25% of the investigative resources expended, but only produced 1% of the issue-relevant information.

Among all four agencies examined, there was very little difference in the number of character reference interviews conducted for clean cases compared to cases containing issues of security concern. The authors concluded thus may have been the result of Federal Investigative Standards that mandate the same minimum scope investigation for all cases.

As previously noted, the researchers also assessed the concept of a phased reinvestigation in which information collected in Phase I is used to determine what investigative steps, if any, should be taken in Phase 2. One of the goals in Phase 1 is to identify clean cases in which further investigative follow-up is highly likely to be unproductive. When the researchers assessed the impact of including all sources currently being used in the periodic reinvestigation except listed and developed reference interviews, residence interviews, and residence records checks in phase 1, they found:

In about 70% of the 4,721 cases, Phase 1 sources provided no issue-relevant information, so the investigation would have been closed after completing that phase for those cases. Phase 2 investigative follow-up would have been initiated on the remaining 30% of the cases.

The phased reinvestigation missed minor or moderately adverse information in only 9 of the 4,721 cases, or an average of 2 out of every 1,000 cases.

No information at all was missed in any case in which an agency took any form of adverse adjudicative action. In other words, no essential or critical information would have been missed. The phrase "adverse adjudicative action" used by the authors was not limited to revocation or suspension of clearances; it included warnings, reprimands, assignment to a monitoring program, and other comparable actions.

Had the phased investigative strategy being assessed been employed, the investigative workload would have been reduced by 11,757 interviews, or an average of 2,486 reference interviews per 1,000 cases.

The authors recommended implementing phased reinvestigations and redeploying the resources saved by doing fewer resource-intensive interviews in clean cases. They indicated the saved resources should be used to improve investigative quality in issue cases, to conduct more frequent records checks to identify some issues earlier, and/or for other measures that reduce personnel security risk.

Follow the Money

An informant named "Deep Throat" told one of the reporters from the Washington Post investigating the Watergate break-in to "follow the money". That same advice can prove just as effective when attempting to uncover or investigate many other forms of public trust betrayal.

A study conducted by the Department of Energy (Brown, 1988) indicated that since World War 11 the principal motivation for committing espionage was financial gain/greed (58 out of 92 cases examined). More recent studies by PERSEREC (e.g., Wood & Wiskoff, 1992) and the FBI also found money has played an important role in most spy cases during the last 50 years. In many of the cases involving motivations other than money (e.g., revenge, non- monetary desires, compromise, ideology) financial payment was still provided by the foreign intelligence service involved.

Payment of funds to betrayers serves several purposes. It rewards the person for providing useful information. It increases the likelihood the individual will continue to willingly provide information in the future and will attempt to provide the most valuable information accessible in order to receive the most funds. It also makes the offender more vulnerable to coercion should that person want to stop committing espionage in the future, because both the money trail and mercenary nature of the offense would increase the likelihood and severity of punishment if the traitor's identity were to be released.

Many of the Americans who betrayed their country sought or received relatively small amounts for their first attempt at espionage. In most of those cases other indicators were present that signaled a high potential for security problems (e.g., financial distress, statements voicing strong displeasure with how they felt they were treated, etc.). In addition, it appears that those willing to betray their country for paltry sums tend to be relatively unsophisticated in their attempts, and consequently, may be more detectable by conventional counterespionage practices and procedures.

In most of the undercover and thwarted first-attempt cases it is also difficult to forecast how much money those individuals would have eventually been paid had they been able to sell classified information on a continuing basis. Cases involving long-term espionage operations usually involve much larger sums of money, such as Ames (9 years, $2,000,000); Chin (33 years, $1,000,000), Conrad (15 years, $2,000,000), Hall (7 years, $300,000), Walker (18 years, $1,000,000), and Whitworth (7 years, $320,000) cases. The motives for, and telltale signs of, many forms of police corruption also involve money. One sign that police personnel might have a tendency to engage in impulsive, irresponsible, or improper behaviors to acquire monetary goods or services that they cannot afford is serious credit problems. Not all serious credit problems, however, reflect issues of security concern. Sometimes people who behave in a responsible manner have credit problems. They may have been faced with medical bills that were not covered by their insurance plan; care giving expenses for their children, parents, or other relatives; spouses being laid off from work; divorce; or other financial setbacks that may not have been their fault. More important than having credit problems is what caused them and what actions the person took after they surfaced.

A small subset of people in positions of trust would engage in acts of betrayal for profit rather than face what they perceive constitutes a humiliating loss of certain goods or services deemed essential for maintaining the lifestyle they feel compelled to present to others. In a classic study of convicted embezzlers, Cressey (1953) found many of the chronic trust betrayers he interviewed in prison rationalized that their first violation would be just a one-time occurrence that they needed to get them out of a problem they wanted to keep hidden from others.

Not all people who betray trust for profit were facing serious credit difficulties when they began their acts of betrayal. Regardless of whether acquiring illegal payments was motivated by need, greed, or some other reason where money is just a secondary benefit, unexplained affluence is often a telltale sign of corruption. Many positions of trust involve incumbents having unsupervised control of information, goods, services, enforcement activities, or selection decisions that certain people would to pay substantial sums of money to illegally acquire or influence. Police personnel can obtain payoffs or bribes for not making arrests or writing tickets, for providing restricted police information to individuals not authorized to receive it, for selling drugs and other contraband that has been confiscated, for modifying their testimony, for not reporting the illegal activities of fellow officers to Internal Affairs units, for providing "special" police services or coverage for individuals or organizations willing to offer payment, and for many other acts linked to their position.

Funds acquired from corrupt acts can be used for a variety of purposes. Cowles, Anderson & Shostack (1992) reported that if the payments are large or frequent, offenders often use the funds to pay for expensive luxury items, such as:
1. "Big ticket" Purchases (e.g., expensive homes, vacation homes, remodeling, cars, boats, planes, other recreation vehicles, jewelry)
2. Lifestyle Support Services (e.g., domestic help, private school tuition)
3. Debt Relief and Investments (e.g., paying down debts, stock purchases, bank accounts, off-shore investments)
4. Recreation (e.g., travel, gambling, exclusive club membership, expensive restaurants)
5. Mistress (e.g., rent, jewelry, clothing, vehicles, monthly allowance)
6. Illegal drugs

Signs of unexplained affluence, such as those listed above, do not necessarily mean the person has engaged in acts of corruption. The funds might have come from inheritances, moonlighting, spousal income, lottery winnings, judgments, insurance payments, investments, or many other legal sources. Given that offenders will almost always claim their funds came from legal sources, it will be necessary to differentiate between those telling the truth and those proving a false cover story. Fortunately, legal sources of income typically leave abundant corroborating records and witnesses, while illegal payments are often made in cash. Specific tools and techniques for identifying signs of unexplained affluence are presented below.

Automated Credit System

In 1994 the Defense Security Service implemented the Automated Credit System. Prior to that, credit information was purchased through a "middleman" organization. The automated credit system enabled DSS to acquire credit information directly from the three national providers (Experian, Trans Union, and Equifax). The system also provided the information desired in a user-friendly format, drew information from multiple vendors when needed, eliminated duplicate account information, and electronically identified the cases of possible security concern based upon existing investigative case expansion criteria. The Automated Credit System reduced credit information acquisition costs for personnel security purposes within the Department of Defense by over 75%. It also significantly decreased the manual effort needed to review and categorize the credit information. Large police departments or collective groups of law enforcement departments might benefit from similar software and direct volume discounts.

Credit reports reflect signs of both financial distress and unexplained affluence. Signs of financial distress include bad debts, collections, repossessions, foreclosures, garnishments, late payments, large credit card balances that are at or near their maximum authorized amount, and low bankruptcy prediction scores. Sign of unexplained affluence may include expensive vehicle, home, or other "big-ticket" purchases; paying off or down debts without selling the objects the loans were used to purchase or taking out debt consolidation loans; and being able to "pay as agreed" extremely high monthly installment loan payments.

Financial Disclosure Forms & Automated FDF Analysis System

In 1996 a special financial disclosure form was developed with input from PERSEREC, IRS, CIA, NSA, FBI, and the Federal Law Enforcement Training Center's Financial Fraud Institute. Unlike most financial disclosure forms, which are designed to help identify conflicts of interest, this form was designed to help identify and prosecute people in positions of trust who acquire funds through illegal means. The US Customs Service and certain segments of the Intelligence Community have implemented the form for people occupying certain national security positions.

A prototype automated system for analyzing the aforementioned financial disclosure form data and for verifying the self-reported entries reflected on it has been developed by PERSEREC. Among the benefits of both the form and the analysis system are:

a) Increasing the level of deterrence against employees considering engaging in betrayal for profit by 1) reminding people who complete the form that resources have been devoted to identify and punish individuals who engage in illegal acts for money and 2) making them feel the information they provide on the form would make it more likely that they would be caught and punished if they engage in those behaviors.

b) Reducing the motivation of potential offenders by making it more difficult for offenders to enjoy the financial profits that they would receive from engaging in crime for money without significantly increasing the chances that they would be caught and punished.

c) Forcing respondents who have acquired significant assets through illegal means to go on the record and either divulge those assets or deny their ownership.

d) Helping identify criminals whose truthful responses on the form indicate that they have acquired significant levels of unexplained affluence by comparing their level of wealth (or increase in wealth since the last form) to their legal income.

e) Facilitating the identification of criminals who intentionally fail to list assets on the form. This is achieved by using secondary data sources to verify the entries and by asking for sufficiently detailed information on the form to be able to identify when discrepancies between the self-report and the second or third party information occur.

f) Facilitating the identification of actual and fictitious external sources of capital that might explain apparent excessive wealth (e.g., insurance settlements, gifts, inheritances, etc.)

g) Facilitating efficient and effective investigations by providing an immediate set of leads for certain income, asset, and liability information (e.g., names, addresses, account numbers, dates, claimed amounts, etc.).

h) Serving as a potentially valuable piece of documentary evidence in the event of criminal prosecution.

i) Serving as a possible vehicle for identifying employees who are headed for serious financial difficulty. If deemed appropriate, those employees could be provided with optional or mandatory financial employee assistance or security clearance counseling before the issue turns into a security matter.

Use of financial disclosure forms like the one described above should be limited to positions where its use would truly be justified by a clear and present threat of corruption for profit. If people do not have unsupervised control over the types of decisions, information, or materials that people are known to be willing to pay substantial sums of money to influence or obtain, then they should not be subjected to this type of requirement.

FinCEN

The Financial Crimes Enforcement Network (FinCEN) is a unit within the Department of the Treasury. Its mission is to "support law enforcement investigative efforts and foster interagency and global cooperation against domestic and international financial crimes; and to provide U.S. policy makers with strategic analyses of domestic and worldwide money-laundering developments, trends and patterns." FinCEN is willing and able to provide direct case support to state and local law enforcement agencies.

Through FinCEN's Gateway program, state and local law enforcement agencies are given direct, on-line access to records filed under the Bank Secrecy Act (BSA) and the Suspicious Activity Reporting System (SARS). Those records identify financial transactions involving cash sums of $10,000 or more (checks are not considered cash). Given that most payments for acts of police corruption are made in cash, this source of information can prove invaluable to Internal Affairs Units.

Follow the Computer Logs

Computerized activity logs can serve as a very useful source of information for identifying and investigating acts of trust betrayal. Almost all databases and computer systems provide an electronic means of auditing usage. One form of corruption that can sometimes be identified with the help of these features is the unauthorized release of restricted information. Among the possible indicators of a potential problem are:

a) Accessing restricted files that pertain to locations, people, or incidents that do not appear relevant to the person's assigned duties.

b) Accessing restricted riles at a much higher frequency than would be expected given the nature of the person's assigned duties.

c) Accessing restricted files during times, from locations, or through means that would not have been expected given the nature of the person's assigned duties.

Just because the person's use of computer systems is atypical does not mean that the person has been engaging in criminal or improper activities. Often, harder-working and more creative, knowledgeable, and successful employees with impeccable integrity will utilize computer systems more extensively than their coworkers. However, so will people who receive benefits from providing restricted information without authorization to criminals, lawyers, private detectives, and other people who improperly seeking restricted information. Often, supervisors of the people in question are in good positions to help Database Administrators and Internal Affairs personnel differentiate between computer use patterns that show positive initiative from those that reflect criminal behavior because the supervisors will have first-hand knowledge of the employee's assignments, duties and work habits.

Computer logs can also be used to help identify officers who have used racist, sexist, or other types of inappropriate comments in e-mails and other forms of electronic communication. Workstations can be identified that were linked to sexually graphic websites during working hours. When these types of techniques are employed, however, care needs to be taken to ensure that the person who was actually using the equipment inappropriately is the same person whose name appears in the computer log. Sometimes people will leave their workstations unattended before automated "locking out" procedures take effect. Other people leave their computer password out in the open, permitting their workstation to be used by anyone with access to it.

Certain departments have the ability to track vehicle and communication devise transmissions by time and location. Analysis of officer radio transmission recordings and activity logs, with or without locator information, can be used to help identify officers who may have been engaging in certain types of inappropriate acts during their shift, such as sleeping on the job, having romantic liaisons, making inappropriate comments, etc.

Follow the Injuries and Complaints

Acts of police brutality are another form of public trust betrayal. As with atypical computer use, it is sometimes difficult to differentiate between officers who bring honor to the department from those who disgrace it based solely upon certain potentially relevant indicators. Officers who are assigned to the roughest neighborhoods during high crime prone hours or to dangerous undercover assignments and are willing to place themselves at risk to come to the aid of others or effect arrests are more likely to be injured and to injure others than their counterparts who face potential dangerous conflict situations less frequently. It is often difficult to determine whether officers used sound judgment and the least amount of force necessary or were being abusive based upon injuries alone.

Abusive responses may be repeated when similar triggering conditions emerge without effective inhibitors being present. This means that officers who engage in acts of brutality are likely to be repeat offenders unless successful interventions take place.

Sometimes abusive acts by police officers are not limited to the people they encounter on patrol during their work hours. The acts can be directed at coworkers, spouses, children, friends, and others the officers encounter when they are not on duty. Alcohol, drugs, perceived disrespect, hatred, stress, and failure or setbacks may increase the likelihood people with violent tendencies and poor impulse control will act out in an inappropriate manner.

Among the potential indicators of a problem are a history of assaults, problem drinking, protective orders, frequent injuries to self and family members, and allegations of abuse in divorce records. Booking officers can be a good source of leads, as can citizen complaints, law suits, and feedback from the rank and file regarding which precincts are most likely to have these types of problems surface.

As with almost all behavioral problems encountered in the workforce, the tendency to respond in an inappropriate manner can be successfully treated in many cases. However, without identification and treatment, officers having these tendencies are likely to bring disgrace to the department, dishonor to themselves, and increased distrust of police and unnecessary physical harm to others. Additional tools and techniques that may be helpful for identifying signs of abusive officers are included in the next section.

Additional Tools and Sources of Information for Identifying Problems

At the heart of all effective betrayal of trust prevention programs are a) clear ethics polices that are known and understood by the personnel to which they apply, b) effective monitoring, and c) consistent enforcement. Personnel need to be told specifically what acts are unacceptable and what are the consequences if they are caught violating that policy or law. Take, for example, accepting gifts from people and organizations that are offered at least in part because of the intended recipient's position and what that person could do or has done as a result of serving in that position that is of potential benefit to the "gift" giver. Without a policy that draws a clear fixed line between acceptable and unacceptable behavior, it is likely that a) there will be far more misunderstanding of what the policy means, b) it will be much harder to discipline personnel for violations and c) the policy will be subject to far more behavior erosion over time as personnel push the limits of that policy. Is it appropriate for an officer or a chief to accept a free dinner at a professional organization where that person has been asked to speak? How about a free round of golf? How about a free all-expense-paid trip for that person and/or the person's spouse? Is a 10% discount on merchandise given to all police personnel acceptable? How about an 80% discount?

The Internal Revenue Service once had a policy where its employees could accept all the free non-alcoholic beverages offered to them as a result of their official role but that if they accepted anything else of value they would be in violation of the policy and would be punished if caught. Under that policy accepting a doughnut, fruit or anything else of value was "over the line" and subject to punishment. While that policy may seem extreme, it did serve to draw a clear line between acceptable and non-acceptable behavior. Today there are dollar thresholds on the value of gifts and awards that can be accepted, which are applicable to all Federal employees. These policies also specify the requisite conditions that must be present for Federal employees to even accept low-cost items.

Ethics policies are undermined if personnel believe there is no effective means available for identifying instances when they are violated or if they believe those polices are not being applied to all personnel regardless of their rank or popularity. A few of the techniques for detecting behaviors of security concern that are sometimes used with personnel granted access to classified information are presented in this section. Some of those tools monitor databases that reflect whether people have been arrested for criminal acts, been convicted of serious traffic offenses (e.g., driving under the influence), been reported and/or disciplined for departmental policy infractions, etc. The value of those tools for identifying problem police personnel can be greatly undermined by officers "extending professional courtesy" to other police personnel by not arresting or reporting them when violators "with badges" are caught engaging in inappropriate acts. This can be especially problematic if the same people have been "extended professional courtesy" on multiple occasions, which may not be known to officers identifying new incidents or to the offending officers' supervisors, especially if the offending officers were caught jurisdictions other than where they work. Larger police departments may also need to establish policies and procedures that will help ensure command personnel and supervisors are immediately notified whenever departmental employees are arrested by other officers in their organization.

Protective Order Databases

Many victims of domestic violence seek protective orders. They may be short-term, emergency protective orders, or orders that stay in effect for longer periods that are issued after a hearing. Protective orders typically prohibit the alleged aggressor from having contact with the victim and from going to specific places where the victim routinely spends time during the period the order is in effect.

The length of time protective orders stay in effect varies considerably from state to state. In some states they are valid only for three months unless the court extends the order due to the circumstances. In other states, an order may be valid for up to three years. Judges can also have the Order entered into the FBI's National Crime Information Center (NCIC). It can either be entered as a "Temporary Protective Order," which expires in 45 days or less, or entered into the system as a "Permanent Protective Order" which is never removed from the computer database.

Many states (e.g., Georgia, Louisiana, and Kentucky) also have statewide protective order registries. In addition, numerous jurisdictions have also implemented protective order registries at the county level.

When protective orders are filed against police officers or applicants, they may signal the individual has or has had a tendency to respond to conflicts in an inappropriate manner. Protective order databases provide police departments and background investigators with another means for identifying these types of issues.

Immediate Notification of Arrest

The FBI presently offers near real-time identification of arrests for its own personnel and for selected other positions within the Justice Department. Not surprisingly, it finds this service valuable. It currently does not have the capability to offer that service on a widespread basis to other law enforcement agencies. California and certain other states have the ability to provide immediate notification of arrest to police departments and licensed security service employers in their respective states. It is recommended that police departments seek to have their personnel included under these flagging systems whenever possible.

Currently, only FBI criminal history fingerprint files are typically checked when the FBI runs fingerprint identification queries. Not checking the civilian fingerprint files means that unless officers who are arrested were previously arrested or divulge that they are law enforcement personnel, their arrests might escape detection by their home department. Immediate arrest notification programs can prevent the department from hearing about embarrassing revelations for the first time in public. They can also help ensure the appropriate administrative actions are taken immediately with personnel who are arrested in other jurisdictions.

National Driver Register

The National Driver Register is a Department of Transportation database that draws information from all fifty states. Motor vehicle departments in each state provide the names of residents who have lost their license or been convicted of serious driving issues. The register identifies people who have been convicted of engaging in the following seven driving-related acts: 1) driving under the influence of alcohol or controlled substances, 2) reckless driving, 3) racing on the highways, 4) vehicular homicide, 5) driving license suspension, 6) failure to provide identification when involved in an accident, and 7) perjury or knowingly making a false affidavit or statement. The database is often checked by state and Federal agencies when people apply for a license or certification to operate planes, ships, trains or other vehicles. Employers of motor vehicle operators also may check the database for employment screening purposes.

While Police Department and security clearance background investigators sometimes check Department of Motor Vehicle records, each check is limited to a single state. Serious driving-related offenses like DUI may also appear in criminal history databases that are checked during the course of conducting background investigations. However, criminal history repositories at the state and national level often fail to include traffic-related offenses because they are either not forwarded to them for posting by the arresting agencies or do not meet requirements for inclusion in those databases. The result is labor-intensive, sporadic checks being conducted that often miss serious driving- related offenses even when they are run on police applicants and officers who have committed those offenses. Checking the National Driver Register on a periodic basis would a) reduce the cost and time needed to conduct these checks, b) cover all 50 states, and c) be far more likely to detect serious driving-related issues when they are present.

Random Drug Screening

One of the most successful programs for combating use of illegal drugs has been the random drug-screening program implemented by the military. Random drug screening not only facilitates deterrence by identifying drug policy violators for punishment, separation, or treatment, it also helps pinpoint the level of drug use within the population being tested. After the military adopted its random drug testing program and "get-tough" policies, drug use in the military quickly plummeted and has remained at low rates compared to populations comprised of people having similar characteristics where drug testing has not been adopted.

Testing based upon urine or hair samples can provide police departments with a means for identifying officers and applicants who have used drugs within a certain range of time. The period of possible detection varies greatly by drug for urine-based tests (i.e., certain drugs will only be detectible for a day or two after use, while other drugs will be detectible for a month or longer). The implementation of random drug screening programs within police departments is likely to be met with considerable resistance, especially during the period just before and after its initial implementation. Often these types of programs are only considered after drug-use scandals involving police officers become public. To minimize the negative reaction by officers, command personnel must be included in the program, and every effort should be taken to ensure the program treats the personnel covered with dignity and minimizes the likelihood that either false-positive or falsenegative tests will occur. Evaluating programs at other departments and adopting the best practices will greatly increase the likelihood that implementation of this type of program would be successful. In the event departments do not want to adopt this type of program for all personnel, they might want to consider making participation in a random drug screening program a condition for certain voluntary assignments, such as undercover drug duties.

Random or Periodic Polygraph Testing

Many of the comments applicable to random drug tests are applicable to random or periodic polygraph testing. Polygraph programs have been successfully employed for many years at both the Central Intelligence Agency and the National Security Agency, which deal with some of our nation's most sensitive intelligence matters. If departments do not feel random or periodic polygraph tests are warranted for all personnel, they might want to consider their use for either certain voluntary assignments or when specific allegations or concerns have arisen.

Disciplinary Problems

As noted earlier in this chapter, PERSEREC's police integrity study (O'ConnorBoes, Chandler, & Timm, 1997) found that the presence of post-hire disciplinary problems is a much better predictor of police corruption than personality dimensions. Disciplinary problems were the most predictive when they a) were volitional (as opposed to the result of accidents or incompetence) and b) reflected possible character problems, such as prejudice, dishonesty, intolerance, violent tendencies, etc. It was recommended that police departments seek to extend their probationary period as long as possible and seek to remove probationary candidates from service if they show clear signs of these types of character flaws.

It is also important to develop systems and procedures to identify personnel who display signs of possible character flaws who are no longer in their probationary period. There are clear signs of problems when formal punishments, reprimands, and warnings are issued. These signs are likely to stand out even more when they are included in databases and reports that contain other positive and negative information that may be relevant to assessing personnel, such as absenteeism rates, the number of Mondays and Fridays the officer called in sick (if assigned to a Monday-Friday schedule), citizen complaints, law suits, misdemeanor and felony arrests made by the officer, traffic tickets issued, calls for service responses, commendations, etc.

Tips from Officers and Supervisors

Few Americans like to report negative information about their coworkers unless they have a strongly personal dislike for them. While police officers are often singled out for their failure to report adverse information about fellow police officers, they are not alone. From an early age Americans learn it is not desirable to be considered a "tattletale", "snitch", or '(stoolpigeon". Students seldom report on other students who they know are cheating on tests or are engaging in criminal or high-risk behavior. Many adults feel the same way about informing on others. Coworker and supervisor interviews conducted for personnel security background investigations yield far less derogatory information than record checks and subject interviews. However, if an espionage or security incident occurs, coworkers are often quick to describe warning signs they observed the subject display before the incident or arrest.

Reporting incidents of either corruption or security concern can be increased by: 1) informing personnel what behaviors or acts are critical to report, 2) why it is each person's duty to report them and who they would be letting down by not doing so, and 3) providing a wide variety of means for reporting those matters, including means that do not require individuals providing the information to identify themselves and/or the suspected offenders by name. Each time an effective security briefing is given to a large audience, it is likely to result in leads being provided. Presentations by command or internal affairs personnel at roll calls from time to time may serve to clarify and reinforce ethics policies, as well possibly serve to trigger post-presentation reporting of corrupt acts. One-on-one sessions with immediate supervisors covering the same topics may also prove valuable, especially when conducted in concert with group presentations.

Exit Surveys and Interviews

Exit surveys are questionnaires given to employees during their final working days with an organization or unit. Traditionally, exit surveys and interviews are used to uncover problems with labor-management relations or policies that may have contributed to voluntary separation. Giacalone (1993) expanded the use of those instruments to the security arena. In addition to identifying a method for constructing security-related exit surveys, he developed and tested an instrument that identified the items, location, procedures, actions, and events that facilitated theft from a government facility. In every case he found non-separating personnel reported that it was more difficult to steal than did separating personnel. Giacalone attributed this phenomenon to non-separating personnel wanting to underplay security risks in order to minimize further inquiries and potential change or to protect their interests or those of their friends.

Exit surveys and interviews could be developed or modified to help ensure officers leaving their department or unit are also asked questions about possible ethics violations that may be occurring. If people are leaving under adverse conditions, they may want to use this opportunity to strike out against one or more individuals. Consequently, their responses may or may not be based upon factual information. As long as the responses are only treated as leads, this weakness should not prove to be a problem. In what may be a related phenomenon, ex-spouses have been found to be an excellent source of information in background investigations conducted for national security purposes. Barbara Walker called the FBI and told them her ex-husband, John Walker, was engaging in espionage activity. Her report was initially not treated as seriously as it should have been by the FBI because of the animosity between her and her ex-husband. Hence, even though people reporting acts of public trust betrayal may have a grievance against the people or organization they are informing on, this does not mean the information they provide will be inaccurate.

Adjudication

Personnel security and police officer selection, retention, and special assignment decisions are dependent upon two factors—the quality of the information about the person in question and the quality of the decision based upon that information. If either are lacking, an improper outcome may result. One approach used to improve the quality of personnel security decisions involving sensitive U.S. Intelligence positions is the "whole person test".

Although the whole person test is applicable to all personnel decisions (e.g., termination, promotion, demotion, and retention), it is used most frequently in hiring, making assignments, and granting access to sensitive information, facilities, or materials. The whole person test takes into account:

1. both the positive and the negative aspects of the person's background and manner of behavior.
2. the specific position or assignment for which the person is being considered (the possible and likely benefits and harm that could result if the person is given that position or assignment and the person's suitability for that specific job), and
3. the probability that the individual's positive and negative behaviors will continue.

Consider, for example, the position of custodian at a police department. Competent, responsible custodians can prevent accidents by cleaning up hazards, reduce losses by detecting and reporting problems and suspicious activities, and help to ensure that a clean, pleasant, and safe work environment is maintained. Because custodians are typically granted unsupervised access to practically all areas of a facility, a disreputable person in that position could significantly damage the reputation of that organization. Accordingly, custodians with a recent history of criminal activity would be poor choices for cleaning areas where drug evidence, sensitive documents, or weapons are available, regardless of their cleaning ability. Hiring a jail consultant who was going to have little or no unescorted access to restricted areas with a similar background, however, might be worth the risk (depending on the amount of potential risk) if his or her potential for significantly contributing to the organization were high.

Also taken into account by the whole person test is the relationship between the individual's strengths and weaknesses and the nature of the particular position in question—that is, the person's suitability for the job. For example, to assign people with serious gambling problems to positions where they would likely come into frequent contact with people who would be offering them large bribes, pay-offs, or kickbacks would show extremely poor judgment.

Among the basic assumptions underlying the whole person test are (a) people's pasts are the best predictor of their future performance, (b) that people change over time, and (c) that change is often likely to follow certain major events in people's lives. The recency, frequency, duration, and nature of an individual's decision pattern to either engage in or to abstain from the act in question, when opportunities for its manifestation have arisen, are important aspects to consider when attempting to predict the related future actions of a given individual.

Among the events that often result in significant behavioral changes are being exposed to a different peer group, acquiring an important position, getting married, having children, getting divorced, and losing one's position. Unless they experience major setbacks or problems with addiction, most people tend to become more responsible as they grow older. Consequently, people who have previously engaged in wrongdoing may be acceptable candidates, even for sensitive positions or assignments, if there is sufficient evidence to believe they have permanently changed their behavior. Similarly, those excluded from consideration or employment at one point in time because of prior misconduct may later be worthy candidates, if they can demonstrate that they have maintained an appropriate lifestyle for a suitable length of time given the level and type of their prior misconduct.

Adjudicative Desk Reference

The Adjudicative Desk Reference (ADR) is an electronic tool developed by PERSEREC to assist in the adjudication process. It provides convenient access to the following information:

Adjudicative Guidelines: This is the official U.S. Government policy that guides decisions about an individual's eligibility for a Federal security clearance.

Supplemental Information to the Adjudicative Guidelines: This is a large compendium of background information and reference materials on the diverse human behaviors covered by the adjudicative guidelines. It is intended to serve as a job aid for assisting adjudicators and other security personnel in making informed judgments.

Policy Documents: Executive Orders 12968 and 10450 and Director of Central Intelligence Directive 6/4 are the principal national-level policy documents that guide the U.S. Government personnel security program and security clearance determinations.

While the ADR was developed to assist personnel security adjudicators, investigators, and security managers, many of its sections would be applicable for people assigned to make law enforcement selection, retention, and special assignment decisions. Free Internet access to the ADR is available at the following web address:

www.dss.mil/training/adr/adrl.htm

Copies of the ADR on CD can be obtained for free by writing to PERSEREC at 99 Pacific Street, Building 455E; Monterey, CA 93940.

Thinking beyond one's jurisdictional boundaries

This section addresses some of the steps departments, states, and national law enforcement organizations might want to consider pursuing collectively to improve the efficiency, effectiveness, and fairness of law enforcement vetting and internal affairs efforts. For example, new police applicants may initially apply to several police departments within their respective geographical areas. If each department conducted a separate background investigation on those applicants, there could be a tremendous waste of resources. To prevent that waste from occurring, departments in certain regions of the country have banded together and conduct only one investigation, which is accepted by all of the participating departments. This may also result in the participating departments collectively reviewing the sources and methods used during the background investigation to help assure that appropriate investigation standards are being met.

Numerous other examples can be cited where similar benefits may be possible through collective law enforcement action. The field of economics has long recognized that production on a large-scale can make certain economies possible. For example, a small police department that conducts its own credit checks on applicants and/or incumbents may require certain software and equipment to perform those functions; however, those same resources may be capable of providing credit checks for every police department in the entire state. Instead of each police department having to also pay a separate maintenance fee to the software provider, only one fee would be charged if departments funneled their requests through a single requester. In addition, instead of each department paying higher rates for its credit checks, high volume discounts might also apply. While some of these same benefits can be accrued through credit report acquisition companies who achieve similar benefits by funneling the credit needs of many clients, some of the resulting savings would constitute profit as opposed to being passed on to their customers. Whereas, all savings achieved through collective law enforcement action could be passed on to participating departments.

Economies of scale also apply to the actions of background investigators. One factor that often adds considerably to the cost of performing this function is travel time and travel expense. Consider the cost if each Department of Defense contractor had its own background investigators who were required to travel to each source of background information applicable to people being considered for work on classified contracts. Those individuals would probably have to travel across the nation and, in some cases, across the world to conduct the required interviews and checks. By pooling those checks, organizations like the Defense Security Service can have people stationed in areas within every state so their travel distance is minimized. In addition, instead of having 100 different investigators traveling to same record repository each day, by pooling the investigations, one person can be sent to that repository to gather the records for 100 cases.

Another advantage of large economies of scale is the ability to have certain employees specialize in certain aspects of their work that they could not have done in smaller organizations or without working in a collective manner. Forensic computer and accounting skills are often helpful in certain types of corruption investigations. It is unlikely that smaller departments will have the luxury of having investigators with those skills working on their staff and, if they do, that those employees would have sufficient workloads requiring those specialized skills to maintain their level of proficiency.

Collective law enforcement actions can do more than just help save money and enable specialization. They can facilitate:

a. increased consistency,

b. fairness,

c. officer acceptance, and

d. the appropriateness of

    1. disciplinary policies and actions,

    2. due process rights, and

    3. adjudication.

This type of collective police department application is not new. In 1959 the California Legislature established the Commission on Peace Officer Standards and Training (POST) to set minimum selection and training standards for California law enforcement. Hundreds of other state, federal, and professional organization examples exist where collective action by police departments has lead to law enforcement advancements.

One area where collective action may be particularly important is disciplinary policies and actions. O'Connor-Boes, Chandler & Timm (1997) found considerable variation in how police organizations responded to acts of departmental misconduct, as well as how they punished substantiated cases of corruption. Undoubtedly, some of the variation was justified by case facts. However, it is also likely that some of the variation was not warranted. The authors recommended that the law enforcement community seek more common standards for punishing their personnel, perhaps resulting in a non-binding document similar in nature to the Federal sentencing guidelines used by judges. Those standards would probably be more appropriate and universally accepted by officers if they were set for, and by, law enforcement organizations with input from organizations representing both command personnel and lower ranking officers and deputies.

It was also recommended that a study be conducted to assess whether police officers who were fired or asked to resign from one jurisdiction have been hired by other law enforcement organizations without disclosing that fact. If so, additional steps should be taken to prevent that problem from occurring, such as having a central registration file of all current and former sworn officers that departments could check during their background investigation process. The utility of that type of index could be expanded if it also included applicants for law enforcement positions and identified the departments where each applicant had applied.

Countless other individual and collective law enforcement actions could be initiated that would improve the efficiency, effectiveness, and fairness of law enforcement vetting and internal affairs efforts. Regional, state, and Federal-level professional law enforcement associations provide an excellent means for helping to refine and implement ideas. However, it is up to individual police officers, criminal justice academicians, and other citizens to identify and pursue those approaches. Given that vetting done for law enforcement and for national security purposes have similar goals and procedures, it is likely that the two disciplines could benefit greatly from learning about the best practices employed by each other's counterpart.

Endnotes
[1] The opinions, findings, conclusions, and recommendations expressed in this chapter are those of the author and do not necessarily represent the official position of the U. S. Department of Defense.

References

Brown, G. B. (1988). *Profile of espionage penetration.* Albuquerque, NM: Sandia National Laboratories

Collins, J. M. (1991). *White collar criminality: A prediction model.* (Defense Technical Information Center AD-A242 480 / 91-14919). Alexandria, VA: U. S. Department of Defense.

Commission on Protecting and Reducing Government Secrecy (Moynihan Commission) (1997). *Report of the Commission on Protecting and Reducing Government Secrecy (Senate 105-2). 103rd Congress.* U.S. G.P.O., Washington, D.C.

Cowles, E. L., Anderson, D. B., & Shostak, J. (1992). *A report on a study to explore the characteristics of offenders committing financially motivated crimes related to the acquisition, use and disposal of illegal funds.* Monterey, CA: Defense Personnel Security Research Center.

Cressey, D. R. (1953). *Other people's money.* New York: Free Press

Director of Central Intelligence. (1998). *Directive 614: Personnel security standards and procedures governing eligibility for access to sensitive com partmented information (SCI).* Washington, DC. Author.

Giacalone, R. A. (1993). *Developing an exit survey instrument for identifying and decreasing theft susceptibility risks in the Department of Defense: The results at SIMA, Norfolk.* Monterey, CA: Defense Personnel Security Research Center.

Heuer, R. J., Crawford, K.S., Kramer, L. A., & Hagen, R. R. (2001). *A new approach to the SSBI-PR: Assessment of a phased reinvestigation.* Monterey, CA: Defense Personnel Security Research Center.

Joint Security Commission (1994). *Redefining security: A report to the Secretary of Defense and the Director of Central Intelligence.* Washington, D.C.

O'Connor-Boes, J; Chandler, C. J.; & Timm, H. W. (1997). *Police integrity: Use of personality measures to identify corruption-prone officers.* Monterey, CA: Defense Personnel Security Research Center.

Security Research Center. (1999). *Recent espionage cases: 1975-1999.* Monterey, CA: Defense Personnel Security Research Center.

Timm, H. W. (2000). *Estimated impact of the proposed automated continuing evaluation System (ACES) on personnel security resources and effectiveness: A preliminary feasibility assessment.* A paper presented at the OPM Security Professionals' Seminar. Roslyn, VA. November 2000. [Published 2001. Monterey, CA: Defense Personnel Security Research Center.]

U. S. Department of Defense. (1985). *Keeping the nations secrets: A report to the Secretary Of Defense by the Commission to Review DOD Security Policies and Practices.* Washington, DC: Author.

Webster, W. (December, 1985). *Presentation at the National Press Club.* [Reported in Associated Press News Release, Byline: Lee Bird, Headline: Webster calls for fewer communist diplomats in the U. S., Section: Washington Dateline. Date: December 10, 1985.1

Wood, S. & Wiskoff, M. F. (1992). *Americans who spied against their country since World War II.* Monterey, CA: Defense Personnel Security Research Center.

Part II
Monitoring and Early Warning

Assessments of police according to their psychological, social, economic and community ties has indeed improved over the past half century, although the predictive validity of any of these independent measures has yet to be conclusively established. Creating and implementing internal as well as external methods to monitor the police has helped to create boundaries around issues of police integrity—both in how it is displayed in the day-to-day actions of police officers, as well as how the community at large understands such actions and the rationale for them. Internal "early warning" or "early intervention" systems are becoming more common in policing as an internal means of monitoring and responding to officer behavior and performance.

Early warning systems have generally been police initiated, although police unions typically oppose the concept, and, more importantly, the language of early warning. Nonetheless, many police agencies are attempting to systematically analyze application, personnel, and field monitoring systems to better understand the behaviors of police officers—inferring ethical lapses from misbehavior. Two readings are included in this section that look at particular aspects of monitoring within specific agencies.

In *Police Integrity: Exploring the Utility of a Risk Factor Model,* Hickman, Piquero, and Greene examine officer histories in the Philadelphia Police Department from the point of application, through the academy, to assignment on the street and subsequent performance. They conclude that the wide range of data resources concerning officer histories (present in many police agencies), if linked together in the context of early warning systems, can provide a powerful management tool to provide a deeper understanding of how and why some groups of officers may be more likely to evidence problem behavior.

In *Armed and Dangerous,* Lersch and Mieczkowski explore police drug-related corruption and use of drugs in the pseudonymous "Eastern City Police Department". In addition to a thorough review of drug-related police scandals, prior drug-related corruption studies, and extant explanations for police drug use and drug-related corruption, they look at various attempts to monitor drug use among the police. They then present drug test data from nearly 20,000 officer trainees and nearly 50,000 sworn officers over a 10-year period in "Eastern City," demonstrating that while positive drug screens are very rare, there was a small group of officers who were identified as drug users during this time period. The implications for officer and agency integrity are discussed, as well as preventative strategies agencies may employ to promote ethical conduct.

4

Police Integrity: Exploring the Utility of a Risk Factor Model

Matthew J. Hickman, U.S. Department of Justice Bureau of Justice Statistics Alex R. Piquero, University of Florida Center for Studies in Criminology and Law Jack R. Greene, Northeastern University College of Criminal Justice

This research was supported in part by a grant from the National Institute of Justice (98-IJ-CX- Points of view are those of the authors and do not necessarily represent the official position of the U.S. Department of Justice.

Introduction

In recent years, the related topics of police integrity and accountability have captured the attention of both police agencies and police researchers (Walker, 2000). In particular, police agencies have been collaborating with academic and private research groups to study the relationship between police behavior and public trust in the police. In many cases, these groups have been collecting and analyzing departmental data resources, and trying to develop practical strategies for supporting integrity and accountability. Police agencies across the nation are actively seeking new ways to organize and analyze information, monitor personnel, and respond to the public demand for integrity and accountability.

The terms "integrity" and "accountability" are often used without much consideration for their meaning. *Police integrity* can be thought of as the product of both actual police behavior and the public perception of that behavior. Police behavior within particular neighborhoods, throughout cities, and across the states is interpreted and reacted to by the citizens served. The public can view police behavior as being respectful of the awesome and necessary power entrusted to them, or as a violation of that trust. Police integrity at any place and time is strong when both actual and perceived behavior are trustworthy in nature, and weak when either actual or perceived behavior is not deserving of public trust.

Related to police integrity, *police accountability* can be thought of in terms of two questions; whether the behavior that the public views as a violation of trust is acknowledged by the agency and governing bodies as a violation of public trust, and whether something is being done to correct the problem. Police accountability at any place and time is strong when the answers to these two questions are in the affirmative, and weak when they are not.

One of the key ingredients in the mix of police integrity and accountability is the monitoring of police behavior. The strong public demand for police services that are free of brutality and misconduct (linked with the potential legal and financial consequences that may result when these public demands are not met) is undoubtedly a key determinant of the priority assigned to the monitoring of officer behavior. This is not meant to imply that police agencies are generally uncommitted to the monitoring of their personnel; to the contrary, police agencies around the country are actively seeking new ways to organize and analyze information, monitor personnel, and respond to the public demand for integrity and accountability. Current emphasis is on developing new methods for monitoring and responding to negative police behaviors before they grow into more serious problems.

There are a couple of key trends in policing and, more broadly, in criminology that together have a strong potential to inform agencies committed to supporting and maintaining integrity and accountability. First, a growing trend in policing is the development and use of "Early Warning Systems" (EWS) to identify negative behavior patterns before they develop into more serious problems. In essence, an EWS is nothing more than a data management tool. The general idea behind EWS is that by continuously collecting and analyzing information about officers, potential problems can be averted. Many agencies have adopted a kind of "three-strikes" approach to EWS; for example, the generation of three citizen complaints in a short period of time may trigger a flag, suggesting that an officer may be having problems and may need assistance in the form of counseling, training, or in the words of an anonymous police manager, a "swift kick in the ass."

Ideally, agencies should collect information on all types of officer behavior, including information on uses of force, complaints, disciplinary action, internal investigations, and the like. Many agencies currently collect this information. The next step is for agencies to link this data together such that any measure for any one officer is easily accessible and can be related to all other measures. Police agencies also have a significant amount of additional information about their officers that may help in the monitoring process: background records, personnel records, academy records, etc. A system that links all of this information together has the potential to be a powerful management and analysis tool. But what kinds of specific information are useful or likely to be useful in this regard?

The second trend mentioned above is growing movement toward adopting the "risk factor prevention paradigm" in criminological research (Farrington, 2000). The idea of risk factor prevention is fairly straightforward and familiar to most people. As an example, a physician will estimate a patient's likelihood for developing heart disease based on certain risk factors (e.g., smoking, being overweight, having a poor diet) and then prescribe preventative treatment (e.g., stop smoking, exercise and lose weight, switch to a less fatty/salty diet). The physician's knowledge of risk factors for the development of heart disease is based on accumulated medical research demonstrating that heart disease tends to be more prevalent among patients who exhibit certain factors, as compared to patients who do not exhibit those factors. Thus, the presence of each factor, both alone and in combination, increases a patient's likelihood of developing heart disease. Most commonly, the increased risk associated with a given risk factor is expressed in terms of an "odds ratio," which is the probability (or "odds") of the outcome in a group having a given risk factor divided by the probability of the outcome in a group that does not have the risk factor.

In an effort to explore the utility of this model for police integrity research, we attempted to isolate risk factors for various police behaviors and outcomes as part of a study of police integrity in the City of Philadelphia. It is important to note that the risk factor prevention approach is a familiar concept to the Philadelphia Police Department (PPD). In fact, as part of the PPD's eight-hour "Corruption Detection and Prevention for Police Supervisors" in-service training curriculum (1995), police supervisors are introduced to "Signs and Symptoms of Corruption" (Handout #1) and "Proactive Measures for Prevention of Police Corruption" (Handout #2). As an example, among the listed signs and symptoms of corruption are "officers getting an inordinate amount of record checks or NCIC checks on license plates or on persons not in custody" and "officers consistently making arrests in districts where they are not assigned." The relevant proactive measures to prevent corruption are to "... prevent subordinates from remaining inside longer than necessary" and to conduct "random personnel observations of field operations." The underlying assumption is that officers are more likely to engage in corrupt activities when they work in environments that permit or facilitate such activity. The preventative response is to create a work environment that does not permit or facilitate such activity.

Our focus is primarily on individual officer characteristics (although we also consider contextual factors), such as their background history and academy performance, that may help to inform the recruitment, screening, selection, and monitoring process. Of the information readily available to the department, what kinds of information are useful in understanding the likelihood of different behaviors of interest? At the outset, we want to emphasize a strong element of caution in conducting, reporting, and interpreting this type of research. It is simply unrealistic to think that any one factor or series of factors will perfectly predict who is or isn't, or who will or won't be, a problem officer. Even in the medical example given above, it is recognized that not every overweight smoker with a poor diet will develop heart disease. Perhaps the most feared type of prediction error occurs when a person is identified as a problem when in fact they are not (i.e., a "false-positive"). The opposite kind of prediction error, when a person is identified as not a problem when in fact they are (i.e., a "false-negative"), is also of concern. For these reasons, risk factors should always be used as indicators suggesting that additional attention may be warranted, and not as absolute indicators of a problem or potential problem. Importantly, the cautions associated with a risk factor approach are also familiar to the PPD; perhaps the single most important piece of information presented in the departmental training material referenced above is the admonition that "the important thing to remember is that these signs and symptoms must be kept in the supervisor's mind as a sort of reasonable suspicion on which to examine a subordinate a little more closely" (Handout #1).

Background

In July of 1996, the National Institute of Justice (NIJ) and the Office of Community Oriented Policing Services (COPS) jointly held the first National Symposium on Police Integrity. A primary purpose of this conference was to call attention to the need for policy-oriented research addressing the problems of officer misconduct and corruption, during a time when police agencies were beginning to recognize the need for increased public accountability. Indeed, as police departments continue to embrace organizational shifts toward a more expansive role (i.e., from traditional methods of policing to community or problem-oriented policing), "new forms of old problems" (NIJ, 1997: 1) become a focal concern. A secondary goal of this meeting was to help foster relationships between police agencies and research organizations by providing a forum of open communication. The conference attendees, including a broad range of law enforcement personnel, labor representatives, community and political figures, and researchers, had a unique opportunity to collectively identify and discuss potential issues, concerns, and solutions to negative police behavior and diminishing public trust in the police. The present research is one example of the types of collaborative relationships that grew out of these early discussions.

One of the core components of community and problem-oriented policing, the formation of partnerships, depends on the existence of mutual trust between the police and the community. For agencies that want to move toward these methods of policing, the relationship between police integrity and community and problem-oriented policing becomes apparent: How can a police agency implement community-oriented strategies when the citizens served don't trust the police? Despite evidence of an eroding public trust in the police (Vicchio, 1997), police agencies continue to implement various programs, strategies, organizational "philosophies," or other changes fueled by the rhetoric of community policing. While individual agencies might not see an integrity problem, the public clearly does (Vicchio, 1997). Unless steps are taken to improve police behavior and the public's perception of police behavior, departmental efforts guided at the development of community or problem-oriented policing (predicated on a community which trusts the police) may be fruitless.

While many departments rely upon a code of ethics linked with existing internal systems of discipline as a means of addressing problems of integrity, this reactive approach, building on the officer's fear of departmental sanction, is inadequate under a community model of policing. Police officers operating in the context of a community problem-oriented policing role must be a priori individuals of strong character and integrity, and oversight must be proactive if community partnerships built on mutual trust are to be successful. One proactive step is the development of EWS and training designed to help officers before severe sanctions become necessary. When officers are fearful of departmental sanctions rather than confident in the support of their agency, and when public trust in the police wanes due to actual or perceived police integrity problems, the community and problem-oriented enterprise is doomed to failure. As Vicchio (1997:13) suggests,

> If we believe that community policing is the most effective way to protect and to serve the public, and then we put officers who operate from the fear of punishment in more direct contact with the community, then the community will not find officers of integrity but, rather, people who know the rules and regulations and keep them simply because they are afraid of getting caught.

In recent years, the PPD has faced both internal and external scrutiny over officer misconduct and corruption. One of the most "public" examples of recent times involved charges of brutality, robbery, and procedural violations committed by officers of Philadelphia's 39 th Police District. Although not as recent, one need only mention MOVE to conjure images of law enforcement personnel in a helicopter dropping a duffel-bag full of explosives onto the roof of the MOVE headquarters, causing a fire that razed several blocks in West Philadelphia.

As a result of these and other highly publicized incidents, the PPD has been characterized, perhaps unfairly, as being riddled with integrity and accountability problems. Wether fair or not, perceived or actual, several special- interest groups have reacted to the PPD's history of conflict with the community. This reaction is most noticeably evident in discussion of recent litigation (Jordan and Ciesler, 1998: 1-2):

> In September of 1996, the City of Philadelphia entered into a wideranging agreement settling reform litigation instituted by the National Association for the Advancement of Colored People, the American Civil Liberties Union, and the Police-Barrio Relations Project. This litigation followed, and was prompted by, the joint federal-city investigation into corruption and misconduct in the 39 th District of the PPD prior to 1992, which resulted in the conviction of six corrupt former members of the Department, and led to the overturning of more than 15 0 criminal convictions and the expenditure of millions of dollars to settle lawsuits brought by individuals whose civil rights were violated. In the Settlement Agreement, the City committed to undertake numerous reforms designed to improve police accountability, reduce the potential for police corruption and misconduct, and enhance the confidence of the people of Philadelphia in the integrity and fairness of their Police Department.

The collaboration that resulted in this research was initiated for the purpose of helping to develop integrity oversight processes in furtherance of the Department's commitment to the Settlement Agreement. Over the course of a series of discussions with executives in the Department's Internal Affairs Division, we mapped out a research agenda focused on linking available data resources to identify any possible indicators of negative police behavior that could potentially inform the screening, selection, and monitoring processes, and in a larger sense to help think about ways to identify officers who may be having problems and that may need help. In order to address these kinds of issues, it was clear that research staff would need to have access to a great deal of sensitive information about active police officers. Somewhat surprisingly, and probably due in no small part to the immediate need for such a study, we were provided with broad access to departmental resources. Of course, the Internal Affairs Division (and other departmental bodies) maintained oversight of our activities. We held regular committee meetings to report on our progress and activities, as well as to communicate preliminary findings. More importantly, we used these committee meetings to get the kind of help that only comes with the unique experiences and special knowledge and insight of Philadelphia police officers. Our advisory committee was composed of members of the Internal Affairs Division, Labor Relations Unit, Fraternal Order of Police, Integrity and Accountability Office, as well as representative members of the Department of various ranks and assignments, such as Patrol and Investigations. In the next section, we discuss the methods and data that emerged from our ongoing work with this group.

Methods and Data

Our data collection was designed to track officer histories from the point of application, through the academy, to assignment on the street and subsequent performance. Our goal was to be able to construct a picture of an officer's career using readily available departmental data, and then compare it to other officers' careers. We started by examining the front-end of officer careers, and then moving through all the subsequent stages up to and after assignment on the street. We briefly review this process below.

When an individual applies to become a Philadelphia Police Recruit, they begin by filling out the necessary application forms and then taking an entrance examination. An eligibility list of applicants is then provided to the Background Unit. Qualified applicants are given a Personal Data Questionnaire (PDQ) and a date for an interview. The PDQ collects self-reported background information, including the applicant's identifying information, family background, residence history, educational history, employment history, credit history, military record, motor vehicle history, adult and juvenile criminal history, and drug use history.

The applicant is then interviewed with regard to the information provided in the PDQ by a member of the Background Unit. A polygraph exam is then administered, and each applicant is allowed two opportunities to pass the polygraph. If successful, a background investigation is conducted, and, if deemed acceptable, the file is reviewed by a final acceptance committee. The candidate is then subjected to a medical exam, followed by a psychological exam. Provided all goes well, the applicant completes forms for city employment, and reports to the

Police Academy.

In the academy, recruits go through several training and evolution phases. Numerous exams are taken and scores recorded. Recruits are also subject to a disciplinary code specific to the academy. Demerits and/or extra duty tasks are assigned when a recruit commits an infraction, and an excessive number of demerits ultimately results in expulsion from the academy.

After successfully completing academy training, these individuals are appointed throughout the department to begin their work as officers on the street. There are 23 different police patrol districts in the City of Philadelphia, and there is great variation in the characteristics of these districts. Some are large, some are small. Some have many annual offenses and arrests, others have fewer offenses and arrests. The residents in some districts are very different demographically from those in other districts.

Finally, subsequent to their appointments on the street, some of these officers will generate citizen complaints, some will become the targets of internal investigations, and possible departmental discipline. Most will generate no problems whatsoever.

All of the information discussed thus far is valuable data of importance to this and similar studies. We collected background data, academy performance data, departmental records concerning citizen complaints, internal investigations, uses of force, and departmental discipline, as well as contextual data (i.e., Census data and other information relevant to the district-level work environment, collected and aggregated via GIS) for nearly 2,000 Philadelphia police officers representing 17 academy classes. In addition, attitudinal data was collected via a survey instrument administered to a random sample of 499 patrol officers. Measures included cynicism, attitudes toward ethics, and estimations of the seriousness of various behaviors, likely punishment, and willingness to report. These data were aggregated to the district-level to examine potential organizational/cultural correlates.

The general approach used in this study is best described as a risk factor model, becoming increasingly popular as a tool in criminological research. A two-step method is used: first, individual correlates are identified by running a series of logistic regressions for each of the independent variables; second, the effect of multiple factors is examined by creating indices from the correlates identified in the first step, and calculating odds ratios and confidence intervals.

The academy sample (n=1,935) is about two-thirds (66.8%) male. With regard to race, 44.5% of the sample is white, 45.9% black, 7.4% hispanic, and 2.1% classified as "other." The majority of recruits were single (68.7%) at the time of sampling, and 21.0% were married. The average age in the sample is 26.7 years old, with a range of 18 to 55 years.

Physical context data relating to the 23 police districts were collected using Census overlays and aggregated information compiled via GIS, and then linked to the other data being compiled for the study. Within the 1,935 officers for whom academy and background data was available, 181 had missing or conflicting district assignment information. For these cases, we replaced the missing contextual data with the mean values. An additional problem is that officers do occasionally move to different districts. Unfortunately, given the available departmental data, we are unable to account for these moves. This is a clear limitation in assessing the effect of the contextual variables. However, based on interviews with district Captains and other departmental personnel, we learned that these moves are surprisingly rare in Philadelphia due in no small part to the extensive paperwork and justifications necessary (often referred to by interviewees as a "headache" to be avoided if possible). We were also informed that officer requests for transfers are almost always denied unless there are special circumstances. As such, we feel comfortable that our data represent a relatively reliable "snapshot" of context for the vast majority of the officers contained in the study.

There is great variation in the socio-geographic context of policing in Philadelphia, and this data is critical to understanding officer behavior throughout the city. For example, the total land area encompassed by police districts varies from a low of 1.29 square miles to a high of 16.3 3 square miles, with a mean of 5.81 square miles. Percent black ranges from a low of 1% to a high of 96%, with the mean value equal to 41%. Unless otherwise noted, these variables were dichotomized using the value at the 75 th percentile as a cutoff.

Attitudinal context variables relating to the 23 police districts were also aggregated from the survey data. Cynicism was measured using Regoli's (1976) 20-item, modified version of Niederhoffer's (1967) cynicism scale. Attitudes Toward Ethics was measured using a modified 15-item version of Krejei et al.'s (1996) attitudes toward ethics scale. Both scales used 5-point Likert response choices. Cronbach's Alpha for the cynicism scale was .67, and for the attitudes toward ethics scale, .80. The survey data were aggregated to the 23 police districts. The mean cynicism score across districts was 32.88, ranging from 27.92 to 38.72. Higher scores indicate lower levels of cynicism. The mean attitudes toward ethics score was 59.10, ranging from 53.88 to 63.00. Higher scores on this scale indicate weaker attitudes toward ethics.

The background and academy variables used in the study include demographics (age at application, race, sex, years of schooling, marital status), employment history (number of jobs held, any length of unemployment, ever been fired, ever applied to PPD, number of times not hired by law enforcement agencies), financial background (behind on bills, excessive loans/debts, total consumer debt, mortgage/rent, bankruptcy, judgements), military experience (ever in military, military disciplinary action), family background (children, adoptive parents, parent was/is in law enforcement, brothers/sisters, family members arrested), home residence (number of addresses in past 10 years, own/rent), motor vehicle history (license suspensions/revocations, accidents, traffic tickets), application history (number of applications, rank, deceptive polygraphs), drug use and sales history (types and recency), firearm ownership, criminal history and contact with the criminal justice system (arrests, convictions, fines, investigations, complaints), and academy performance (test scores, disciplinary action).

The dependent variables of interest for this study are presented below. We focus here on physical abuse complaints, verbal abuse complaints, police shootings, and departmental discipline. As can be seen, only a very small proportion of the sample has generated more than one count within any particular variable. This is due in part to the fact that our academy sample is relatively recent (post-academy exposure ranges from 3 to 58 months). For analytic purposes, the variables are coded dichotomously as either zero or one-plus. The most frequent category is departmental discipline (30.6% of the sample), followed by physical abuse complaints (16.6%). About ten percent had verbal abuse complaints, and the least frequent category was police shootings, involving 5.4% of the sample.

Variable	One or more n (%)	Two or more n (%)	Three or more n (%)
Departmental discipline	592 (30.6)	190 (9.8)	63 (3.3)
Physical abuse complaints	322 (16.6)	68 (3.5)	12 (0.6)
Verbal abuse complaints	190 (9.8)	19 (1.0)	2 (0.1)
Police shootings	104 (5.4)	13 (0.7)	1 (0.1)

Summary of Findings

Several individual correlates were identified for each of the outcome variables. Selected correlates are summarized in **table 1**, organized by officer demographics, background/academy variables, and work environment variables.

With regard to physical abuse (PA) complaints, 22 of the 77 background/academy variables were significantly related to PA complaint generation while controlling for exposure. Officers who were younger than 26 years old at the time of application (OR=1.43) and male officers (OR[female] =0.29) were more likely to generate PA complaints. Non-white officers (OR=0.70), officers who had any length of unemployment prior to application (OR=0.76), who had previously applied for jobs with the City of Philadelphia (OR=0.75), and those who had previously not been hired by the City (OR=0.76) were less likely to generate PA complaints. Officers who were behind on their bills at the time of application (OR=0.76) were less likely to generate PA complaints. With regard to military experience, those who had ever been in the military (OR=1.61) and those who had ever been the subject of military discipline (OR=2.32) were more likely to generate PA complaints. Officers having children (OR=0.73) were less likely to generate PA complaints. Officers renting their primary residence at the time of application (OR=1.67) were more likely to generate PA complaints, while those having a mortgage (OR=0.68) were less likely. Officers whose driver's license had ever been suspended or revoked (OR= 1.38) were more likely to generate PA complaints, as were those who had received traffic tickets within the past 5 years (OR=1.38). Officers whose rank on the eligibility list fell in the lowest quartile for

Table 1. Selected correlates

Physical Abuse Complaints	Police Shootings
Demographic	*Demographic*
White	Non-white
Male	Male
Young at time of application	
Background/Academy	*Background/Academy*
Military experience	Military experience
Military discipline	Military discipline
Renting primary residence	Parent was/is a law enforcement officer
Driver's license ever suspended / revoked	Driver's license ever suspended / revoked
Traffic tickets past 5 years	Traffic tickets past 5 years
Ever been arrested	Ever been arrested
Ever owned or purchased firearms	Ever been subject of private criminal complaint
Ever obtained or applied for gun permit	Ever had to pay any fine
Deception indicated on polygraph	Ever under court order to pay judgements
Work Environment	*Work Environment*
High % residents w/o H.S. education	High % black residents
High number of annual offenses	High % female heads of household w/ children
High number of annual arrests	High % unemployed males
	High % child poverty
	Higher mean level of cynicism
	Lower (weaker) mean attitudes toward ethics

Verbal Abuse Complaints	Departmental Discipline
Demographic	*Demographic*
(none)	Non-white
	Young at time of application
	Not married
Background/Academy	*Background/Academy*
Behind on bills at time of application	Previously not hired by City of Philadelphia
Driver's license ever suspended / revoked	Military discipline
Traffic tickets past 5 years	Renting primary residence
Ever used solvents or inhalants	Adopted
Possessed marijuana past 6 months	Low score on Human Relations (academy)
Ever obtained or applied for gun permit	Low score on Orientation (academy)
Ever been arrested	Low score on handling violent people (academy)
Academy discipline	Academy discipline
Work Environment	*Work Environment*
Large area (square miles)	Large area (square miles)
	Higher mean level of cynicism

the group (OR=0.66) were less likely to generate PA complaints. Officers who had one or more deceptive polygraph results in their application history (OR=1.36) were more likely to generate PA complaints. Officers who had ever owned or purchased firearms (OR=1.63) and those who have ever obtained or applied for a gun permit (OR=2.05) were more likely to generate PA complaints. Officers who had ever been placed under arrest (OR=1.38) were more likely to generate PA complaints. Finally, officers who scored relatively lower on section of academy training related to orientation (OR=0.72), law (OR=0.57), and patrol procedures and operations (OR=0.55) were less likely to generate PA complaints.

Additive indices were created using the individual correlates identified above. Variables with OR's greater than 1.00 were retained. The race, sex, and children variables were reversecoded and retained. An additive index of these 13 background/academy variables was constructed. Scores could range from 0 to 13, and actual scores ranged from 0 to 11. Three categories were created based on approximate thirds, including 0 to 3 factors, 4 to 5 factors, and 6 or more factors. The group having six or more factors had roughly four times greater odds (OR=4.29) of generating physical abuse complaints, as compared to the group having zero to three factors. About 24% of the six or more factors group had generated physical abuse complaints, as compared to about 7% of the zero to three factors group, and the sample baseline of about 17%.

Number of risk factors	n	Physical abuse complaints (%)	OR	95% C.I.
0 to 3	613	7.2	--	--
4 to 5	649	18.3	2.83	1.95, 4.10
6 or more	655	23.5	4.29	2.98, 6.17

Note: 18 cases had missing data.

Six contextual variables were also significant predictors of physical abuse complaints. Officers working in districts where residents are predominately black (OR=0.74), where there is a higher proportion of individuals aged 18 to 24 years (OR=0.69), and where there is a higher proportion of renters (OR=O. 7 1) as compared to other districts, were less likely to generate physical abuse complaints. Officers working in districts where there is a higher proportion of residents without a high school education (OR=I. 7 1) and in districts with a higher number of annual total offenses (OR=1.97) and arrests (OR=1.88) as compared to other districts, were more likely to generate physical abuse complaints. As might be expected, strong correlations were found among some of the contextual variables. Variables with OR's greater than 1.00 were combined and dichotomized to the presence of zero or one- plus, and split-sample descriptive analyses were performed. In sum, the group having the highest percentage of physical abuse complaints (26.2%) is the group having 6 or more background/academy and one or more geographic factors. The groups having the smallest percentage of physical abuse complaints (7. 1 % and 7.2%) are the groups having zero to three background factors (geographic factors seem to make no difference here). Interestingly, the effect of geographic factors is most pronounced among the groups having 4 to 5 background/academy factors (12.6% versus 22.9%).

Number of risk factors	Total n	Zero geographic factors		One or more geographic factors	
		n	Physical abuse complaints (%)	n	Physical abuse complaints (%)
0 to 3	613	257	7.2	312	7.1
4 to 5	649	250	12.6	280	22.9
6 or more	655	236	20.3	265	26.2

Note: 18 cases had missing data.

With regard to police shootings, 12 of the 77 background/academy variables were significantly related to involvement in police shooting incidents while controlling for exposure. Non-white officers (OR=1.51) were more likely to be involved in police shootings. Female officers (OR=O. 19) were less likely to be involved in police shootings. Officers under court order to pay judgements against them at the time of application (OR=2.57) were more likely to be involved in shooting incidents. With regard to military experience, those who were ever a member of the military (OR=2.07) and those who were the subject of military discipline (OR=2.45) were more likely to be involved in shooting incidents. Officers who had a parent who is/was employed as a law enforcement officer (OR=1.79) were more likely to be involved in shooting incidents. Officers who had family members who had ever been arrested (OR=0.62) were less likely to be involved in shooting incidents. With regard to motor vehicle history, officers whose driver's license had ever been suspended or revoked (OR=1.79) and those who had received traffic tickets within the past 5 years (OR=1.84) were more likely to be involved in shooting incidents. Finally, in terms of contact with the criminal justice system, officers who had ever been placed under arrest (OR=1.71), ever had to pay a fine (OR=1.52), or had ever been the subject of a private criminal complaint (OR=3.2 1) were more likely to be involved in shooting incidents.

An additive index of 11 background/academy variables was constructed (variables with OR's greater than 1.00, and sex was included reverse-coded). Scores could range form 0 to 11, and actual scores ranged from 0 to 9. Categories were created based on approximate thirds, including 0 to I factor, 2 to 3 factors, and 4 or more factors. The group having four or more factors had roughly five and a half times greater odds (OR=5.78) of becoming involved in shooting incidents, as compared to the group having zero to one factors. About 10% of the four or more factors group had been involved in shooting incidents, as compared to about 2% of the zero to one factor group, and the sample baseline of about 5%.

Five contextual variables were also significant predictors of police shootings. Officers working in districts where residents are predominately black (OR=2.32), where there is a higher proportion of female heads of household with children (OR=1.95), where there is a higher proportion of unemployed males (OR=1.89), and where there is a higher proportion of children living in poverty (OR= 1.5 1) as compared to other districts, were more likely to be involved in police shooting incidents. However, somewhat counter-intuitively, officers work-

Number of risk factors	n	Shooting incidents (%)	OR	95% C.I.
0 to 1	552	1.8	--	--
2 to 3	758	4.7	2.64	1.30, 5.38
4 or more	604	9.6	5.78	2.92, 11.42

Note: 21 cases had missing data.

ing in districts where there is a higher proportion of residents receiving public assistance (OR=0.26) were less likely to be involved in shooting incidents. Strong correlations were found among the contextual variables. Variables with OR's greater than 1.00 were combined and dichotomized to the presence of zero or one-plus, and split-sample descriptive analyses were performed. In sum, the group having the highest percentage of police shootings (13.5%) is the group having 4 or more background/academy and one or more geographic factors. The group having the smallest percentage of police shootings (0.6%) is the group having zero to one background factors and no geographic factors.

Number of risk factors	Total n	Zero geographic factors		One or more geographic factors	
		n	Shooting incidents (%)	n	Shooting incidents (%)
0 to 1	552	315	0.6	237	3.4
2 to 3	758	435	2.3	323	8.0
4 or more	604	330	6.4	274	13.5

Note: 21 cases had missing data.

Finally, two attitudinal variables were related to officer involvement in police shootings. Officers working in districts exhibiting higher levels of cynicism (OR=1.52; marginal significance) and weaker attitudes toward ethics (OR=1.86) were more likely to be involved in shooting incidents.

With regard to verbal abuse (VA) complaints, 11 of the 77 background/academy variables were significantly related to generation of VA complaints while controlling for exposure. Officers who were behind on bills at the time of application (OR=1.39) were more likely to generate VA complaints. With regard to motor vehicle history, officers whose driver's license (OR=1.88) or license from another state (OR=2.77) was ever suspended or revoked, and those who had received traffic tickets in the past 5 years (OR=1.76), were more likely to generate VA complaints. With regard to drug use and sales, officers who had ever used solvents or inhalants (OR=1.79) and those who had possessed marijuana within the last 6 months prior to application (OR=2.65) were more likely to generate VA complaints. Officers who had ever obtained or applied for a gun pen-nit (OR=1.93) were more likely to generate VA complaints. Officers who had ever been place under arrest (OR=1.66) were more likely to generate VA complaints. Officers who scored relatively lower on sections of academy training dealing with law (OR=0.36) and investigations (OR=0.49) were less likely to generate VA complaints. Finally, those who had been the subject of academy discipline (OR=1.64) were more likely to generate VA complaints.

An additive index of the 9 background/academy variables with OR's greater than 1.00 was constructed. Scores could range form 0 to 9, and actual scores ranged from 0 to 6. Categories were created based on approximate quartiles, including 0 factors, I factor, 2 factors and 3 or more factors. The group having three or more factors had roughly five times greater odds (OR=5.02) of generating verbal abuse complaints, as compared to the group having zero to three factors. About 16% of the three or more factors group had generated verbal abuse complaints, as compared to about 4% of the zero factors group, and the sample baseline of about 10%. In addition, one contextual variable (area in square miles, OR=1.39) was related to generation of verbal abuse complaints.

Number of risk factors	n	Verbal abuse complaints (%)	OR	95% C.I.
0	365	4.4	--	--
1	602	7.1	1.79 (ns)	0.99, 3.24
2	493	11.2	3.02	1.69, 5.39
3 or more	465	15.7	5.02	2.83, 8.91

Note: 10 cases had missing data.

With regard to departmental discipline, 15 of the 77 background/academy variables were significantly related to whether an officer became the subject of departmental discipline while controlling for exposure. Officers who were less than 26 years old at the time of application (OR=1.48), non-white officers (OR=1.31), and officers not married at the time of application (OR=1.35) were more likely to become the subject of departmental discipline. Officers previously not hired by the City of Philadelphia (OR=1.29) were also more likely to become the subject of departmental discipline. Officers with loans or debts exceeding $1,000 (OR=0.74), total consumer debt exceeding $8,750 (OR=0.75), and those having a mortgage (OR=0.67) were less likely to become the subject of departmental discipline. With regard to military experience, officers who were the subject of military discipline (OR=1.79) were more likely to become the subject of departmental discipline. Officers who were adoptees (OR=1.28; marginal significance) were more likely to become the subject of departmental discipline. Officers renting their home at the time of application (OR= 1. 5 8) were more likely to become the subject of discipline, which corresponds with the negative effect reported for the mortgage variable. Somewhat counter-intuitively, if the officer had ever sold or given a narcotic (OR=0. 7 1) they were less likely to become the subject of departmental discipline. Officers who scored relatively low on the law enforcement orientation section of academy training (OR=1.42), the human relations section (OR=1.3 1), and in the section relating to the handling of violent and/or dangerous people (OR=1.44) were more likely to become the subject of departmental discipline. Finally, officers who were the subject of academy discipline (OR=1.68) were more likely to be the subject of departmental discipline.

An additive index of I I background/academy variables was constructed using those variables with OR's greater than 1.00. Scores could range form 0 to 11, and actual scores ranged from 0 to 9. Categories were created based on approximate quartiles, including 0 to 3 factors, 4 factors, 5 factors and 6 or more factors. The group having six or more factors had roughly two and a half times greater odds (OR=2.77) of becoming the subject of departmental discipline, as compared to the group having zero to three factors. About 43% of the six or more factors group had been the subject of departmental discipline, as compared to about 21% of the zero to three factors group, and the sample baseline of about 31%.

Number of risk factors	n	Departmental discipline (%)	OR	95% C.I.
0 to 3	622	20.9	--	--
4	479	29.0	1.64	1.23, 2.17
5	396	34.1	2.00	1.50, 2.67
6 or more	434	43.1	2.77	2.10, 3.66

Note: 4 cases had missing data.

In addition, one contextual variable was related to departmental discipline. Officers working in larger districts (area in square miles, OR=1.26) were more likely to become the subject of departmental discipline. Finally, one attitudinal variable was related to departmental discipline. Officers working in districts exhibiting higher levels of cynicism (OR=1.35) were more likely to become the subject of departmental discipline.

Conclusion

The purpose of this paper was to apply a risk factor model to the study of police integrity. We used data from a large sample of police officers from the City of Philadelphia Police Department to isolate the risk factors, both individual and contextual, that accounted for various police behaviors and outcomes. Specifically, we started by examining the front-end of officer careers, from the point of application through entrance into the Academy, and moving through all the subsequent stages up to and after assignment on the street.

The key outcome variables in our risk factor analysis focused on physical abuse complaints, verbal abuse complaints, police shootings, and departmental discipline. Several findings emerged from our effort. First, a number of demographic, background/academy, and work environment risk factors were related to complaints and discipline. Second, additive indices that combined important individual correlates showed that the probability of complaints and discipline was highest with the highest collection of risk factors. Third, in the case of physical abuse complaints and police shootings, a high number of individual risk factors and geographic factors combined to create higher probabilities of complaints.

In sum, our results indicated that the background characteristics and academy performance that an officer brings with him-/her-self to the street may be indicative of later performance. Although we caution readers in the sense that the possession of certain characteristics should not be viewed in a deterministic fashion, we believe that the risk factor model has the potential to be useful in understanding how and why some groups of officers may be more likely to evidence later problems.

Future studies should attempt to examine how the constellation of risk factors varies across certain officers and over time within the Department. It may be that the risk factors that were important today may change in the future. More importantly, we believe that officers do not operate in isolation to the areas in which they patrol. That is, police patrol both people and places (Smith, 1986). As such, researchers and police-makers should continue to pay close attention to the interaction between individual and environmental characteristics in producing police behavior.

References

Farrington, D.P. (2000). "Explaining and Preventing Crime: The Globalization of Knowledge—the American Society of Criminology 1999 Presidential Address." *Criminology*, 38:1-24.

Jordan, J. and E. Ciesler. (1998). *Second Report* Philadelphia: Philadelphia Police Department, Integrity and Accountability Office.

Krejei, P., J. Kvapil, and J. Semrad. (1996). "The Relation Between Job Satisfaction, Job Frustration and Narcissism and Attitudes Toward Professional Ethical Behavior Among Police Officers." In M. Pagon (ed.), *Policing in Central and Eastern Europe*. Slovenia: College of Police and Security Studies.

National Institute of Justice. (1997). *Police Integrity: Public Service with Honor*. Washington DC: U.S. Department of Justice.

Niederhoffer, A. (1967). *Behind the Shield*. NY: Doubleday.

Regoli, R. (1976). "An Empirical Assessment of Niederhoffer's Police Cynicism Scale." *Journal of Criminal Justice*, 4:231-241.

Smith, D.A. (1986). "The neighborhood context of police behavior." In A. J. Reiss, Jr., & M. Tonry (Eds.), *Communities and Crime*, Crime and Justice: A Review of Research, Volume 8. Chicago: University of Chicago Press.

Vicchio, S. (1997). "Ethics and Police Integrity: Some Definitions and Questions for Study." Keynote address at the National Symposium on Police Integrity, July 1996. In National Institute of Justice, *Police Integrity: Public Service with Honor*. Washington DC: U.S. Department of Justice.

Walker, S. (2000). *Police Accountability: The Role of Citizen Oversight*. CA: Wadsworth.

5

Armed & Dangerous: Exploring Police Drug Use & Drug Related Corruption

Kim Michelle Lersch Tom Mieczkowski
University of South Florida Department of Criminology

Introduction

In the early 1980s, a small group of police officers assigned to one of the most crime ridden areas in New York City became known as the "Buddy Boys." These officers were involved in a variety of misdeeds, including receiving protection money from dealers; stealing drugs from dealers; falsifying arrest reports; committing perjury in court cases; and on- and off-duty use of marijuana, cocaine, and other substances (Kappeler, Sluder, and Alpert, 1994). Of particular interest was the admitted use of drugs by the officers. McAlary quoted one of the officers, Henry Winter, who justified his use of drugs while on duty:

> I never touched coke until I got to the precinct. And I just wanted to see what the hell it was. I wasn't an addict or anything. It's like—say you're doing an eight-to-four tour, and you wind up going through the four-to-twelve to the midnight-to-eight, then you come back, you work and do another eight-to-four. You're tired. You do some coke. It was a nice feeling. Kept you up, kept you aware, kept you awake (McAlary, 1987:108, cited in Kappeler, Sluder, and Alpert, 1994:191).

While the Buddy Boys case was highly publicized and resulted in disciplinary actions against nearly 40 officers, only a few years later a similar incident took place in a nearby New York City precinct. In this case, Officer Michael Dowd was ultimately convicted of federal charges stemming from his drug dealing and other illegal activities. Dowd's criminal career began with drinking on duty and fixing traffic tickets, but escalated to stealing money from corpses, selling drugs confiscated from dealers and crime scenes, accepting pay-offs from dealers for information related to departmental raids and surveillance, and shaking down street level dealers. He claimed earnings from his illegal activities of $4-$5,000 per week. He drove a new Corvette, went on expensive vacations, and purchased several new homes-all on a salary of $400 per week. Dowd also claimed that he would regularly use cocaine while on-duty, sometimes sniffing it off of the dashboard of his marked police cruiser (Turning Point, 1994).

Acts of drug related police corruption are not confined to the New York City Police Department. Other agencies have had similar experiences, such as the Miami, Florida Police Department. From 1981 to 1982, there was a virtual hiring frenzy in the MPD. A total of 714 officers were hired, more than doubling the size of the agency in a very short time. Standards for employment were relaxed and as a result, individuals who would previously have been denied employment were now welcomed on the police department. Individuals with poor work histories, credit problems, poor driving records, and criminal records were now offered positions with the MPD.

Among the new officers recruited by the MPD during the hiring blitz under the lax standards was a group of 19 Hispanic officers who became known as the 'River Cops.' The criminal careers of the River Cops began by stealing drugs and cash from motorists stopped for traffic violations, and culminated in major drug rip-offs (Dombrink, 1988). In a highly publicized incident, one of the officers, Osvaldo Coello, was arrested in his Lotus after a high speed chase with a Florida Highway Patrol trooper. The Trooper found $4,500 in cash and a small amount of cocaine in Coello's pocket. The cocaine was placed on top of the Lotus, where a handcuffed Coello leaned forward and ate the evidence (Mancini, 1996).

The River Cops were accused of a variety of state and federal crimes, including using the MPD as a racketeering enterprise to commit acts of felony murder, threats involving murder, civil rights violations, robbery, possession of narcotics, and various conspiracy charges. Ultimately, the officers were convicted of varying charges from murder to conspiracy, and were given prison sentences that averaged 23 years (Mancini, 1986).

The decade of the 1990s did not bring much relief in the area of drug related corruption. Police agencies from a number of large cities have come under federal scrutiny, including Atlanta, Chicago, Cleveland, Los Angeles, New Orleans, Savannah, and Washington D.C. (United States General Accounting Office, 1998). At the writing of this chapter, one of the largest corruption scandals in the history of the Los Angeles Police Department is still unfolding. What began with six pounds of cocaine missing from the LAPD property room has evolved into a major investigation involving allegations of harassment and brutality, planting of drug evidence, perjury, and evidence tampering. While the investigation continues to unfold, to date 28 officers and 3 sergeants have been suspended, fired, or have quit as a result of the investigation. Another 70 officers are currently under investigation for their illegal conduct or for failure to reports such acts. Nearly 100 criminal cases, mostly involving false drug or weapons charges, have been thrown out of court due to questionable evidence, and scores of convictions have been overturned. Public defenders estimate that thousands of cases could ultimately be affected (Cohen, 2000).

These sorts of deviant acts are not confined to large metropolitan police departments. Members of the Delta squad, an elite drug interdiction team at the Manatee County Sheriff's Office in Florida, have pled guilty to a number of federal charges including conspiracy to distribute crack cocaine and conspiracy to violate civil rights (Caldwell, 2000). Nationwide, from fiscal years 1993-1997, a total of 640 officers were convicted as a result of corruption investigations led by the Federal Bureau of Investigation. Of those officers convicted, nearly half were involved in drug-related offenses (United States General Accounting Office, 1998).

The purpose of this chapter is to explore issues related to drug related police corruption with an emphasis on drug use by police officers. Very little empirical data exist on the extent of drug related police corruption and police drug use. We will discuss various explanations for how such misdeeds may occur, and present data from a large police agency regarding drug use by currently employed law enforcement officers. Finally, we will present various control mechanisms for drug related police misconduct.

Drug related corruption

First, we begin with a discussion of drug related police corruption. There is a great deal of disagreement among scholars and policing experts as to what sorts of behaviors are included under the term 'corruption.' Some definitions of 'police corruption' are very broad and include a variety of behaviors, such as taking bribes or gratuities, verbal abuse on citizens, acts of brutality, and even homicide (Kappeler, et.al. 1994; United States General Accounting Office, 1998). 'Traditional' police corruption was typically marked by a relationship that was mutually beneficial for both the officer and the citizen involved. A motorist may offer an officer a bribe in exchange for the officer ignoring his traffic violation, or a prostitute may trade cash for immunity from arrest. Barker and Carter (1986) define acts of corruption as follows: the act is forbidden by some law, rule, regulation or ethical standard; the act involves the misuse of the officer's position; and the act involves some actual or expected material reward or gain. While Barker and Carter define the gain in terms of money, goods, services, and/or discount, others have broadened the definition to include psychological gains in the form of vindication, recognition, or commendations (see, for example, Radelet and Carter, 1994).

In the special cases of drug-related police corruption, the acts in question can become more serious. In his analysis of a number of police agencies, Carter (1990) identified the following behaviors as 'typical' of drug related corruption:

- Accepting bribes from drug dealers / traffickers in exchange for 'tip' information regarding drug investigations, undercover officers, drug strategies, names of informants, etc.
- Accepting bribes from drug dealers / traffickers in exchange for interference in the justice process such as non-arrest, evidence tampering, perjury, etc.

- Theft of drugs by the officer from property rooms or laboratory for personal consumption of the drug or for sale of the drug.
- Street 'seizure' of drugs from users/traffickers without an accompanying arrest with the intent of converting the drug to personal use.
- Robbery of drug dealers of profits from drug sales and/or the drugs for resale.
- Extorting drug traffickers for money (and sometimes property such as stereos, televisions, etc.) in exchange for non-arrest or non-seizure of drugs (Carter, 1990:90-91).

Drug Corruption and Police Drug Use

"The policeman never rubs off on the street; the street rubs off on the policeman" I Researchers have identified several dangers for corruption involving police officer drug use. One is that officers who are "recreational" drug use are at risk for entering what Carter (1990a) identified as a "user driven cycle" of corrupt behavior. It usually begins when a drug-using officer ceases to buy drugs from suppliers and instead confiscates drugs, either from dealers whom he or she apprehends, or else from the evidence locker or storage areas where seized drugs are held. As Carter has pointed out, officers virtually universally describe how easy it is to seize drugs with a minimum of personal risk. The motivation is straightforward. First, stolen drugs are cost-free to the officer. Second, officers who attempt to buy drugs in the "regular retail drug market" run the risk of identification and possible blackmail, so it is often functionally safer for them to seize drugs encountered during arrests and keep them for their personal use rather than buying them. Carter believed that the pressure for drug-using officers to move towards this technique was inexorable:

> From officer interviews and inferences that can be drawn from
> depositions or statements, it appears that the progression from use
> to corruption is an evolutionary process, eventually affecting most
> drug-abusing officers to some degree ... Most typical, the corruption
> involves the confiscation of drugs for personal use. (p. 89)

Furthermore, Carter observed that many of these officers engaged in a series of articulated rationales for their behavior, denying in effect that it was corrupt behavior. Often they see their seizure of drugs from street dealers as accomplishing the intent of the law ("getting drugs off the street"). 2 Officers also characterized this behavior as "not being theft" (since the drugs are contraband they cannot be legally "owned" like property), and as not being corrupt behavior (since no cash was exchanged between the citizen and the officer). These sentiments were echoed by the NYPD 'Buddy Boys,' who would regularly rob street level dealers. At first, the officers would destroy the contraband that they recovered. The officers felt that their illegal searches were justified, since this was an effective manner of keeping the harmful drugs out of the hands of the public. Later, once they realized the enormous profits that could be derived from the drugs, the officers turned to selling the confiscated drugs (Kappeler, et al., 1994).

Although little has been researched and almost nothing is empirically known about the extent of police drug use, it cannot be assumed that it is insignificant. Even drug use on the job itself is a possibility that must be considered when evaluating the corrupting influences of drug use on police performance. There appears to be only one published study to report both quantitative and qualitative data on police on-duty drug use. Kraska and Kappeler (1998) described the level of on-duty drug use in a small to medium size police department, and the rationales and attitudes of officers engaged in this form of deviance. The authors were hired as officers for other than research purposes and report their drug data as a 'serendipitous finding' of drug use on the job by fellow officers. The data was derived from 49 unstructured interviews, official records, and participant observation. " On-duty drug use" was defined as drug use twice or more while on duty within the last 30 days prior to the interview. Kraska and Kappeler reported that 30 percent of the officers reported using marijuana on duty and 10 percent used other drugs, consisting of illicit hallucinogens, barbiturates, or stimulants. Twenty-eight percent of the on-duty marijuana users were relatively young officers (21-30 years of age) and 27 percent were 'older' officers (31-38 years of age). All of the officers had at least 4 years of experience with the agency.

Explanations: The Prevalence of Drug Use in Society

A number of explanations have been offered for drug use by police officers. Arguably, first and foremost is the fact that substance abuse is fairly common among the general population. Since drug use is relatively widespread socially, it is expected that police will reflect to some degree these general societal patterns. According to self- report data from the Substance Abuse and Mental Health Administration (SAMHSA) Office of Applied Studies, 88 million Americans age 12 and older reported the use of an illegal drug at least once in their life. This equates to 40 percent of our nation's population. Nearly 25 percent of respondents age 18-25 reported using marijuana within the past 12 months and 5 percent reported the use of cocaine within the past 12 months (http://www.ojp.usdoj.gov/bjs/def/du.htm)).

The level of certain types of drug use is even higher among high school and college students. In the *Monitoring the Future Study*, high school seniors were asked about their use of drugs or alcohol during the past 12 months. Alcohol use was the most prevalent, with 73.2 percent of the students reporting use. This was followed by the use of marijuana (36.5 percent), stimulants (10.5 percent), hallucinogens (8.1 percent) and other opiates (7.0 percent). Nearly half of the high school students (48.8 percent) reported using marijuana or hashish at some time in their life. As noted by the data source, the levels of drug use reported by the high school seniors more than likely do not accurately reflect the drug use of 17-18 year old youths. These data do not include the use patterns of high school dropouts or students who were truant on the day of the survey, thereby under-reporting the use of drugs by this age group (available at http://www.ojp.usdoj.gov/bjs/dcudu.htm).

In 1998 and 1999 the percentage of college students reporting the use of marijuana within the last year was at the highest level reported over the previous decade, with 35.5 percent reporting use. Cocaine use also appeared to be more popular. In 1998/1999 nearly 5 percent of college students reported the use of cocaine within the past 12 months, which was the highest level since 1990. Since high school seniors and college students are the target population for police recruits, clearly the increasing level of drug use presents a serious concern for officer recruitment ().

If agencies had the option, applicants with drug use in their past would be eliminated from the pool of qualified applicants. The police application process, with its reliance upon background checks and polygraph examinations, rests on the philosophy that the best predictor of future behavior is past behavior. Following this logic, the assumption is that individuals who have used illegal substances in the past are more likely to use drugs in the future. Furthermore, given the nature of police work, previous drug use may lead to involvement in even more serious deviant activity. As noted by Walker (1999:300) " ...there is evidence that people with any kind of drug involvement history are far more likely to become corrupt."

Given the widespread use of illicit drugs, it is not possible to automatically exclude applicants with a prior history of drug use. Instead agencies have turned to accepting applicants with a history of 'experimentation' with certain types of drugs, while also taking into consideration how much time had passed since the prospective officer' s last use. When recruiters from local agencies have visited our college classrooms, students were told that experimental use of marijuana (which as defined as a maximum use of 12 times) would not automatically eliminate applicants from the pool as long as the experimentation took place at least 12 months prior to the filing of the application. Cocaine use was unacceptable under any circumstances, although students were encouraged to speak with the recruiter. Some applications were reviewed on a case-by-case basis, especially if the applicant was female and/or a member of a minority group.

Of course, these standards can rise or fall based on the number of applicants and the need for police officers. In a conversation with a local Internal Affairs investigator, he noted his deep concerns with the quality of the new recruits that his agency was hiring. The agency was facing massive retirements and was recruiting nationwide for qualified applicants. Applicants who previously would have been denied employment consideration due to their previous drug use, criminal histories, unstable employment histories, or credit problems were now being welcomed on the agency. This agency is not alone in its struggle to attract qualified, drug free applicants. As previously noted, the roots of the River Cops scandal of the Miami Police Department may be traced to relaxed hiring standards, as can the troubles reported by the Rampart Division of the LAPD. Washington D.C. has also paid a price for hiring unqualified applicants (Walker, 1999).

Drug use as a Consequence of the Job Characteristics

As noted by Carter (1990b), it has been argued that drug use by police is essentially a consequence of their unique position as police officers. Due to the high level of stress experienced by police officers as well as the nature of their job assignments (especially in narcotics enforcement), officers may turn to drug use to cope. With respect to the influence of job-related stress on drug use, Kraska and Kappeler (1988) explored this issue in their study of on-the- job drug use patterns of police officers. Under this explanation, drug use can be a coping response to stress, and represents an extension of the elevated alcohol consumption patterns of police officers as a group.

Policing has often been perceived as a very stressful occupation, with higher than average rates of suicides, divorces, alcoholism, and on-the-job deaths. Carter (1994) identified a number of different sources of police stress, which included:

Life threatening stressors: Police officers continually face the grim reality of a potential encounter with a violent and possibly armed person. While violent police citizen encounters are rare, the fear exists.

Social isolation stressors: Police officers tend to segregate themselves from mainstream society. Since officers must enforce laws that control social and leisure activities of the community (such as public drinking, parties, etc.), and since many officers sometimes engage in some of these same activities and behaviors, the officers tend to segregate their social lives from ordinary citizens. Police clubs, sporting teams, and organizations whose memberships are exclusive to officers are common (Stark, 1972).

Organizational stressors: The paramilitary organizational structure of the typical police agency may be a source of stress. Martelli, Martelli, and Waters (1989) discussed the influence of authoritarian, non-participatory management styles, citing lower moral among rank and file officers. Additionally, opportunities for advancement in police agencies may be extremely limited, which may also contribute to officer stress (Walker, 1999).

Functional stressors: This may include such elements as the use of discretion, role conflict, and the enforcement of the law. While role conflict has always been a source of stress for police officers, arguably the emphasis on community policing has caused even greater ambiguity concerning the role that police officers must play in our society. A patrol officer may be asked to assume conflicting roles as crime fighter, problem solver, or friend multiple times on the same shift, or even while handling the same call for service.

Personal stressors: While all professionals experience stress related to their personal life, police officers are at special risk because of the somewhat unique nature of their employment. Again, because of the rare but ever present risk for serious injury, officers' families are at increased risk for stress. Additionally, police officers tend to work unpredictable, long hours. Shift work is common, and in some agencies the rotation schedule may itself be a source of stress. In one local agency, patrol officers would work two days on the day shift, followed by two days off. Next came two afternoon shifts, followed by two days off. Finally, the officers worked two midnight shifts followed by three days off. Then the cycle repeated itself.

Physiological stressors: Marshal, Vena, and Violanti (1986) noted a number of physiological correlates of stress among police officers including lack of exercise, high use of alcohol, and smoking. Additionally, shift work may also contribute to the physiological stressors by forcing officers to eat and sleep at irregular times.

Psychological stressors: Stephens and Miller (1998) explored the effects of a number of different types of stressors on a sample of New Zealand officers. Officers were asked to identify the experiences that had the worst effect on them. Experiences involving sex by force, horrific homicides, serious accidents, and chronic distress at work were the most commonly reported. Other identified unpleasant experiences included body recoveries (especially if the body was decayed), suicides (especially those with shotguns), and the death or abuse of a child.

As a result of the high exposure to stress, officers may turn to the use of alcohol or drugs. Alcohol use is common among police officers and as many as 25 percent of police officers may have serious alcohol problems (Dishlacoff, 1976). The subculture of policing encourages and reinforces the use of alcohol. As discussed by Arrigo and Garsky (1999), when new recruits are introduced to the informal police culture, alcohol consumption 'may serve as a test of trustworthiness, loyalty, and masculinity (1999:621).' Officers who do not drink may be regarded as deviant and viewed with skepticism. Drinking after work or even on the job may become common behavior for some officers, which leads to norms of acceptance for such actions (Davey et al., 2000).

While some have argued that the pattern for the use of drugs by police officers is similar to the use of alcohol, others dismiss this explanation. Carter (1990b) maintains that far from being a stress-reducer, the use of drugs by police officers would serve to cause an even higher level of stress for the police officer. While alcohol use may be commonplace, norms of acceptance may not surround the use of drugs. Carter (1990b) described the case of a patrol officer employed by a large municipal police agency who was found using cocaine while on duty. Interestingly, the officer felt that if his fellow officers suspected that he was an alcoholic (as opposed to a drug user), they would 'cover for him.' Therefore, whenever he used cocaine, he would also use alcohol. While his fellow officers might suspect that his behavior was being affected, the odor of the alcohol would provide an acceptable justification for poor performance. It appears that in this particular agency, the use of alcohol while on duty was accepted, while the use of drugs was not.

The research on police stress is extensive, and while there is no evidence to support the notion that police drug use is linked to on-the-job stress, there is no evidence to dismiss this relationship (Carter, 1990b). If one accepts the idea that the policing occupation is very stressful, then programs and management strategies designed to reduce stress would be advantageous for employee retention and a healthier workplace environment. Researchers have suggested a number of initiatives to promote a lower stress environment, such as promoting participatory management and greater participation in decision making processes; establishing specific stress-reduction programs, such as relaxation techniques and exercise programs, health/nutrition programs, and peer counseling; developing spouse and family support groups; and training recruits and currently employed officers in stress awareness (for a discussion of stress reduction strategies, see for example Ayers, et al. 1990; Farmer, 1990).

Before leaving this discussion of officer stress and drug use, it should be noted that there is some debate whether or not police work is more stressful than other demanding professions. Patterson (1992) found that correctional officers reported higher levels of stress than did police officers. While some researchers have reported higher levels of suicide among police officers (Friedman, 1967) others have found suicide rates among police officers were no different than the rate for the general population (Andrews, 1996).

The Police Subculture

An oft-cited sociological explanation that has been proposed for police misconduct involves the subculture of policing. Proponents of this perspective (Skolnick, 1966; Stark, 1972; Westley, 1970) discuss the police officer as being affect by the norms, values, expectations, and regulatory principles of their occupations. While the term 'subculture' is usually applied to lower class youth gangs, a subculture may be defined as a group that maintains a distinctive set of values, norms, and life-styles which sometimes differs from the overall culture of society. For a variety of reasons, the distinct occupational characteristics of the police officer tend to be in conflict with and isolated from the community in which they are employed to protect and to serve.

From the beginning of their employment as officers, young recruits find themselves in a different lifestyle from most of their non-departmental friends. Because they are low in seniority, many rookies must work the night shift. At a time when most young couples or individuals are developing friendships and socializing, the pool of available people declines due to the odd hours that the police officer works. Officers are forced to rely heavily on their co-workers for companionship, which further serves to isolate them from society. In Skolnick's analysis (1966), 35 percent of the 700 friends listed by 250 police officers were officers as well. Further, 54 percent of the officers had attended 3 or more police banquets or dinners in the past year. Skolnick contrasted this figure to that given by a sample of printers in a similar study, in which 54 percent of the printers had not attended any sort of organized social function with their co-workers in the past 5 years.

Further, the dangerous nature of police work fosters an environment based on friendship and trust. Danger is always present, and the authority of the officer is always being challenged (Skolnick and Currie, 1970). Officers must rely on each other for protection; norms that stress the importance of teamwork, cooperation, and mutual responsibility are extremely high among officers (Westley, 1970; Stark, 1972). Officers turn to each other for support and understanding. Mainstream society is viewed as unsympathetic and hostile against officers, and the officers must have someone to turn to in order to alleviate the stress of their occupation (Stark, 1972).

Arguably, the influence of the police subculture is strongest among those officers assigned to narcoti cs enforcement, especially those who operate in plain clothes or undercover modes. Narcotics units are characteristically comprised of a small, cohesive group of individuals that are under a great deal of pressure, both external and internal, to produce results. Individuals assigned to the narcotics unit are often socially and professionally isolated from other officers, especially when working undercover. Narcotics officers are immersed in a world marked by large amounts of cash, drugs that are tempting both for use and easy sale, and the deviant lifestyles of informants as well as users and dealers targeted for arrest and prosecution.

Girodo (1991, p 361) in his evaluation of police undercover officers noted that "although drug use is forbidden for police, it is not uncommon among under-cover investigators." Girodo observed that undercover officers are always challenged by drug dealers who pro-offer drugs under the belief that police officers will not and legally cannot consume drugs unless facing a life-threatening situation. Girodo notes that "In response, some police intent on making a case, and with knowledge that they may be tested this way, dispense with an attempted dis-simulation, and pre-empt the target's tactic and gain credibility by being the one's to initiate and use drugs." (p. 362) In his assessment of 271 federal sworn law enforcement personnel, Girodo found that of the officers in his study, undercover officers had high levels of neuroticism and low levels of impulse control. He concluded that his findings add to "the accumulating evidence connecting social-role problems, adverse psychological health, behavioral maladjustment, and job dissatisfaction to accumulated undercover assignments" (p. 368) This is of critical concern because undercover assignments are very commonly utilized in narcotics enforcement operations.

Generally, it has long been recognized that there are a number of psychological risks linked with undercover work. As Gary Marx (1988) noted, long-term undercover assignments are associated with high potential for erosion of the undercover officer's values and standards that differentiate legal and illegal behavior. Furthermore, prolonged undercover work is associated with increasing feelings of comradeship and sympathy for the criminal elements under investigation. Farkas (1986), for example, has argued that corruption in undercover narcotics work is linked to the development of "friendship and loyalty" to the investigated criminal group, and is characterized by "actual criminal activity" while working undercover. Marx, for example, cites police graffiti he observed in a precinct station locker room:

"To Bust a Doper Be a Smoker"

These assignments tend to have corrosive effects on the individual officers, including in some cases, a collapse of the officer's ethical and psychological barriers to engaging in the very behavior they are charged with preventing. As Marx notes, one officer in a joking manner told him, "we're here to enforce the law, not obey it".

Exploring the Prevalence of Drug Use

Police departments typically have drug-testing policies, and consequently several common points or circumstances at which drug testing is likely to be carried out. It is common, for example, to find that police departments test job applicants for sworn positions, or to test on a regular or randomized basis officers involved specifically in vice and narcotics operations. The most universal application of drug testing as it is currently practiced in policing agencies is in the testing of job applicants. Data on the use of drug testing by state agencies published by the Bureau of Justice Statistics reveals that of all 50 state-level law enforcement agencies, 42 use a drug screen for applicants or new officer recruits. There are eight states that do not routinely test new applicants (Colorado, Kentucky, Maine, Nebraska, Oklahoma, South Carolina, Vermont, and West Virginia). Examination of local law enforcement agencies (cities, counties, townships, etc.) reveals that in excess of 80% of local law enforcement agencies also test applicants.

In 1986 McEwen, Manili, and Connors published data from a National Institute sponsored survey on employee drug testing policies in 33 police departments around the United States (McEwen, Manili, Connors, 1986). They reported that at the time 24 of the 33 departments (72.7%) had testing programs. These 24 all tested job applicants. All 33 departments had a written policy and procedure to follow in the event they suspected drug use by an officer. The McEwen et al. 1986 data is reported in **Table 1**.

Generally, they identify three situations that were identified as "testing points". These are:

- Testing job applicants
- Testing probationary officers
- Testing tenured officers in special circumstances

Table 1

The 1986 McEwen Survey on Drug Testing Practices by 33 Police Departments Job Categories and Events Tested in Surveyed Departments

Job Categories and Events Tested	Number of Departments	Percent
Job Applicant	15	62.5
Probationary Officers	5	20.8
Officers Seeking Transfer to Sensitive Jobs	3	12.5
Officers in Sensitive Jobs	4	16.7
Officers Suspected of Drug Use	18	75
After Auto Accidents	2	8.3
Scheduled Testing	1	4.2

Once an agency decides to test its employees for substance use, there are a number of different types of drug screens that may be used in their testing process. Most agencies employ urinalysis as the drug screen of choice; however, hair analysis is becoming more popular, especially in larger agencies. The difference between hair and urinalysis testing technologies for drug screening is the test specimen and the amount of retrospective time that the test can provide. Both technologies use very similar technical analytic procedures, but use different specimens. Urine testing is very good for short-term detection, having a time window of roughly 48 to 72 hours for rapidly excreted drugs (e.g., cocaine, heroin, amphetamine) and a week or two for slowly excreted drugs like cannabinoids and PCP. Because of the rapid turnover of urine in the body, urinalysis does not do well at detecting long-term patterns of drug use. This is compounded in situations where the person tested can anticipate the testing requirement, and abstain from drug use for several days prior to testing. For example, if a person is a regular cocaine user but abstains from use for 4 or 5 days prior to the administration of a urine test, then the test would almost certainly render a negative result for cocaine. This is obviously problematic in the detection of "true" drug use among police officers, if the officers know in advance the date when they will be asked to produce a urine specimen.

Hair analysis provides a better alternative to the detection of long-term drug use and is more difficult to evade by simple countermeasures. Hair assays cannot detect drugs until typically 3 to 5 days after ingestion, since the hair must emerge above the epidermis (For testing purposes, the hair is cut from the scalp or body and *not* pulled). Normally, unless or until the hair is removed from the body or chemically dissolved and destroyed, the drug can be detected even several months after ingestion (e.g., see Baumgartner and Berka, 1989; Mieczkowski, Newel and Wraight, 1998; Mieczkowski, 2001).

"Eastern City Police Department"

In the following section, we present data obtained from a large municipal police agency regarding the number of currently employed sworn law enforcement officers who tested positive for drug use. Since the agency requested anonymity, we shall refer to the agency as "Eastern City Police Department." It should be noted given the nature of this particular data source, if an officer did have a positive drug screen it could not be ascertained whether the drug use was on or off duty.

The data set consists of 68,347 individuals subdivided into two subsets: officer trainees (19,643), and sworn officers (48,704). This data set represents data gathered over a 10-year period from 1989 to 1999. During different periods within this time span, different drug assay technologies were used. The structure of the data for Eastern City is described in **Table 2**.

Table 2
Data Structure for Trainees and Sworn Officers

Eastern City Category	Total Number of Subjects	Test Context	Drug Assay Type	Numbers of Subjects per Assay	Years Collected
Trainees	19643	Semi-Announced	Urinalysis	11634	1989-1995
		Semi-Announced	Hair Assay	8009	1996-1999
Sworn Officers	48704	Random	Urinalysis	48704	1990-1999

Testing Trainees at the End of Training Period

A characteristic of police recruitment is the training process, which normally includes a formalized training experience such as an academy or institute, typically followed by a probationary or trainee period before the person is fully vested as a sworn officer. Normally, this includes a period of time when the officer is put into the field under the control of a training officer, is given progressively increasing autonomy to perform their role, and is ultimately evaluated based on their field experience as the final step in the training process. Eastern City uses this approach in moving officers through their training period, and includes a drug test as these officers approach the end of their probationary period. Eastern City has historically used urinalysis, until several years ago when they introduced hair analysis as the technique for the post-probationary test. Table 3 provides data for the total of positive and negative outcomes by drug for the period 1989 through 1999. The period 1989-1995 represents the results from urinalysis testing, and the years 1996 -1999 represent hair analysis results. As a matter of policy, officers who refuse the test are treated as positives. The outcomes of the testing process are broken down by race/ethnicity. Regardless of test type, very few trainees tested positive for drug use. A total of 7 trainees tested positive through the use of urinalysis in the period from 1989-1995, while 35 trainees tested drug positive using hair analysis from 1996-1999.

Table 3
End of Training Period Testing, Urinalysis and Hair Analysis

Ethnicity	Urinalysis 1989-1995			Hair Analysis 1996-1999		
	Number Tested	Number Positive	%Pos.	Number Tested	Number Positive	%Pos.
White	7986	5	.06	5254	19	.36
Af. Amer.	1418	1	.07	1112	14	1.26
Hispanic	2098	1	.04	192	2	.14
Other	132	0	0	192	0	0
Total	11,634	7	.06	8,009	35	.44

Random Urinalysis for Sworn Officers

Eastern City has a policy that all officers are subject to random testing by urinalysis regardless of rank, seniority, etc. **Table 4** presents 10 years of data (1990-1999, inclusive) from the random urinalysis screening program.

Table 4
Urinalysis Results, Random Screening, Sworn Officers, 1990-1999

Ethnicity	Number Tested	Number Neg.	Cocaine Pos.	Cocaine & Marijuana Pos.	Cocaine Pos.	Refused Testing	Pos. Any Drug
White	34,162	34,081	56	19	3	3	81
Af. Amer.	6,287	6,237	46	3	0	1	50
Hispanic	7,664	7,643	16	4	0	1	21
Other	591	590	1	0	0	0	1
Total	48,704	48,551	119	26	3	5	153

As can be seen in Table 4, a small number of officers were found to test positive for drug use, with the majority of these officers testing positive for cocaine use. While the number of officers testing positive is low-only .31 percent of the total number of officers tested-the number is still somewhat surprising in that these officers were aware that, an any time, they could be asked to submit to a urinalysis drug screen. Arguably, the numbers may be higher in agencies that do not employ such random drug screening.

Table 5 makes the overall outcome comparisons for status (trainee officer and sworn officer) for Eastern City and to the extent data are available, the outcomes for the assays used in the screening process.

Table 5
Comparison of Percent Positive Drug Tests by Job Status

Status	Test Type	% Pos. Any Drug	% Cocaine Pos.	%Marijuana Pos.	Pos. for 2 Drugs or Refused
Trainees	Urinalysis	0.06%	0.026%	0.017%	0.017%
	Hair Assay	0.45%	0.37%	0.062%	0
Sworn Officers	Urinalysis	0.31%	0.24%	0.053%	0.016%

Clearly, the most striking finding is the substantial cocaine differential between hair assay and urinalysis outcome for trainee officers. These officers are called in without advance notice at the end of their training period. Although they know they are going to be tested, they do not know precisely when, and thus they have less chance—if they are using drugs—to "prepare" for the test. When comparing urinalysis to hair analysis, hair analysis uncovers far more drug use than does urinalysis. There is a fourteen-fold difference in cocaine positive outcomes

(.37% hair vs. .026% urine), and a 3.6-fold difference in marijuana detection (.062 hair vs. .017 urine). Overall, comparing the trainee rates for any drug positive outcome, hair analysis has a detection rate 7.5 times that of urinalysis.

It is also interesting to compare the sworn officers' random urinalysis outcomes to the trainees. Sworn officers do much worse than trainees. Whether one looks at positive for any drug, or at specific drug types, sworn officers are much more likely to test positive than trainees. For example, sworn officers are positive for any drug at five times the rate of trainees, and are dramatically different from trainees at rates for cocaine positive urinalysis (0.24% sworn officers vs. 0.026% for trainees)—a rate than is nine times higher. Since trainees are much more likely to test cocaine positive by hair than by urine, it is an interesting speculation to imagine what the rate for sworn officers would be if hair analysis was added as a part of the random testing program. It may also be true that trainees are, so to speak, "on their best behavior". When they enter and spend time in the field as fully sworn officers, they may engage in acts that do not appear as risky or problematic to them at this later stage of their career.

Summary of the Data

It should be emphasized that a positive drug screen result was a very rare event, regardless of whether or not the individual tested was a sworn officer or probationary trainee. Out of 68,347 individuals tested, a total of 42 probationary officers and 153 full officers tested positive for any drug - and this was over a 10-year period. Because of the low number of positive drug screens, it is important to keep the results in perspective. The vast majority of police officers tested negative for drugs. However, there was a small group of sworn officers and probationary officers who did in fact test positive for drugs.

These findings should also be viewed in light of the fact that all of the Eastern City officers, regardless of their job status, were fully aware that at any time that could be asked to submit to a drug screen. For probationary officers, their continued employment rested on a negative result. Under these circumstances, it is somewhat surprising that a drugusing individual would continue in this line of work knowing full well that their use could be exposed at any time. Furthermore, the reader is reminded that not all agencies routinely test probationary officers or currently sworn police officers. According to the McEwen et al. data (1986) only 21 percent of the surveyed agencies regularly tested probationary officers, and 16.7 percent regularly tested officers in sensitive jobs. One can only imagine how many positive drug screens would be found in an agency with no threat of detection of the substance abuse.

What can be done? Policy Implications

It goes without saying that substance abuse by police officers is a very serious issue. While it may not be a major issue if the person working behind the counter at the local convenience store is drug-free, clearly the concerns with drug use by police officers especially while on duty—are much more salient. Furthermore, while drug use by police officers does not automatically lead to acts of drug-related police corruption (and vice versa—some officers engaged in acts of drug related police corruption never use drugs themselves), it has been argued there is some relationship between the behaviors. Therefore, the policies designed to discourage drug related corruption among police officers may also be useful in discouraging drug use and, more generally, other acts of misconduct. In its report on drug- related police corruption, the United States General Accounting Office (1998) recommended a number of practices to prevent and reduce police corruption. At the hiring and recruitment phase, the following steps were recommended (USGAO 1998:21-22):

- Better candidate screening
- Raising the age of recruits
- Raising educational standards
- Incorporating integrity training into police academy curricula
- Reviewing police officers' integrity as part of probationary period evaluations
- Extending the probationary period.

Unfortunately, given the current employment conditions, many police agencies are experiencing great difficulty in recruiting prospective officers. The number of qualified candidates applying to agencies is down. Further, due to the time lag between the application for employment and hiring, many qualified individuals find employment elsewhere. It is difficult for agencies to raise standards given the low supply of interested applicants. Consider, for example, the area of educational standards. In 1967 the Presidents' Crime Commission recommended that the bachelor's degree should be the minimum requirement for the hiring of police personnel. However in the state of Florida, while several state-level law enforcement agencies require a bachelor's degree for employment consideration, only one police department required a four-year degree. Because of the high number of vacancies coupled with few interested recruits, this agency was forced to re-considering this requirement. In the state of Florida, as is the case in many states, a 19-year old with a G.E.D. may be hired as a sworn police officer.

Beyond the recruitment and initial training phase, it is essential that agencies maintain the high level of integrity that has been instilled at the academy. The USGAO (1998:22) suggested the following techniques to prevent the occurrence of drug related police corruption:

- Integrity training as part of the continuing education of officers
- The inclusion of integrity assessments in in-service evaluations
- A consideration of integrity assessments when determining promotion
- Rotational assignments, to reduce pressures from personal ties that may lead to opportunities for corruption

The general notion is to promote and reinforce norms that advocate ethical behavior. It is not enough that an agency include a brief statement of the importance of integrity in its mission statement; officers must be keenly aware of the departmental stance on corrupt activities and truly adopt this high standard of behavior as part of their own code of ethics. While in some agencies, the police subculture may encourage deviant activities, in others the informal norms may serve to promote a higher standard of ethical behavior.

In the special case of the prevention of drug use, agencies need to test not only probationers, but fully functioning sworn personnel as well. Given the fact that police officers tested positive at a higher rate than probationers, it is clear that testing beyond the initial employment phase is a necessity. Furthermore, this testing should be done at random and not as part of a scheduled protocol. Scheduled testing has been the least objectionable from the perspective of infringement of individual rights, but is the easiest for a determined drug user to evade. For most drugs abstinence for just a few days prior to the scheduled test will assure a negative result. A random test protocol (that is, an officer can potentially be asked to produce a urine specimen at any time) is more effective in identifying drug use. However, random testing programs have raised the most serious objections by personnel and unions, and when legally challenged have been the least sympathetically viewed by the courts.

Additionally, agencies may wish to consider using hair analysis as their drug screen of choice. Oftentimes the decision concerning which test to use comes down to a simple   issue of cost. Urinalysis is cheaper than hair analysis on a per-test basis. Urinalysis in the general marketplace can range in price from $4 to $7 per test. In contrast, hair analysis can range from $35 to $50 per test. Police agencies may initially view hair testing as being cost prohibitive. However, it is important to bear in mind that hair testing, while appearing to be more expensive, may provide more information for the money spent. A urine test costing $6 'buys' three days of information on cocaine use, for a per-day information cost of $2. An analysis of a 1.5" length of scalp hair at $50 'buys' 90 days of information on cocaine use, for a per-day information cost of $1.80. Of course, this is dependent on the assumption that 1.5" of scalp hair is recoverable from the officer being tested (which may not be the case) and it is also premised on the notion that the agency would consider this additional information useful.

For agencies that would like to use hair analysis but are facing budgetary concerns, there is an alternative to using hair analysis to screen every probationary officer or randomly selected sworn officer. Agencies could initiate a process that would make regular use of urinalysis but also include a random subset of samples tested by hair analysis. The mere threat of a hair test, with its longer window of detection for the use of rapidly excreted drugs like cocaine, amphetamines, and heroin, may be enough to encourage some drug-users to find a different line of work. However, as evidenced by the Eastern City probationers who knew that they would be tested by hair analysis at the end of their probationary period, not all drug users will self-select out of law enforcement.

Conclusion

Clearly there is a justifiable concern with the use of drugs by police officers. As has been noted in this chapter, police officers are a part of the society and will reflect the society's norms and values, both good and bad. Drug use is a concern because it can impair an officer's ability to function appropriately and effectively, because it heightens possibilities of corruption, because it represents and ethical and legal breach of trust, and because it corrodes the public's confidence in the police and their integrity. Data presented in this chapter demonstrated that there was group of individuals who were employed as police officers and were using various illegal drugs. While the vast majority of police officers are not involved in drug use, the actions of the minority cannot be ignored. Agencies must take steps to prevent and detect the use of drugs by their officers.

References

Ayres, R.M. Flanagan, G.S., and Ayres, M.V. (1990). *Preventing Law Enforcement Stress: The Organization's Role*. Washington DC: The National Sheriff's Association and Bureau of Justice Assistance, 1990.

Arrigo, B. and Garsky, K. (1997). Police suicide: A glimpse behind the badge. In R.G. Dunham and G.P. Alpert (eds.) *Critical Issues in Policing* (3rd ed.) pp. 609-626. Prospect Heights, 11: Waveland Press, Inc.

Barker, T. and Carter, D.L. (1986). *Police Deviance* (Ist ed.). Cincinnati, OH: Anderson Publishing Co.

Barker, T. and Carter, D.L. (1994). *Police Deviance* (3rd ed.). Cincinnati, OH: Anderson Publishing Co.

Baumgartner, W., Berka, C. 1989. Hair Analysis for Drugs of Abuse. *Therapeutic Drug Monitoring: American Association of Clinical Chemistry*10(8):7-21.

Caldwell, A. (2000, June 18). Crime, in the name of the law. *St. Petersburg Times*, pp. 1A, 10A.

Carter, D.L. (1994). Theoretical dimensions in the abuse of authority by police officers. In T.L. Barker and D.L. Carter (eds.) *Police Deviance* (3rd ed.) pp.276-277. Cincinnati, OH: Anderson Publishing Co.

Carter, D.L. (1990a). Drug-related corruption of police officers: A contemporary typology. *Journal of Criminal Justice*, 18, 85-98.

Carter, D.L. (1990b). An overview of drug-related misconduct of police officers: Drug abuse and narcotic corruption. In R. Weisheit (ed.) *Drugs, Crime, and the Criminal Justice System* (79-110). Cincinnati, OH: Anderson Publishing Co.

Cohen, A. (2000, March 6). Gangsta cops. *Time*, pp. 30-34.

Crank, J. and Caldero, M.(1999). *Police Ethics: The Corruption of Noble Cause*. Cincinnati, Anderson Publishing.

Davey, J.D., Obst, P.L, and Sheehan, M.C. (2000). Work demographics and officers' perceptions of work environment which add to prediction of at risk alcohol consumption within an Australia police sample. *Policing: An International Journal of Police Strategies and Management*, 21 (1): 69-81.

Dishlacoff, L. (1976, January). Drinking cop. *Police Chief*, 43(l): 32,34,36, 39.

Dombrink, J. (1988). The Touchables: Vice and police corruption in the 1980's. *Law and Contemporary Problems,* 51, 201-232.

Farkas, G.M. (1986). Stress in Undercover Policing. In J.T. Reese H. A. Goldstein (eds.), *Psychological Services for Law Enforcement* (pp. 433-440), Washington, DC, U.S. Government Printing Office.

Farmer, R.E. (1990). Clinical and managerial implications of stress research on the police. *Journal of Police Science and Administration,* 8(2): 205-218.

Girodo, M. (1991). Drug Corruption in Undercover Agents: Measuring the Risk. *Behavioral Sciences and the Law,* 9: 361-370.

Josephson, F.L. and Reiser, M. (1990). Officer suicide in the Los Angeles Police Department: A twelve-year follow-up. *Journal of Police Science and Administration,* 17, 227-229.

Kappeler, V.E., Sluder, R.D., & Alpert, G.P. (1994). *Forces of deviance: Understanding the dark side of policing.* Prospect Heights, II: Waveland Press, Inc.

Kraska, P. and Kappeler, V. (1988). Police On-duty Drug Use: A Theoretical and Descriptive Examination, *American Journal of Police.,* 7(l), 1-28.

Marx, G. (1988). *Undercover: Police Surveillance in America,* U. of Cal. Press, Berkley.

Mancini, C. (1996). *Pirates in Blue.* Miami, FL: National Association of Chiefs of Police.

Marshal, J.R., Vena, J.E., and Violanti, J.M. (1986). Disease, risk, and mortality. *Journal of Police Science and Administration,* 10, 17-23.

Martelli, J., Martelli, T.A., and Waters, L.K. (1989). The police stress survey. *Psychological Reports,* 70, 267-273.

McAlary, M. (1987). *Buddy Boys: When good cops turn bad.* New York: G.P. Putnam's Sons.

McEwen, T., Manili, B,. Connors, E. (1986). Employee Drug Testing Policies in Police Departments, *National Institute of Justice Research in Brief,* October, Washington, D C.

Mieczkowski, T., Newel, R., Wraight, B. (1998). Evaluating Drug Use Prevalence Among Juvenile Offenders Using Hair Analysis. *The International Journal of the Addictions* 33(7):1547-1568.

Mieczkowski, T. (2001) Drug Screening Technologies: A Review of Capacities, Limits, and Issues Influencing Interpretation of Drug Tests in Clinical and Field Settings, *Addiction Recovery Tools: A Practitioner's Handbook* (R. Cooms, Ed.), Sage Publications, Newbury Park, CA.

Patterson, B.L. (1992). Job experience and perceived job stress among police, correction, and probation/parole officers. *Criminal Justice and Behavior*, 19: 260-285.

Radelet, L.A. & Carter, D.L. (1994). *The police and the community* (5th ed.). Englewood Cliffs, NJ: Prentice Hall.

Skolnick, J. (1966). *Justice Without Trial. Law Enforcement in Democratic Society*. New York, NY: Wiley.

Skolnick, J.H. and Currie, E. (1970). *Crisis in American Institutions*. Boston, MA: Little, Brown, & Co.

Stark, R. (1972). Police Riots: Collective Violence and Law Enforcement. Belmont, CA: Wadsworth Publishing Company, Inc.

Stephens, C. and Miller, 1. (1998). Traumatic experiences and post-traumatic stress disorder in the New Zealand police. *Policing: An International Journal of Police Strategies & Management* 21(1): 178-191.

Turning Point (14 September, 1994). *The Tarnished Shield*. New York: American Broadcasting Company.

United States General Accounting Office (1998, May). *Law enforcement: Information of drug-related police corruption*. Washington, D.C.: United States General Accounting Office.

Wagner, M. and Brzeczek, R.J. (1983). Alcoholism and suicide: A fatal connection. *FBI Law Enforcement Bulletin* (August), 8-15.

Walker, S. (1999). *The police in America: An introduction* (3rd ed.). Boston, MA: McGraw-Hill College.

Westley, W.A. (1970). *Violence and the Police: A Sociological Study of Law, Custom, and Morality*. Cambridge, MA: MIT Press.

Part III
Force, Coercion, and Integrity

The issues of force, coercion, and integrity are so intimately inter-twined within the study of police officer attitudes and behaviors that researchers can hardly talk about one without acknowledging the others. Police use of force and coercion are important theoretical, empirical, and policy concerns. Oftentimes, however, research on these issues takes the form of high-profile case studies and does not demonstrate a full appreciation of prevalence, causes, and remedies. On the other hand, police integrity reflects the underlying values and ethical attachments of police officers and how these values and ethics influence police behavior. Although integrity has many meanings, the research tradition on this score has been slow to develop. In this section, four readings present relevant information concerning police use of force, coercion, and integrity.

In *Patterns of Police Use of Force as a Measure of Police Integrity*, Garner, Maxwell, and Heraux argue that questions of police integrity are raised when the average amount of force used by police officers against racial minorities is higher than the average amount of force used against whites. In general, these authors seek to identify the extent to which police behavior reflects conscious or unconscious patterns that violate professional, moral, or legal standards.

In *Citizen Behavior and Police Use of Force: An Examination of National Survey Data*, Smith provides an in-depth examination of the population experiencing force in the U.S. Specifically, he examines information regarding the circumstances of the incident and the conduct reported by the citizen as well as their description of police actions. The largest survey of its kind to look at citizen contacts with the police, drawing information from about 80,000 persons aged 16 years or older, these data provide researchers with National estimates of police-citizen contacts. Among the many survey findings, Smith reports that most citizens experiencing force reported they had done nothing at all, or were in some way disobeying the officer, and that less than half of those experiencing police force were actually arrested, suggesting that the police may indeed use force as a means of "street justice" independent of arrest decision making.

In *Toward a Better Understanding of Police Use of Nonlethal Force*, Terrill and Mastrofski review the state of research on police coercion, focusing on what is currently known about the extent, intensity, and causes or predictors of coercion. Their analysis of the limitations of past research leads them to consider three challenges for advancing future research and evaluation: (1) the need to incorporate workable normative standards for the use of force into the analytic framework, (2) the need to capture more fully the subtleties of police coercive practice, and (3) the need to incorporate the dynamics of the police-citizen interaction into the analysis of police coercion. After identifying these challenges, the authors suggest ways to meet these challenges and provide an illustration of one approach that attempts to deal with all three issues.

In *Third Party Policing: Considering the Ethical Challenges*, Mazerolle and Prenzler examine police integrity in the context of "third party policing," or police efforts to persuade or coerce non-offending persons, such as property owners, parents, and business owners, to take some responsibility for preventing crime or reducing crime problems. In this chapter, the authors describe the dimensions of third party policing and provide examples of how third party policing is utilized by the police in both ethical and potentially unethical ways. In the second section of their essay, Mazerolle and Prenzler examine potential ethical challenges of third party policing. In response to the issues raised, the authors conclude by presenting a set of ethical guidelines for a best practice approach to third party policing.

6

Patterns of Police Use of Force as a Measure of Police Integrity

Joel H. Garner *Joint Centers for Justice Studies, Inc.
Christopher D. Maxwell Michigan State University and
Cedrick Heraux Michigan State University

*Direct all correspondence to Joel Garner, Joint Centers for Justice Studies, Inc., 13 Willowdale
Drive, Shepherdstown, WV 25443-3514. E-mail: igamer@jcjs.org, Phone (304) 876-3460.
Research supported under Grant No. 95-IJ-CX-0066 from the National Institute of Justice, Office
of Justice Programs, U.S. Department of Justice. Opinions in this report are those of the authors
and do not necessarily reflect the official position or policies of the U.S. Department of Justice, the
Joint Centers for Justice Studies, Inc., or Michigan State University.

Conceptions of Integrity

Police integrity is often conceived as a trait of an individual officer. This traditional conception emphasizes concrete acts that are identified in law, policy or professional standards as policy integrity. Absence of police integrity is often identified by an incident or a pattern of incidents that involve illegal, unethical, or unprofessional behavior, although it can also involve the failure to act according to professional standards to protect and to serve (Criminal Justice Commission, 1997).. In the 19th and 20th centuries, law enforcement officers in many large U.S. cities became associated with incompetence, corruption, and brutality. The police were believed to have routinely taken payoffs from saloon-keepers, pimps, and gamblers in return for selective nonenforcement, and from peddlers and small business owners in exchange for protection. Free meals from restaurant owners became the norm in many areas and many officers established reputations for being especially tough on immigrants and minorities (Forst, 2000). Although this notion of police integrity covers a wide range of behaviors, it emphasizes the underlying moral fiber and explicit behavior of individual officers. From this perspective, it is the individual officer's behavior that lacks integrity. The most popular theory of officer misconduct is the rotten-apple theory, which emphasizes individual moral character and behavior. Walker and Katz (2002, p. 329), however, point out that the latter explanation has several failings, including its failure to explain: (1) the long history of corruption within policing, (2) why some honest officers become corrupt, and (3) why some departments have extensive and enduring corruption while others are relatively free from these problems. Common approaches to addressing lapses in individual integrity involved improved recruitment, selection, training, management, and disciplining of individual officers.

There is a second dimension of police integrity—the role of law enforcement organizations as active agents in the illegal, unethical, or unprofessional behavior of their officers (Conditt Jr., 200 1). In this conception, the lack of integrity is an organizational, as well as a personal, trait. This can involve the coordinated behaviors of a large number of individual officers and, in some well documented incidents, the active behavior of management officials. In addition, the organizational integrity of law enforcement agencies has also been challenged for their failure to identify, deter, or effectively discipline officers who engage in illegal or unethical behavior. Pedersen (2001), for example, speaking from the view of the practitioner, notes that police unions and police administrators routinely ignore minor corruption in order to protect their officers. Williams (1986) concurs, arguing that organizational misconduct is perhaps most dangerous, as both administrators and officers are involved in a systematic pattern of corruption. Indeed, Hanewicz (1985, p. 45) calls for

> more attention [to] be directed to the organizational environment of
> policing, where administrative policies and regulations are formed to
> guide the day-to-day activity of police officers.

Common approaches to promoting organizational integrity involve the selection of outside leadership and the enhanced use of independent oversight and discipline (Finn, 2002).

One indicator of the lack of police integrity at either the individual or the organizational level is the amount and severity of force used by the police. For instance, Williams (1986, p. 27) notes that "police corruption can appropriately, but broadly, be defined to include 'acts of brutality and excessive force, the display of prejudice and other uncivil conduct, [or] the unequal distribution of police service... "' At the individual level, a particular instance of unnecessary or excessive force is inappropriate use of an officer's power. As an organizational concept, integrity can be violated by a systematic collusion of officers to engage in such inappropriate behavior, often with the tacit approval of mid-level managers within the department. Questions of police integrity are raised at both the level of the individual officer that commits excessive force and at the level of police organizations that condone or do not address inappropriate or illegal uses of force.

Measuring Police Integrity

In this chapter, we identify a different issue of police integrity. We argue that questions of police integrity are also raised when the average amount of force used by police officers against racial minorities is higher than the average amount of force used against Whites. Unlike the individual and organizational notions of police integrity, which are both derived from individual behaviors that are illegal, unethical or unprofessional, this approach to understanding law enforcement integrity examines individual behaviors which in themselves may be, or at least appear to be, beyond reproach. This approach to operationalizing police integrity seeks to identify the extent to which police behavior reflects conscious or unconscious patterns that violate professional, moral or legal standards.

Suspect Race and Sex and Police Use of Force

It has been frequently noted that regardless of the reality of widespread police misconduct, the perception is clearly that the police engage in illegitimate use of force disproportionately against minorities, particularly young minority males (NELSON, 2000; Williams, 2000; Walker & Katz, 2002). One needs simply to glance at newspapers from several large cities to discover that somewhere an officer is accused of engaging in improper behavior based on the race or (albeit slightly less so) the sex of the suspect. Indeed, Bell (2000, p. 88) provides a representative example of the sentiments of those who feel targeted by the police, arguing that "the steady stream of reported instances of police harassment of Blacks from [the 1960s] to the present serves as both a portent of a Black holocaust in America and a divergence of that too awful fate." Similarly, Russell (2000, pp. 137, 140) notes that the "public face of a police brutality victim is that of a young man who is Black or Latino... [and] is tacitly treated as a Black thing [by the public]." The frequency and vehemence with which these concerns are stated establishes the importance of this concern but does not establish the existence or extent of differential police behavior.

We have identified eight studies that have measured either the prevalence or the seventy of force and used multivariate statistical methods to test for the independent effects of suspect race or sex on the amount of force used by the police (see Engel, Sobol & Worden, 2000; Friedrich, 1980; Garner, et al., 1995; Garner, Maxwell & Heraux, 2003; Kavanagh, 1994; Smith, 1986; Terrill & Mastrofski, 2002; Worden, 1995). As a group, these studies include substantial differences in the sampling procedures employed, the nature and size of the data collected, the measures of force used, the type of multivariate statistical analyses employed, and the substantive findings concerning the role of suspect race and sex (see Table 1).

The use of diverse samples, data sources and measures of force limits our ability to synthesize the substantive findings from these eight studies. Except for Kavanagh (1994), each of these analyses reports that the police use more force against racial minorities than against White suspects. In three of the nine studies in Table 3 (see Smith, 1986; Terrill & Mastrofski, 2002; Worden, 1995) these effects are statistically significant. Five studies (see Engel, et al., 2000; Friedrich, 1980; Garner, et al., 1995; Garner, et al., 2002; Kavanagh, 1994) report that the effect of suspect race is not sufficiently large to be statistically significant. In six of these studies, race is measured as a simple dichotomy—White and nonwhite. In three studies (see Kavanagh, 1994; Garner, et al., 1995; Garner, et al., 2002), suspect race is a three-category measure-White, African-American, and Hispanic.

Table 1: Samples, Data, Models, and Reported Findings about Suspect Race and Sex

Authors	Nature of Sample	Data	Statistical Model	Suspect Race	Suspect Sex
Friedrich (1980)	1,091 police public encounters in high crime precincts in Chicago, Boston and Washington, D.C. in the Summer of 1966	IO	OLS	Not Significant	Not Significant
Smith (1986)	762 nondangerous suspect encounters in 60 neighborhoods in Rochester, St. Louis, and Tampa/St. Petersburg, Summer of 1977	IO	Probit	p < .05	P < .05
Kavanagh (1994)	1,512 arrests in New York Bus Terminal for year beginning July 1990	AR	Logistic	Not Significant	Not Significant
Worden (1995)	1,528 suspect encounters in 60 neighborhoods in Rochester, St. Louis, and Tampa/St. Petersburg, Summer of 1977	IO	MNL	Not Significant	P < .05
Garner et al. (1995)	1,585 adult custody arrests in Phoenix during two weeks in June, 1994	OSR	Logistic /OLS	N.S.	P < .05
Engel, et al. (2000)	1,461 non-traffic suspects in Rochester, St. Louis, and St. Petersburg in 1977	IO	Logistic	Not Significant	Not Significant
Terrill and Mastroski (2002)	3,116 suspect/disputant encounters in high crime precincts in St. Petersburg (Summer, 1997) and Indianapolis (Summer, 1996)	IO	Ordered Probit	P < .05	P < .05
Garner et al. (2002)	7,512 adult custody arrests in six mostly urban jurisdictions during the summer, fall and winter of 1996-1997.	OSR	Logistic/ GLR	Not Significant	P < .05

Data Notes: AR=Arrest reports; IO=Independent observations; OSR=Officer self-reports.

Model Notes: GLR=Generalized Linear Regression; LR =Logistic; MNL=Multinominal logistic; OLS=Ordinary least squares;OP=Ordered probit; P=Probit

Reported Effects: N.S. = Not Statistically Significant; N.R. =Not Reported; p < .05 = statistically significant at p <.05 level.

Table 2: Models of Police Use of Force

Suspect Characteristics	Model 1 (No Race/Sex) B	Sig.	Model 2 (Race Only) B	Sig.	Model 3 (Sex Only) B	Sig.	Model 4 (Race and Sex) B	Sig.
Known to be Assaultive	-0.10	0.79	-0.10	0.78	-0.14	0.72	-0.14	0.71
Known to Carry Weapon	-2.08	0.00	-2.08	0.00	-1.97	0.00	-1.98	0.00
Suspect is Intoxicated	-0.32	0.10	-0.31	0.11	-0.29	0.14	-0.28	0.15
Victim Relationship to Arrestee (Stranger)								
Friend	-1.23	0.00	-1.20	0.00	-1.18	0.00	-1.17	0.00
Family	-1.48	0.00	-1.47	0.00	-1.47	0.00	-1.47	0.00
Victim Not Identified	-0.84	0.00	-0.83	0.00	-0.82	0.00	-0.82	0.00
Nature of Bystanders (No Bystanders)								
Unknown Relationship	0.92	0.00	0.91	0.00	0.92	0.00	0.91	0.00
Stranger to Suspect	0.51	0.06	0.51	0.06	0.52	0.05	0.52	0.05
Friend of Suspect	0.42	0.15	0.42	0.15	0.44	0.12	0.44	0.12
Suspect Family	0.06	0.86	0.05	0.88	0.11	0.77	0.10	0.78
Age of Suspect	-0.07	0.81	-0.03	0.93	-0.08	0.78	-0.05	0.87
Suspect Resistance (Civil)								
Antagonistic	1.12	0.00	1.12	0.00	1.10	0.00	1.11	0.00
Physical Resistance	7.30	0.00	7.30	0.00	7.30	0.00	7.30	0.00
Race of Suspect (White)								
African-American			0.05	0.82			0.02	0.91
Hispanic			0.44	0.13			0.34	0.23
Other			-0.06	0.92			-0.09	0.87
Missing			0.09	0.82			0.06	0.89
Female Suspect					-0.87	0.00	-0.85	0.00
Explained Variance (Eta Squared)	32.2%		31.5%		32.5%		31.8%	

Note: Reported findings based on multivariate tests with an additional 38 encounter level characteristics. See Garner, et al. (2002) for details.

Separate comparisons are reported between White and African-American and White and Hispanic suspects, with similar results.

All of these multivariate studies report that the police use more force against males than females. In five studies (see Garner, et al., 1995; Garner, et al., 2002; Smith, 1986; Terrill & Stephen D. Mastrofski, 2002; Worden, 1995) these effects reach statistical significance and in three studies (see Engel, et al., 2000; Friedrich, 1980; Kavanagh, 1994) they do not. Overall, three studies consistently report statistically significant race and sex effects (see Smith, 1986- Terrill & Mastrofski, 2002; Worden, 1995) and three consistently report non-significant effects (Friedrich, 1980; Kavanagh, 1994; Engel et al., 2000). Garner et al. (1995) and Garner et al. (2002) report statistically significant effects for sex but not for race.

Only the Terrill and Mastrofski (2002) study went beyond statistical significance tests to assess the relative size of the effects of suspect race and sex: they report slightly larger differences in the predicted probabilities of force for male and for non-white suspects. Depending on how police use of force is conceived and measured, these studies use ordinary least squares, logistic, and probit statistical methods. In these analyses, the effects of suspect race and sex are considered as separate, independent measures. None of these analyses report if or how the observed effects of race or sex interact, or if this interaction changes the amount of explained variance in models with and without variables for suspect race or sex.

Despite the fact that suspect race and sex are the two characteristics most consistently tested in the published literature of police use of force, in none of these studies is suspect race or sex the central focus. Friedrich (1980) and Worden (1995) are primarily concerned with the organizational characteristics of the police agencies. Smith's (1986) focus is on neighborhood effects. Engel, et al. (2000) emphasize suspect demeanor. Suspect sex and race are just two of many suspect traits analyzed by Kavanagh (1994), Garner, et al, (199 5), Garner et al. (2002) and Terrill and Mastrofski (2002) and these suspect characteristics are given no special attention or meaning in their conclusions. In general, this literature recognizes the social salience of race and the inappropriateness of its use as a policy or practice in any aspect of policing, but there is considerably less attention to the meaning of suspect sex and whether increased use of force against males is as inappropriate as increased use of force against racial minorities.

Other Racial and Sexual Patterns of Police Behavior

The use of force is not the only area in which police integrity has been challenged based on complaints that the police behave differently based on the sex or the race of victims or suspects. Research during the 1970s and 80s identified potential problems with how the police were responding to domestic violence cases, particularly those incidents involving females assaulted by their husbands. Several scholars documented policies and reported on research that suggested that police were not arresting male suspects when the victim or complainant was an intimate partner (Elliott, 1989; Ferraro, 1989). In addition, several successful liability lawsuits against police departments found that police in several cites had policies or practices that lead their officers not to make domestic violence arrests. Questions have also been raised about the use of racial profiling by police officers to initiate legitimate police activities (Harris, 1999). In this context, racial profiling is seen as police-initiated actions that use race, ethnicity, or national origin as the basis, rather than an individual's behavior, or an officer's prior knowledge about the individual (Ramirez & Farrell, 2000). While other studies and analyses of these studies have called into question the validity of these early findings (U.S. General Accounting Office, 2000; McMahon, et al, 2003; Felson and Ackerman, 2000), the point is that in a number of areas-police use of force, domestic violence, and traffic stops— police integrity has been tested by the use of statistical analyses of the effects of race and sex on police behavior.

Patterns as a Measure of Police Integrity

Our concept of police integrity is related to the terminology and definition of police integrity used by the Public Integrity Section of the U.S. Department of Justice. The Violent Crime Control and Law Enforcement Act of 1994 prohibits governmental authorities from engaging in "a pattern or practice of conduct by law enforcement officials" that deprives persons of "rights, privileges, or immunities secured or protected by the Constitution or laws of the United States" (42 U. S. C. § 14141(a)). Whenever the Attorney General has reasonable cause to believe that a violation has occurred, the Justice Department is authorized to bring legal action "to eliminate the pattern or practice." (42 U. S.C. § 14141(b)). Based on this authority, the Justice Department has investigated complaints against several large urban police agencies. Despite the increasingly common use of the term "pattern or practice" neither the Crime Control Act of 1994 or the related case law has provided a clear determination of what constitutes a "pattern" or a "practice" (Livingston, 1999). Suits and threats of suits arising from these investigations have resulted in a number of consent decrees between the Justice Department and a variety of jurisdictions but these legal actions have not resulted in a consistent understanding of this term. The U.S. Supreme Court, in interpreting previous legislation using similar language, has ruled that

> [A] pattern or practice would be present only where the denial of rights consists of something more than an isolated, sporadic incident, but is repeated, routine, or of a generalized nature.... Single, insignificant, isolated acts of discrimination by a single business would not justify a finding of a pattern or practice.(International Brotherhood of Teamsters v. United States, 431 U.S. 324, 336.)

Based on his reading of the Justice Department complaints in these suits and judicial rulings in earlier legislation using similar language, Miller (1998) suggests that a few related rights violations may be sufficient if accompanied by evidence of organizational policies or practices condoning these violations. He also suggests that a larger pattern of police behavior would be needed without evidence of organizational practices

Our conception brings social scientific standards to defining a pattern. We rely not on the existence of a few instances of allegedly brutal, corrupt or illegal behavior by some police officers, but a pattern of behavior detected in a systematic review of officer behavior in an entire agency. This conception may be a more stringent and a more lenient criteria for determining a pattern of police misconduct. It calls for the examination of a representative sample of police behavior but it considers behaviors, such as the normal use of force, which would not normally be considered in Department of Justice suits. Our definition is similar to that used by Harris (1999) and others to establish the existence of racial profiling in police traffic stops. We differ from Harris's approach in that we would go beyond the use of simple bivariate analyses of suspect race and police behavior and use contemporary scientific standards for multivariate tests of competing explanations of police behavior before determining that an inappropriate pattern of police behavior existed.

Testing for Patterns in Police Use of Force

Based on a sample of 7,512 adult custody arrests in six urban U.S. jurisdictions, the analyses reported here rely on the confidential self-reports from police officers to measure the amount of force used by and against a suspect. Using a detailed checklist, arresting officers reported after each arrest what they said (commands, shouts, cursing, or conversational voice), what types of restraints they used (handcuffing, leg cufs, hobbles or other restraints), which weaponless tactics they used (gentle hold, grabbing, pushing, shoving, wrestling, hitting, punching, kicking, or control holds), and which weapons they used or threatened to use (baton, chemical agent, flashlight, canine, handgun, rifle or shotgun). We did not record whether officers searched or patted down suspects and this information is not used in our measure of the severity of force.

In this research, we measure the quantity or severity of force by capturing the ranking of 5 7 types of police behavior on a scale from one to 100. The ranking used is based on the average ranking provided by 503 police officers from five of the six participating jurisdictions and ranged from a low of 15.6 for 'police speak in a conversational tone' to a high of 81.7 for 'police use handgun'. The average ranking was 30.0 and the modal category was handcuffing ranked at 28.2. We then used these rankings, along with what the police officers reported they did or said., to determine the amount of force in that arrest based on our one to 100 ranking of police behaviors. When officers reported that they engaged in two or more forceful acts, we recorded the highest ranking item, hence the name for the measure of severity of force. Across all 7,512 arrests, the average severity of force measure is 30.4; the modal rank is 28.2— police use of handcuffs. For details on the measurement of police use of force see Garner and Maxwell (1999).

Our research approach differs in four important ways from two other study designs that have been used to measure police use of non-lethal force-independent observations and official use of force reports. The first difference is in the comprehensiveness of the sample studied. Observational studies typically use samples of all police suspect encounters by volunteer officers in high activity precincts, work shifts and days of the week. Studies based on official use of force reports cover all officers, precincts, shifts and days of the week but do not include direct measures of police public encounters that do not involve force. The scope of our research covers all officers, precincts, shifts and days of the week but misses police behavior that occurs without an arrest being made. This design strengthens our ability to assess systematic behavior within a department or across several departments.

The second difference is the independence of the measure of force and incident characteristics. Observational studies are based on the coding and narrative accounts of trained observers that promise confidentiality to the observed officers and our research uses self-reports by officers but also provided confidentiality to police officers. While there is a presumption of higher reliability or at least less bias in independent reporting, no study of police use of force has used multiple types of measures and assessed the extent of the differences between self-report and independent observation.

The third major difference is how force is measured. None of the studies of police use of force research use the same measure of force, even when the analyses are based on the same samples and raw measures (for a detailed comparison see Garner, et al., 2002). Studies that rely on official use of force forms tend to be limited to a small number of higher severity police behaviors, such as weapon use. Our research captures a wide range of verbal and physical actions, all of which are ranked on the one to 100 scale. Observational studies vary greatly among themselves in the range of police behaviors measured and considered to be force and a recent observational study (Terrill, 2000; Terrill & Mastrofski, 2002) has demonstrated that design's potential to included handcuffing, searches and pat downs as uses of force.

The fourth major difference in this study is our emphasis on a variety of encounter level characteristics of the nature of the offense, the arrest location, the mobilization of the police, the police officer and the suspect. The number and range of encounter level considerations in this study exceeds those of other multi-variate studies of police use of force and this lessens the likelihood that our analyses will be incorrect. While most of the prior analyses are also limited to encounter level characteristics, some studies have considered attitudinal characteristics of officers, the organizational characteristics of the law enforcement agencies studied or the characteristics of the neighborhoods in which the police operate and we do not. We control for base level differences in the six jurisdictions participating in this research but we do not incorporate systematic information about the sites into our statistical analyses.

There are strengths and weaknesses to these and other approaches to studying police use of force and no one approach or set of measures is likely to be preferred for all research purposes. In this study, we use one sample, one measure and two statistical analyses to provide empirical tests to illustrate how we address the nature and meaning of the cumulative findings about the association between the suspect's race and the suspect's sex on police use of force. Unlike most of the prior research, we have a large and diverse sample of arrested suspects. While most of the prior research is limited to contrasting White suspects with nonwhite suspects, our design includes a comparison of White suspects with African-American suspects, Hispanic suspects and suspects of other races-Asian, American Indian, etc.. For these reasons, our large and diverse sample makes it possible for us to test for the possibility of any interaction between suspect race and suspect sex. All of the prior multivariate studies of police use of force have been limited to testing for the direct effects of suspect race or sex but never whether there are combinations of race and sex against which the police use increased amounts of force.[1]

In this chapter[2], we report the association of seven suspect characteristics and suspect race and sex with the severity of police use of force. We report these results in four separate models to assess how the additive and joint effect of race and sex impact the patterns of police use of force. This format permits a ready comparison of not only the direction, size and statistical significance of the individual regression coefficients but also the amount of variance explained by models that do and do not consider suspect race or suspect sex.

Among the seven characteristics reported here (**see Model I in Table 2**), four explain some variation in the amount of force used by the police officers. These four measures include: suspect known to carry a weapon, all three categories of the suspect-victim relationship, one of the four categories of the suspect-bystander relationship, and both types of suspect resistance. The level of suspect resistance was the single largest predictor of force. While both types of resistance significantly increased the level of force, the use of physical resistance by the suspect substantially increased the level of force used by the police officers. The suspect's age and their intoxication were not related to the use of force and neither was the police officer's belief that the suspect was present.

The second model in Table 2 adds one additional term, the suspect's race to model 1; the third model adds a term for suspect sex, but does not include suspect race. The last model in Table 2 includes terms for both race and sex in an additive format. The results of the second model show that in our sample of 7,512 arrests in six jurisdictions, when compared to Whites, no other racial category on average had significantly more or less force used against them. The results from the third model show that female suspects when compared to males have significantly less force used against them. When we consider both the suspect race and the suspect sex in Model 4, the results do not change-there are sexual but no racial differences. In an analysis of the ten possible combinations of race and sex (including categories for missing data), we found that, compared to the modal category of White Males, less force was used against African-American Females and White Females. We found more, not less, force used against Hispanic Females but this effect was not statistically significant[3]. In all other comparisons, there were no statistically significant differences in the amount of force used.

In terms of the overall quality of the linear models, neither the addition of race nor sex, nor the combination of these two measures substantially increased the quantity of the explained variance (Eta Squared). Our initial model (**see Table 2**) accounted for nearly 32% of the variance, the addition of the race measure actually dropped the explained variance by 0.7%, while the addition of the sex measure increased the explained variance by 0. 1 %. The combination of both race and sex and the interaction of race and sex, also dropped the quantity of explained variance from the initial model. Thus, adding the suspect's race actually resulted in less model accuracy and the addition of sex increased the model accuracy by only 1%.

Summary and Discussion

In this chapter we sought to expand the idea of studying the "patterns and practices" that has recently developed in the police literature to more fully connect the issues of police use of force and police integrity. We assessed whether there are patterns of inequitable police use of force across sex and racial groups using traditional standards of sociological research. If differences between races or sexes are found, we argue that this calls into question the integrity of the police even though no single instance of force may be unjustifiable. The results of this research are that the quantity or average amount of force used by the police during a typical arrest is about equal across racial categories. We interpret these findings as supportive of police integrity in the departments studied. However, the quantity of force was greater against male suspects when compared to female suspects and we interpret these findings as supportive of the lack of police integrity, especially since we have controlled for a large number of other encounter level characteristics including suspect resistance. Although our interpretation of these findings as a measure of departmental integrity is relatively novel, the findings concerning the effects of suspect race and sex are consistent with the majority of the prior research on police use of force. The cumulative evidence from systematic research on police use of force is that the departmental integrity of the police may be less challenged by the issue of race and more challenged by issue of sex.

Because of the nature of our sample, we were able to diagnose whether there is an interaction between the suspect's race and sex, and we found that there is. We found that the police in our six Jurisdictions, on average, used less force used against the 600 African American women than against the 2,22 1 White males and that these differences were statistically significant. We also found that the 126 Hispanic females in our study experienced more force than the White males. The differences were not statistically significant but this may be due, in part, to the relatively small sample sizes, not the absence of a real effect. These results have implications for investigations of the integrity of police agencies. Although the popular and scientific literature have emphasized the importance of differences between White and African- American suspects in the use of force, our findings suggest that future investigation of the integrity of the police should investigate further whether police departments systematically use more force against Hispanic suspects, especially Hispanic females.

On the basis of our results, we are not arguing that there are no instances of excessive and brutal force used by the police against African-Americans and other racial minorities, or that police regularly use excessive force against male suspects. The newspapers and the T.V. are replete with graphic descriptions of these incidents and police historians describe numerous instances of police brutality against immigrants and minorities over the 150 years of American policing (Escobar 1999; Grimshaw 1969c). We are not saying that there are no additional instances that involve the use of some force by the police that are justifiable in the abstract, but that after further in-depth review may involve strong racial overtones (see for example Crouch 2000; Russell 2000). Furthermore, we are also not claiming that excessive or unjustifiable amounts of force are not more frequently used against minorities than against White suspects. Our study is about the amount of force used, not whether that force was justifiable or excessive and our findings must be understood in that context. Based upon our analysis of more than 7,500 confidential police surveys (and the reports of prior research), we find that there is not a pattern of more force used against minorities during an arrest, but that using the same data and same methodological tests, there is more force used against males than females, even when controlling for the nature of suspect resistance and several dozen other encounters level characteristics.

Using the same data, methods and criteria that were applied to assessing the lack of police integrity with regard to equity between races, our findings with regard to suspect sex suggest the lack of integrity for law enforcement agencies. Our findings and the dominant findings in the prior research are that the use of force by law enforcement agencies is not, on average, provided in an equitable manner for males and females. The existence and size of effects for suspect sex but not race suggest fruitful avenues of empirical, ethical and legal inquiry concerning differences in the existence and import of racial and sexual equity in police operations. For instance, does the existence of statistically significant effects for suspect sex mean the same thing as statistically significant effects for suspect race? To what extent should law enforcement agencies address the question of disproportionate use of force against male suspects. Our empirical findings concerning the effects of suspect race and sex conform to the majority findings of prior research; unlike prior research, we emphasize the importance of these findings in terms of police integrity. While our research and all prior research on police use of force are subject to numerous caveats (See below), we believe that the many strengths of our research puts the balance of the evidence on the issue of suspect race in support of police integrity, but that the balance of the evidence on the issue of suspect sex raises questions about the integrity of contemporary police use of force practices.

Caveats

This research has a number of limitations. First, we sample arrests and do not capture use of force that may occur when an arrest is not made. At the present time, there is no systematic evidence about how much force or what type of force occurs in these non-arrest encounters. However, the possibility that some uses of force in this context are missed in studies, is real. Second, this research is based on officer self-reports and there is a presumption of bias in all self- reports, even under conditions of confidentiality. Again, we have no research which uses multiple sources of data about police suspect encounters to calibrate the similarities and dissimilarities in self-report measures and independent observations or the impact of confidentiality protections. Third, this research was conducted in a small number of volunteer law enforcement agencies. The behavior of police in these jurisdictions may not be easily generalizable to other jurisdictions but this is also true of all research on police use of force that use a small number of jurisdictions. Fourth, this research did not include neighborhood or organizational characteristics that might moderate the effect of race or sex. We believe, however, that the strengths of this research outweigh its potential weaknesses and that our knowledge of police use of force is improved by focusing on the combination of race and sex, while simultaneously considering a number of other suspect and encounter level characteristics. Lastly, although we incorporated a large number and diverse range of encounter level characteristics in our model, it is possible that our basic model of police use of force is not fully specified and that our estimated effects for suspect sex are spurious. While the effects we found for suspect sex were statistically significant, the inclusion of suspect sex did not appreciably increase the amount of variance explained. This suggests that the size of the effect of suspect sex is not large and that the effect for suspect sex might not be found in research with better specified models that use improved measures of police use of force and controls for neighborhood characteristics, organizational characteristics of law enforcement agencies, or encounter level characteristics not considered here.

Endnotes

[1]Our data collection resulted in some arrests where the race or the sex of the suspect was unknown. We retained those arrests in our analyses by creating a category for suspects whose race or sex was missing.

[2]These results were extracted from a larger analysis of the nature of the arrest situation, the location of the arrest, how the police were mobilized and characteristics of the arresting officer and the suspect. For details of these analyses, see Garner, et al. (2002).

[3]This sample included 632 White Females, 600 African-American Females and 126 Hispanic Females.

References

Bell, D. (2000). Police brutality: Portent of disaster and discomforting divergence. In J. Nelson (Ed.), *Police Brutality: An Anthology* (pp. 88-10 1). New York, NY: W.W. Norton and Co.

Conditt Jr., J. H. (200 1). Institutional Integrity: The four elements of self-policing. *FBI Law Enforcement Bulletin* (Washington, D.C.), 18-22.

Criminal Justice Commission. (1997). *Integrity in the Queensland Police Service: Implementation and impact of the Fitzgerald Inquire Reforms.* Brisbane: Author.

Crouch, S. (2000). What's New? The truth, as usual. In J. Nelson (Ed.), *Police Brutality* (pp. 157-168). W. W. Norton & Co: New York.

Elliott, D. S. (1989). Criminal justice procedures in family violence crimes. In L. Ohlin & M. Tonry (Eds.), *Family Violence* (Vol. 11, pp. 427-480). Crime and justice: an annual review of research. Chicago: University of Chicago Press.

Engel, R. S., Sobol, J., & Worden, R. (2000). Further exploration of the demeanor hypothesis: The interaction effects of suspects' characteristics and demeanor on police behavior. *Justice Quarterly*, 17(2), 235-258.

Escobar, E. J. (1999). *Latinos in American Society and Culture* (M. T. Garcia, Ed.). Berkeley, CA: University of California Press.

Felson, R. & Ackerman, J. (200 1). Arrest for Domestic Violence and Other Assaults. *Criminology*, 39:655-676.

Ferraro, K. J. (1989). Policing women battering. *Social Problems*, 36(l), 61-72.

Forst, B. (2000). The Privatization and Civilianization of Policing. In C. M. Friel (Ed.), *Boundary changes in criminal justice organizations* (Vol. 2, pp. 19-79). Criminal Justice 2000. Washington, DC: U.S. Department of Justice, Office of Justice Programs, National Institute of Justice (NCJ 182410).

Friedrich, R. J. (1980). Police use of force: Individuals, situations and organizations. *The Annals of the American Academy of Political and Social Science*, 452, 82-97.

Garner, J. H., Buchanan, J., Schade, T., Hepburn, J., Fagan, J., & Mulcahy, A. (1995). *Understanding the Use of Force by and Against the Police* (Final Report to National Institute of Justice, 92-IN-CX-KO28). Newark, NJ: Rutgers University.

Garner, J. & Maxwell, C. D. (1999). "Measuring the Amount of Force Used By and Against the Police in Six Jurisdictions". (Pp. 25-44) *Use of Force by Police: Overview of National and Local Data*, Washington, D.C.: National Institute of Justice.

Garner, J., Maxwell, C. D., & Heraux, C. (2002). Characteristics Associated with the Prevalence and Severity of Force Used by the Police. *Justice Quarterly*, 19(4) 705-746.

Grimshaw, A. D. (1969). Actions of police and the military in American race riots. In A. Grimshaw (Ed.), *Racial Violence in the United States* (pp. 269-286). Chicago: Aldine Publishing Co.

Hanewicz, W. B. (1985). Discretion and order. In F. Elliston & M. Feldberg (Eds.), *Moral Issues in Police Work* (pp. 43-54). Totowa, NJ: Rowan and Allanheld.

Harris, D. A. (1999). Driving While Black: Racial Profiling on our Nation's Highways. American Civil Liberties Union.

Kavanagh, J. (1994). *The occurrence of force in arrest encounters*. Ph.D. Dissertation submitted to the School of Criminal Justice, Rutgers University, Newark, NJ.

Livingston, D. (1999). Police Reform and the Department of Justice: An Essay in Accountability. *Buffalo Criminal Law Review*, 2: 815-837.

Miller, M. (1999), Note: Police Brutality, *Yale Law and Policy Review*, 17: 149-186.

McMahon, J., Garner, J., Davis, R., & Kraus, A. (2002). *How to Correctly Collect and Analyze Racial Profiling Data: Your Reputation Depends On It*, Final Report for: Racial Profiling-Data Collection and Analysis. Washington, DC: Government Printing Office.

Nelson, J. (2000). *Police Brutality: An Anthology*. New York, NY: W.W. Norton and Co.

Pedersen, D. (2001). Rising above corruption: How to put integrity at the forefront in your department. *Law Enforcement Technology*, 28(10), 136-142.

Ramirez, D., McDevitt, & Farrell, A. (2000). *A Resource Guide on Racial Profiling Data Collection System* (Northeastern University No. NCJ 184768). Washington, D.C.: U.S. Department of Justice (67).

Russell, K. "What Did I Do to Be So Black and Blue?" Police Violence and the Black Community. *In Police Brutality*, edited by Jill Nelson, 135-48. W. W. Norton & Co: New York, 2000.

Smith, D. A. (1986). The neighborhood context of police behavior. In A. Reiss & M. Tonry (Eds.), *Communities and Crime* (Vol. 8, pp. 313-341). Crime and Justice. Chicago, IL: University of Chicago Press.

Terrill, W. (2000). *Police coercion: Application of the force continuum*. Unpublished doctoral dissertation, Rutgers, State University of New Jersey, School of Criminal Justice.

Terrill, W., & Mastrofski, S. D. (2002). Situational and Officer Based Determinants of Police Coercion. *Justice Quarterly*, 19(2), 215- 248

U.S. General Accounting Office. (2000). *Racial Profiling: Limited Data Available on Motorist Stops*. (Tech. Rep. No. GAO/GGD-00-41). Washington, D.C.: Government Accounting Office.

Walker, S., & Katz, C. M. (2002). *The Police in America*. New York, NY: McGraw Hill.

Williams, H. (1986). Maintaining police integrity: Municipal policing in the United States. *Police Studies*, 9(l), 27-3 1.

Williams, P. J. (2000). Obstacle Illusions: *The Cult of Racial Appearance*. In J. Nelson (Ed.), *Police Brutality* (pp. 149-156). W. W. Norton & Co: New York.

Worden, R. (1995). The causes of police brutality: Theory and evidence on police use of force. In W. Geller & H. Toch (Eds.), *And Justice For All: Understanding and Controlling Police Use of Force* (pp. 23 - 5 1). Washington, D.C.: Police Executive Research Forum.

7

Citizen Behavior and Police Use of Force: An Examination of National Survey Data

Steven K. Smith[1], U.S. Department of Justice, Bureau of Justice Statistics

Introduction

During 1999 about 44 million persons in the U.S. said they experienced at least one face to face contact with the police. Among those with personal contact, 422,000 said the police officer used or threatened to use force during the encounter. This chapter takes an in-depth look at the population experiencing police use of force in the U.S. Specifically, the circumstances of the incident and the conduct reported by the citizen as well as their description of police actions are examined. The findings described here are from a Bureau of Justice Statistics nationally representative survey of approximately 80,000 persons aged 16 years or older, the largest survey of its kind to look at citizen contacts with the police. (Footnote: Initial findings from the BPS survey were reported in *Contact between Police and the Public: Findings from the National Survey*, February 2001, NCJ-184957. Note also that, as of this writing, the 2002 Police Public Contact Survey is in the field.) Findings from this national level survey are examined in the context of previous local studies regarding police use of force. A discussion is also provided assessing the methodological issues in using a household-based survey to gather incident-level information on police use of force as arc recommendations for future research directions.

While the authority to use force distinguishes law enforcement from other agencies responsible for delivering public services, it is difficult to capture systematic information about the specific circumstances under which force is used. Although citizen experience with police use of force is relatively rare, it has the capacity to impact police-citizen relations well beyond those immediately involved. Various studies, using a range of methodological approaches, have looked at the numerous elements of police-citizen relations including the prevalence of police use of force, public attitudes towards police performance, and attitudes related to police misconduct. However, systematic national-level data of the magnitude analyzed here, on actual police-citizen contacts and use of force incidents based on data from citizen respondents, has heretofore not been available.

The different methods used to examine police use of force—official agency records, police officer surveys, observational studies, and local citizen surveys—generally concur that, when similarly defined, it is a fairly rare event. Adams (1999), Terrill (2001), and Garner, et al (2002) each provide a useful review of findings from recent studies which have looked at police use of force and the behavior of the citizen. Garner et al (2002) provide a particularly comprehensive and useful review, including Garner's (1996) work in Phoenix, which relied on officer and citizen interviews and officer reports and Mastrofski's (1998) observational studies in Indianapolis and St. Petersburg, Florida. Both studies confirmed that the use of force is fairly rare. Furthermore, prior studies also indicate that the types of force most commonly used by police converge at the less serious, lower end of the force continuum—primarily pushing and grabbing. A national prevalence measure of police use of force against citizens was first generated during the 1996 BPS pilot survey which found about 440,000 persons said they experienced force (Bureau of Justice Statistics, 1997). In 1999, the estimate was 422,000. The difference between these estimates was not statistically significant.

Several local citizen surveys have confirmed these national level findings. For example, Son, et al (1997:156-157) analyzed survey data from 992 Ohio residents and found "only 0.3 percent of all respondents reported that they had personally experienced excessive force or other types of physical abuse from the police in the 12 months preceding the survey."

Methodology

The survey data examined here represent the largest national sample of households that have been queried about their interaction with the police. Approximately 80,000 persons age 16 or older in nearly 40,000 households were interviewed as a supplement to the National Crime Victimization Survey (NCVS) during the last six months of 19992 . The methodology was similar to that used in the 1996 pilot test but was expanded to include a much larger sample of households.

The NCVS relies on a stratified, multi-stage, cluster sample based on housing units across the Nation. The primary sampling units are made up of counties or large metropolitan areas. Within a sampled PSU, clusters of approximately four housing units or their equivalent are selected. The NCVS interviews each resident in the sampled household age 12 or older. (Footnote: For detailed discussion of NCVS methodology see *Criminal Victimization in the United States, 1999 Statistical Tables*, January 2001, NCJ-1 184938.) The 1999 Police-Public Contact Survey appeared as a supplement to the standard NCVS questionnaire and was administered to all sampled household residents age 16 or older. In total, 80,543 persons completed the 1999 PPCS which included 16,424 persons with police contact, and 138 persons who said force was used or threatened against them by the police. Sample weights were applied to the estimates generated by the survey to represent national population figures.

Historical overview of national data collection

The Violent Crime Control and Law Enforcement Act of 1994 provided the Attorney General with the authority "to obtain, through civil action, appropriate equitable and declaratory relief in cases in which police pattern or practice deprived persons of their constitutional rights and privileges." (*Footnote: See 42 USC 14141.*) Furthermore, section 210402 of Title XXI of the Act, Subtitle D, Police Pattern and Practice, directed the Attorney General "through appropriate means [to] acquire data about use of excessive force by law enforcement officers." The Attorney General was also directed to "publish an annual summary of the data acquired under this section."

As part of the response to this legislative directive to gather data on use of force incidents, the Bureau of Justice Statistics (BPS) of the U.S. Department of Justice designed and implemented a national household survey to collect data on people's experience with the police, especially to generate estimates regarding the extent and characteristics of police use of force. (Footnote: In 1996, BPS fielded a pilot test using similar questions for what would later become the national sample in 1999; *Police Use of Force: Collection of National Data*, Bureau of Justice Statistics, November 1997, NC J-165040.) Respondents were specifically asked about any face-to-face contact they may have had with the police during the 12 months prior to the time of interview. Respondents were instructed to exclude any contacts with private security guards, social interactions, or contacts with police that were related to them. Also excluded were regular job-related contacts with the police.

Survey Findings

The nearly 422,000 persons who said they experienced police threat or use of force during a 12 month period primarily described low-level, non-injurious encounters with the police. In fact, about one-quarter of those among the 422,000 said the police only threatened force. Other indicators that force used by police tends to be of a less serious nature include findings displayed in **Table 1** that relatively few persons involved in a force incident reported that they had suffered an injury (15%), sought medical attention (9%), or filed any sort of formal complaint against the officer(s) (14%).

Table 1

Total persons reporting a police use of force incident, by whether they were injured, received medical treatment, or filed a complaint-as a result of the incident, 1999

Total persons with force contact	422,000 (100%)
injured	64,000 (15%)
received medical treatment*	36,000(9%)
filed formal complaint	60,000 (14%)

*includes emergency services, self-treatment, and doctor visits.

Police action

In the 1999 PPCS respondents who said they had experienced police use of force were asked to describe the kind of force or threat of force that the police used. Police have a range of options available to them during face-to-face contacts with citizens. Depending on the nature of the contact, force may be used. The choice of police use of force is generally applied through a continuum that is part of an established agency policy (Desmedt, 1984; Alpert, 1999). In the PPCS, the range of police use of force actions were read to the respondent but were not presented to the respondent as a scale of seriousness (see **figure 1**).

Figure 1:
Types of police use of force actions provided to the survey respondent:

What type of physical force did the police officer(s) use or threaten to
        use during this incident?
Did the police officer(s): Actually push or grab you in a way
        that did not cause pain?
Actually push or grab you in a way that did cause pain?
Actually kick or hit you with the police officer's hand or something held in the
        police officer's hand?
Actually unleash a police dog that bit you?
Actually spray you with a chemical or pepper spray?
Actually point a gun at you but did not shoot?
Actually fire a gun at you?
Threaten to push or grab you?
Threaten to kick or hit you with the police officer's hand or something held in
the police officer's hand?
Threaten you with a police dog?
Threaten to spray you with a chemical or pepper spray?
Threaten to fire a gun at you?

Table 2 presents both police actions and reported citizen behavior. The different actions by police and citizen are arranged by their frequency of occurrence during a force incident. As detailed in Table 2, these actions generally align themselves to most force continua. As one moves across the force continuum from the least serious to the most serious uses of force, the number of citizens reporting that kind of force becomes much smaller. As indicated in Table 2, most people in a force situation reported that the police used force on the lower end of the continuum, that is primarily grabbing and pushing. More than one-third (37%) said they police pushed or grabbed them in manner that did not result in pain. Thirty-five percent said they were pushed and grabbed by the police which did result in pain.

The national household survey did not find any respondents who said that the police threatened them with a police dog or actually unleashed a police dog on them. Furthermore, the use of a weapon by a police officer, or for that matter a citizen, generally considered at the outer edge of the force continuum, was not observed among the 80,000 respondents.

In more than 90% of the police-public contacts in which force was reportedly used, the police officer initiated the contact, usually in a traffic-related context. Among all police use of force cases, it was rare that the contact was originally initiated by the citizen's request for police assistance.

Citizen behavior during force incidents

A variety of studies have examined citizen behavior and demeanor during police contacts to assess their impact on corresponding police action. The effect of citizen demeanor toward the police on police behavior has been examined by Terrill (2002), Engel, et al (2000), and Klinger (1995). Survey data from the PPCS do not provide the opportunity to assess demeanor as do observational techniques. This prevents the data user from establishing a potential cause and effect relationship between the action of the citizen and that of the officer. However, as a proxy, data can be collected directly from the respondent regarding the actions they took during the force incident.

The PPCS recorded citizen action during the incident in two ways. Firstly, respondents were asked directly if they thought anything they might have done during the incident provoked the police into using or threatening to use force against them. Approximately 25% of those involved in a police use of force incident said they thought their own actions provoked the police. Secondly, the survey asked the respondent if, during the incident, they engaged in any of a series of behaviors listed in figure 2, regardless of whether they thought they may have provoked the police.

Figure 2:

List of actions asked of citizens during police use of force incident:

At any time during this incident did you:
argue with or disobey the police officer(s)
curse at, insult, or call the police officer(s) a name
say something threatening to the police officer(s)
resist being handcuffed or arrested
resist being searched or having the vehicle searched
try to escape by hiding, running away, or being in a high-speed chase
grab, hit, or fight with police officer(s)
use a weapon to threaten the police officer(s)
use a weapon to assault the police officer(s)

(Also of interest in the study of police use of force is the percentage of people who said they used physical force against the police and had force used against them by the police. However, this national sample did not contain a sufficient number for analysis of persons who said they used force against the police during an incident in which police used force. Overall four respondents, weighted to 9,999 persons said they used force against the police, preventing a detailed examination of this phenomenon.)

Approximately 48% of the persons involved in a force incident did not report doing any of the listed actions during the police encounter. This does not include drinking or using drugs at the time of the incident. The data do not allow examination of cases in which citizens exhibited certain potentially provocative behaviors and police force was not used because people who did not report a police use of force were not asked about their own behavior during their police interaction.

The types of actions exhibited by the citizens during the force incident are displayed in Table 2. What is the nexus between the behavior citizens reported displaying during the force incident and the force used by police? Half (51 %), or 217,112, of all the persons responding that they had experienced force by the police said they did one of the behaviors listed in figure 2. Of the more than 400,000 persons reporting a force incident with police, the most common scenarios involved the citizen, either reporting that they had done nothing, or that they were arguing or disobeying the officer and the officer pushed or grabbed the citizen which was reported to have caused pain. Three other scenarios which were among the next most common interactions also involved the citizen arguing or disobeying the officer. Citizens who reported a more serious behavior during the police use of force incident were somewhat more likely to have also reported that more than one type of police action or threat of force action was used against them.

However, not all of those that admitted to having done "something" thought that their behavior had provoked the police into using force. Slightly less than half (47%) of the persons who acknowledged doing one or more of a series of listed behaviors also said they thought their actions may have provoked the police. The other half did not think their actions provoked the police.

Formal charges: A force incident with the police did not necessarily mean the person faced formal charges for their behavior. Only about half of the individuals involved in a force incident were formally charged with an offense. This included traffic offenses as well as the more serious charges of resisting arrest and assaulting an officer. Excluding traffic citations, only about one-third were formally charged by the police during the force incident.

Persons who experienced police use of force were not always arrested during the incident. Overall, 42% of those that said force was used against them were also arrested by the police. Within the universe of cases where force was used, half of those persons who said they did any of the actions listed in figure 2 were arrested. Not surprisingly, persons with a force incident that were most likely to be arrested were those that said they resisted being handcuffed or arrested or tried to escape or

Table 2.

1999 Police Public
Contact Survey

Citizen behavior during force incident by type of police use of force reported by the citizen, 1999

Type of Police action	all persons reporting police use of force	persons who did nothing during incident	persons who argued or disobeyed police	persons who cursed or insulted police	persons who said something threatening to police	persons who resisted search by police	persons who resisted handcuffing or arrest	persons who tried to escape or hide from police*	persons who grabbed hit or fought with police*
push/grab, no pain	37%	45%	19%	9%	19%	55%	34%	68%	0
push/grab, pain	35	30	42	47	40	18	67	32	78
point gun, no shoot	15	19%	11	11	7	0	22	0	0
threaten to push grab	13	7%	18	13	14	29	8	0	0
kick or hit	10	6%	7	20	18	8	16	64	19
threatened to hit	8	5%	16	17	35	32	0	0	0
used chemical spray	5	1%	6	16	0	0	0	32	0
threatened to shoot	5	7%	0	0	0	0	17	32	62
threatened to spray	4	3%	6	9	8	0	0	0	0
unleash dog that bit	0	0	0	0	0	0	0	0	0
threaten with dog	0	0	0	0	0	0	0	0	0
fire a gun	0	0	0	0	0	0	0	0	0
total**	131%	123%	126%	142%	141%	150%	164%	228%	159%
total persons	421714	204602	152920	60845	38242	31658	30506	21382	9994

**Totals may exceed 100% as multiple responses were permitted.

*based on less than 10 cases

Source: Bureau of Justice Statistics Police-Public Contact Survey, 1999

Table 3.

Percent of citizens arrested during police use of force incident by type of reported citizen behavior, 1999

1999 Police Public Contact Survey

	total persons reporting police use of force during the force incident, 1999	total argue or disobey	total curse or insult	total say someth threatening	total resist search	total resist hand or arrest	total escape or hide	total grab, hit, or fight officer
total persons	-421,714	-152,920	-60,845	-38,242	-31,658	-30,506	-21,382	-9,994
percent arrested	42%	45%	53%	42%	41%	85%	76%	60%

Source: Bureau of Justice Statistics, Police-Public Contact Survey, 1999

hide from the officer. The rest had an even probability or less of being arrested despite their reported action against the police. Klockars (1995) also reported that an arrest did not necessarily occur in conjunction police use of force. Police may have used force, pushing and/or grabbing, to defuse or de-escalate a potentially violent situation. However, once deescalated, an arrest may not be deemed necessary.

Handcuffing

The 1999 PPCS reported slightly more than I million persons were handcuffed during the 12 month period. As displayed in Table 5, only 19 percent of those who were handcuffed during their police contact also reported having had forced used against them. Likewise, not all persons involved in a force incident with the police ended up being handcuffed. The PPCS found that about half (52%) of the persons in a police use of force situation were handcuffed during the incident. By comparison, about 3% of all the persons who reported being stopped by the police during a traffic stop were handcuffed.

Table 5:
Persons handcuffed by the police by whether they also had forced used against them, 1999

Handcuff only (no force)	955,497 (81%)
Handcuff and force	218,672 (19%)
Total handcuffed	1,174,169 (100%)

Table 6 indicated that somewhat more than half (55%) the people reportedly involved in a force incident were also either handcuffed or arrested, 39% were both arrested and handcuffed.

Table 6:
Percent of citizens involved in a police use of force incident by whether they were also arrested and/or handcuffed, 1999

Total force	(422,000) 100%
Arrested only	3%*
Handcuffed only	13%
Arrested and handcuffed	39%
No other additional action	45%

*based on fewer than 10 cases

Table 7:
Percent of citizens arrested during a police use of force incident that were also charged with a crime, 1999

Arrested during force incident	(175,352)
charged with crime	64%*
not charged with crime	36%
Total	100%

*excludes traffic citations

Overall not everyone involved in a police use of force encounter was formally charged with a crime. About one-third of all the citizens involved in a forceful police encounter were charged. Likewise, as indicated in Table 7 not all citizens who were arrested during a police use of force incident were also formally charged with a criminal violation. About two-thirds (64%) of those arrested during a police use of force incident were eventually charged with a crime.

Use of drugs and alcohol during incident

The frequent involvement of drugs and or alcohol by persons engaged in criminal activity has been documented through a variety of studies including the review of police arrest records and surveys of citizens, arrestees, and inmates (Greenfeld, 1998). The *1999 Police-Public Contact Survey* asked citizens who had force incidents with the police whether they had been drinking or using drugs at the time of the incident. Twenty-one percent said they had been using drugs or alcohol during the police use of force incident. Alcohol and drug users were more likely to have been arrested during a police use of force incident. For example, 60% of those who said they had been using alcohol or drugs at the time of the force incident were also arrested compared to 38% of those who said they had not been using drugs or alcohol.

Police contact with youth

The more serious the level of police contact the younger the persons tended to have been. For example, as displayed in Table 8, the 1999 median age of all persons in the U.S. age 16 or older was approximately 42 years, 36 years for all persons having had a face-to-face contact with the police, 27 years for those arrested, and 23 years for those reporting a force incident.

Although an infrequent occurrence across all age groups, persons with police contact aged 16-19 (2.8%) and aged 20-29 years (1.5%) were more likely to have had force used against them than persons from the older age brackets. Likewise, younger drivers were more likely to be stopped by the police when driving than older drivers. For example, 18% of drivers aged 16 through 19 were stopped at least once during 1999 compared to all other age groups.

Table 8:
Median age and type of police contact reported, 1999

		Median age
Total population 16 and over	209 million	42
Any contact with the police	44 million	36
Motorist stopped	19 million	34
Persons arrested	1.0 million	27
Persons handcuffed	1. 1 million	26
Persons searched	1.7 million	25
Persons reporting force used	422,000	23

Excessive force

A widely-accepted industry standard for "excessive force" has not been devised and the pitfalls in defining excessive use of police force have been fully examined (McEwen 1996). The range of experts consulted during the development of the original *1996 Police-Public Contact Survey* acknowledged the difficulty in identifying excessive force incidents and recommended deferring that assessment to the survey respondent's judgment. Therefore, the 1999 PPCS dealt with the issue of measuring "excessive force" by directly asking the respondent whether they thought the type of force used against them was indeed excessive. The vast majority (76%) of persons who reported police use of force said the force was excessive. Black citizens involved in a force incident were just as likely as white citizens to characterize the force as excessive.

In contrast to those persons experiencing force, the vast majority of citizens in non-force encounters with the police said they were satisfied with the police behavior and thought they acted in an appropriate manner (Langan, et al 2001). Some differences in the level of satisfaction with police behavior were observed by race, which is not inconsistent with overall public opinion data on attitudes toward the police by race. For example, a 2000 Harris poll found that 69% of whites and 36% of blacks though the police in their community treated all races fairly. Likewise, 36% of blacks and 14% of whites said they were sometimes afraid that the police would stop and arrest them when completely innocent (Bureau of Justice Statistics *Sourcebook*. 2001) Also, Wortley, Hagan, and Macmillan (1997) reported from their study that blacks are generally less likely than whites to have a positive attitude toward the criminal justice system or to a specific encounter with the police.

People appeared to assess the excessiveness of the actual force or threat of force in the context of the incident as opposed to whether the force was excessive relative to some other less serious force options. For example, a person may believe that a mere threat by the officer to use force, or indeed any action by the officer, was excessive given the action of the citizen. The survey reported cases in which persons who had experienced minimal force, or simply the threat of force, characterized the force as excessive. Respondents were not asked what level, if any, of force may have been appropriate given the nature of the incident.

Conclusion

Findings from the *1999 Police Public Contact Survey* concur with prior research in that police use force is a rare event and when it does occur it usually does so at the lower end of the force continuum. Likewise, self-reported citizen action in force incidents is also clustered at the lower end of the seriousness scale, most likely arguing, cursing, or disobeying the officer.

How to measure police use of force?

A number of methodological options present themselves to researchers intent on better understanding police use of force against citizens. These methods have been implemented in numerous local studies, and their strengths and weaknesses well-documented (Garner, et al 2002). Observational studies, review of official police records, use of force complaints, citizen surveys, and police officer interview data have each been used to improve our understanding of a complex and sensitive issue that goes the core of police-community relations.

The use of national-level, citizen-based surveys has its own advantages and disadvantages. A national survey can, for example, contact a large sample of households or individuals over a well-defined period of time, using a standardized survey instrument which is administered in similar fashion by uniformly trained interviewers. Of course, a randomly conducted household survey which guarantees the protection of respondent's identification and privacy does not permit the researcher to link citizen responses with a particular event, or to match it with official police agency records. Nor would survey data provide access for the researcher to contact any of the officers involved. (Footnote: Data collections conducted by the U.S. Bureau of the Census operate under 42 USC 3789g and 3735 which protect privacy and identification of respondent.) However, the anonymity provided by a survey can facilitate people's candid response. Such an interview environment may be in stark contrast to those conducted among respondents who are under the custody of the criminal justice system, such as arrestees. Such an environment may constrain the respondent's candor. For example, Garner (1996) found that the reliability of arrestees on reporting whether they used force during their encounter with the police was less than ideal.

The 1999 PPCS data did not provide information on cases in which force may have been justifiably used but was not, depicted as cells C and D in figure 3. In other words, it did not measure what did not happen. Addressing this issue would be a beneficial modification to future surveys. Some of this information can be gleaned from observational studies, but these are generally quite costly to undertake and require a long-term commitment from field staff and the cooperating law enforcement agency.

Figure 3:
Use of force by police or citizen

	Citizen	
	Yes	*No*
Police	X	X
	---	---
	na	na

It is important to understand the chronology of citizen and police behavior during the incident in the context of the force continuum in order to assess the appropriateness of police behavior. Although the temporal sequence of the police use of force situation cannot be easily gathered from a household survey, the survey remains a useful vehicle to collect data directly from citizens. Given the complexity and sensitivity of the police use of force issue all methods should be brought to bear on the topic to provide a better understanding of this phenomenon. Research on police records, citizen complaints, and the use of observational study techniques can be used to complement local and national citizen survey findings.

Endnotes

[1]Steven K. Smith, Ph.D. is Chief of the Adjudication, Law Enforcement, and Federal Statistics Unit at the Bureau of Justice Statistics. Points of view are those of the author and do not necessarily reflect the official position of the US Department of Justice.

[2]The Police Public Contact Survey, 1999 dataset is available from the National Archive of Criminal Justice Data <http://www.icpsr.umich.edu/NACJD>.

References

Adams, Kenneth, et al (1999). *Use of Force by Police: Overview of National and Local Data*, Washington, DC: National Institute of Justice NCJ-176330.

Adams, Kenneth (1995). Measuring the Prevalence of Police Abuse of Force. in *And Justice for All: Understanding and Controlling Police Abuse of Force*, edited by William A. Geller and Hans Toch, Police Executive Research Forum, Washington DC.

Alpert, Geoffrey P. and Roger G. Dunham (1999). *The Force Factor: Measuring Police Use of Force Relative to Suspect Resistance.* In Adams, Kenneth, et al (1999) *Use of Force by Police: Overview of National and Local Data*, Washington, DC: National Institute of Justice NCJ-176330, pp. 61-76.

Bureau of Justice Statistics (2001) Criminal Victimization in the *United States, 1999 Statistical Tables*, Washington, DC. NCJ-1 184938.

Bureau of Justice Statistics (2001) *Sourcebook of Criminal Justice Statistics, 2001.* Tables 2.29 and 2.3 0, Harris Interactive, Inc. Washington, DC. NCJ-190251.

Desmedt. John (1984) "Use of Force Paradigm for Law Enforcement," *Journal of Police Science and Administration* 12 (2) 170-176.

Engel, R., J. Sobol, and R. Worden, (2000) "Further Exploration of the Demeanor Hypothesis: the Interaction Effects of Suspects' Characteristics and Demeanor," *Justice Quarterly*, Vol. 17, No. 2, pp. 235-258.

Garner, Joel H., Thomas Schade, John Hepburn and John Buchanan (1995). "Measuring the Continuum of Force Used by and Against the Police." *Criminal Justice Review* 20 (2) 146168.

Garner, Joel H., John Buchanan, and Thomas Schade, and John Hepburn (1996). *Understanding the Use of Force by and Against the Police*, National Institute of Justice: Research in Brief. Washington, DC.

Garner, Joel H., and Christopher D. Maxwell (1999) "Measuring the Amount of Force Used By and Against the Police in Six Jurisdictions," in Adams, Kenneth, et al (1999) *Use of Force by Police: Overview of National and Local Data*, Washington, DC: National Institute of Justice NCJ-176330, pp 25-44.

Garner, Joel H., Christopher D. Maxwell, and Cedrick Heraux (2002). Characteristics Associated with the Prevalence and Severity of Force Used by Police. *Justice Quarterly*, 19:4, 705-746.

Greenfeld, Lawrence A., Patrick A. Langan, and Steven K. Smith (1997) *Police Use of Force: Collection of National Data*. Washington, DC: U.S. Bureau of Justice Statistics NCJ165040.

Greenfeld, Lawrence A. (1998) *Alcohol and Crime: An Analysis of National Data on the Prevalence of Alcohol Involvement in Crime*. Washington, DC: Bureau of Justice Statistics, NCJ168632.

Klinger, D.A. (1994) "Demeanor or Crime? Why 'Hostile' Citizens Are More Likely to Be Arrested." *Criminology* 32:475-93.

Klockars, Carl (1995) A Theory of Excessive Force and its Control. In W. Geller and H. Tochs (eds.) *And Justice for All: Understanding and Controlling Police Abuse of Force* (pp. I I 30) Washington, DC: Police Executive Research Forum.

Langan, Patrick, Lawrence A. Greenfeld, Steven K. Smith, Matthew R. Durose, and David J. Levin (2001) *Contacts Between Police and the Public: Findings from the 1999 National Survey*. Washington, DC: Bureau of Justice Statistics, NCJ-18495 7.

Mastrofski, Stephen D., Roger B. Parks, Albert J. Reiss, Robert E. Worden, Christina DeJong, Jeffrey B. Snipes, and William Terrill (1998). *Systematic Observation of Public Police: Applying Field Research Methods to Policy Issues*. Washington, DC: National Institute of Justice, NCJ-172859.

McEwen, Tom (1996) *National Data Collection on Police Use of Force*, Washington, DC: Bureau of Justice Statistics, NCJ-160113.

Pate, Anthony M. and Lori Fridell, *1993 Police Use of Force: Official Reports, Citizen Complaints, and Legal Consequences.* Washington, DC Police Foundation.

Son, Soon, et al (1997) "Citizens' Observations of Police Use of Excessive Force and Their Evaluation of Police Performance Force." *Policing: an International Journal of Police Strategy and Management.* Vol. 20 No. 1, pp. 149- 159.

Terrill, William, (2001) Police *Coercion: Application of the Force Continuum,* New York: LFB Scholarly Publishing.

Wortley, S., J. Hagan, and R. Macmillan, 1997. "Just Deserts? The Racial Polarization of Perceptions of Criminal Injustice." *Law and Society Review* 31:637-76.

8

Toward a Better Understanding of Police Use of Nonlethal Force

William Terrill Northeastern University
Stephen D. Mastrofski George Mason University

The defining aspect of the police role is the capacity to use force (Bittner, 1970). Given this, it is not surprising that a substantial number of studies on police use of force have been completed during the past few decades (Bayley and Garofalo, 1989; **Binder and Fridell, 1984**; Bittner, 1970; Black, 1980; Chevigny, 1969; Friedrich, 1977; Fyfe, 1979, 1980, 1988; Garner, Schade, Hepburn, and Buchanan, 1995; **Geller, 1982**; Muir, 1977; Reiss, 1968, 1971; Sykes and Brent, 1983; Terrill, 2001; Terrill and Mastrofski, 2002; Toch, 1969; Westley, 1953; Worden, 1995). This growing body of research provides important insights into this key element in the practice of street-level policing. Past research helps us understand how challenging it will be to gather information on police use of force that will help us understand the causes and consequences of its use and enable us to offer meaningful evaluations of police street- level practices.

In this chapter we review the state of research on police use of force, noting what we know about the extent to which the police apply coercion, the intensity of that coercion, and the causes or predictors of coercion. Our analysis of the limitations of past research leads us to consider three challenges for advancing future research and evaluation: (1) the need to incorporate workable normative standards for the use of force into the analytic framework, (2) the need to capture more fully the subtleties of police coercive practice, and (3) the need to incorporate the dynamics of the police-citizen interaction into the analysis of police coercion. We suggest ways to meet these challenges and provide an illustration of one approach that attempts to deal with all three issues.

Research on Police Coercion

In 1931 the National Commission on Law Observance and Enforcement (Wickersham Commission) brought widespread national attention to the issue of police violence in the form of brutality for the first time. The commission published the *Report on Lawlessness in Law Enforcement* that characterized "third degree" police tactics as a major institutional problem (National Commission on Law Observance and Enforcement, 193 1). Over twenty years later Westley (1953) studied the police and their views toward the application of force. He discovered that officers rely on force because they view it as an effective means to control those in need of control. Westley also found that force was used as a way to gain public and peer respect.

Despite Westley's early insight, it was not until the mid- 1960s that the first wave of scholarly attention was given to police use of force. In many cities throughout the country, riots accompanied claims of excessive police force. The President's Commission for Law Enforcement and Administration of Justice concluded that these allegations of police violence were legitimate. Soon the Law Enforcement Assistance Administration (LEAA) was created with the aim of improving the criminal justice system. The administration also allocated money for research on criminal justice issues, the first large scale federal effort toward such ends. As a result, most of what is known about police use of force has been acquired over the past thirty years.

Researchers have used a variety of methods to study police use of force including observational studies, citizen complaints, surveys, and officer use of force reports. Regardless of the data collection strategy, researchers have concentrated on three aspects of force: how often officers use it, the different types of force employed, and what causes officers to use it.

Frequency of Force

Reiss (1968, 1971) was one of the first researchers to measure the extent of police force systematically. In 1966 he conducted an observational study of police in Chicago, Boston, and Washington D.C. He created an expert panel to review incidents where the "...policeman struck the citizens with his hands, fist, feet, or body, or where he used a weapon of some kind—such as a nightstick or a pistol" to determine if excessive force was used (1968:3). Of 1,565 policecitizen encounters with suspected offenders, 44 involved instances where officers struck citizens in the manner Reiss outlined. Of these 44 encounters, 37 were judged by the review panel to have involved excessive force (2.4% of all cases) (1968). Friedrich (1977, 1980) re-examined Reiss' data. Unlike Reiss, Friedrich relied solely on the observers' classification of whether force was used at all, and if so, whether he or she believed force was excessive. Using this classification method and based on 1,565 police-suspect encounters, he found that reasonable physical force was applied in 51 cases (3.3%) and excessive force in 29 cases (1.8%).

In 1977, another observational study known as the Police Services Study (PSS) was conducted in 24 departments in three metropolitan areas (Rochester, New York; St. Louis, Missouri; and Tampa, Florida). Using PSS data, Worden (1995) analyzed 1,528 police-citizen encounters involving suspected offenders. He concluded that reasonable force was used 2.4 percent of the time and excessive force was applied 1.5 percent of the time. Another police observational study was done in the mid- 1980s by Bayley and Garofalo (1989) in New York City. Of

467 police- citizen encounters classified as "potentially violent," they found some form of physical force was used about eight percent of the time.[1]

As part of a training evaluation regarding police use of force, Fyfe (1988) conducted observational research with the Metro-Dade Police department in Miami, Florida. Of approximately 2,000 potentially violent police-citizen situations, he found that force 'greater than firm voice commands' occurred about twelve percent of the time.[2] Klinger (1995) also examined the Metro-Dade data, but looked at a subset of cases classified as disputes. He found that in 241 dispute cases, some form of physical force was used 17 percent of the time.

In 1996 and 1997, an observational study known as the Project on Policing Neighborhoods (POPN) was conducted in Indianapolis, Indiana and St. Petersburg, Florida. Using data from this study, Terrill (2001) analyzed 3,544 police- citizen encounters involving suspected offenders. He found physical force was used in 21 percent of the observed encounters. The frequency of force increased to 58% when verbal force (e.g., commands and threats) was considered.

Officers' official reports are also used to assess police force. Analyzing 123,500 arrest reports from Rochester, New York between 1973-1979, Croft (1985) found some form of physical force used in approximately two percent of these arrests. In a later study, Croft, along with Austin (1987), examined police use of force in Rochester and Syracuse, New York. Examining data from 1984 and 1985, they found force was used in five percent of arrests in Rochester and in four percent of arrests in Syracuse.[3]

Using force reports from custody arrests over a 12-month period in St. Paul, Minnesota, Lundstrom and Mullan (1987) found force was used in 14 percent of the cases. A few years later, McLaughlin (1992) also looked at use of force reports in approximately 11,000 arrests made by Savannah, Georgia officers. He found physical force was used only one percent of the time. In a study conducted by Garner et al. (1995) in Phoenix, Arizona, they found the highest rate of physical force to date; of 1,585 arrests over a two-week period, officers used some form of physical force 22 percent of the time.

Yet another method to examine use of force is citizen complaints. In 1966 and 1967, Chevigny (1969) examined citizen complaints of the New York City Police department. Of 441 complaints filed, he found that 164 involved allegations of abusive police force. Dugan and Breda (1991) surveyed 165 police agencies in Washington state in 1987 and 1988; analyzing 691 complaints, they found that 123 involved physical force. Although many jurisdictions have recently streamlined the citizen complaint process, measuring use of force through this mechanism is still more limited than reliance on use of force reports because many force incidents do not produce complaints. In the Reiss (1968) data set, of the 37 cases classified as excessive, only one resulted in a citizen complaint.

Finally, surveys are also used to determine the extent of police force. In 1966 Bayley and Mendelsohn (1969) surveyed 806 Denver citizens about police brutality. Of these, fifteen percent of Hispanics, nine percent of Blacks, and four percent of Caucasians claimed that they had personally experienced police brutality.

Campbell and Schuman (1968) conducted a national survey of citizens in 15 cities for the National Advisory Commission on Civil Disorders. When asked whether they had been "roughed up" by police officers, seven percent of the black respondents and two percent of white respondents claimed that they had. A 1991 Gallup poll found that five percent of citizens surveyed reported having ever been physically mistreated or abused by police, while 20 percent reported that they knew someone who had been physically mistreated or abused. Recently a large national survey found that about one percent of people reporting face-to-face contact with police reported experiencing police force (Langan, Greenfeld, Smith, Durose, and Levin, 2001:26).

Based on these studies, experts are now widely agreed on the conclusions of a recent Department of Justice report, stating that what is "known with substantial confidence is that police use force infrequently" (National Institute of Justice, 1999:vii). A close review of these studies suggests that the situation may be more complex. First, force has been defined in a variety of ways, some studies focusing only on physical force, but others including voiced threats. Second, the pool on which percentages are calculated has also varied. Some consider all suspects that were observed in encounters with the police. Others look only at arrestees, and others focus only on the treatment of citizens involved in "potentially violent" situations. And still others place no time limitation on citizens' experiences; they explore whether survey respondents have "ever" been abused and offer separate results by the citizen's race. Thus, the risk of experiencing police physical force has been presented as low as .01 from a national sample of respondents over a one year time period, and as high as .22 for a sample of Phoenix arrestees drawn from police reports. Differences in how force is operationalized, how samples were drawn, where and when they were drawn, and how the population at risk was defined (e.g., suspects versus all citizens contacting police) all undoubtedly contribute to this variation.

While these issues are all amenable to empirical comparison and are at least potentially reconcilable, whether any specific level of risk constitutes a low or "infrequent" level is certainly open to debate. It depends upon one's base of comparison. If we were to observe a sample of obstetricians throughout their workweek, we might observe that the delivery of babies occupies a small percentage of their daily encounters with patients, yet we might be reluctant to conclude that they deliver babies "infrequently," since they deliver far more babies than is typical among the public generally or other occupations. In the case of police, it might be more useful to compare the frequency of their use of force with that of the general population. We expect that doing so would show that the police coerce others far more frequently.

Another issue that has gone unremarked from these studies is the risk of excessive or abusive force by police. Police officers and the general public appear to have achieved a substantial consensus that police abuse of force is relatively rare. Based on a nationally representative survey sample of police officers, researchers have found that the vast majority of officers (78 percent) believe that police in their city seldom or never use more force than necessary to make an arrest (Weisburd, Greenspan, Hamilton, Bryant, and Williams, 2001:15). A 2000 Harris poll found that over three fourths of the American adult public feels that police do a pretty good or excellent job of not using excessive force (Gallagher, Maguire, Mastrofski, and Reisig, 2001:134). One may presume that these estimates are based on a rather broad denominator—perhaps the total population of all police-citizen face-to-face interactions. But an entirely different picture emerges when one focuses only on those circumstances when police force is used for assessing the propriety of police actions. Although three systematic field studies find that excessive force was used against 1.5-2.4 percent of *all* suspects patrol officers encountered, observers have failed to note that when police do use physical force, the risks seem quite substantial that it will be excessive—ranging from 38 to 84 percent, depending on the data set and method of assessing force (Gould and Mastrofski, 2001). This is consistent with the assessments of citizens who report experiencing police force, 76 percent of whom said that the force was excessive in a large national survey of police-citizen contacts (Langan et al., 2001:28). The findings of these four studies suggest that when police resort to (physical) force, there is a substantial likelihood that disinterested trained observers or the citizens experiencing that force will judge it to be excessive. It may be the relative infrequency with which police use force that gives a substantial majority of police and public confidence in the rarity of police abuse of force. While four studies constitute a pretty slender thread on which to hang a conclusion, when abuse of force is framed in this way, such levels might well exceed what the public would find acceptable of police in a democratic society governed by law.

The Amount of Force

Numerous studies have measured variation in the type of force police use. McLaughlin (1992) found that the most common use of police force during arrests involved punching or kicking (34 percent of force incidents). Only eight percent of force incidents involved the use of the baton or mace. Pate and Fridell (1993) conducted a national survey of police departments concerning the extent of force by officers, types of force used, number of citizen complaints, and force reporting procedures. In city departments they found handcuffing to be the most frequently used type of force (490 incidents per 1,000 sworn officers) followed by "bodily force" (272 incidents per 1,000 sworn officers). Both of the above studies highlight that "[N]onlethal force encompasses a wide variety of police actions" (Klinger, 1995:17 1). According to Klinger, "[E]xplicit recognition of the diversity of force that is classified as nonlethal is important not only because it identifies differences in kinds of force but also because it points to differences in severity as well" (1995:171). Klinger (1995) observed that because there are different types of force police use, force can be ranked in terms of severity. Therefore, force can be measured along a continuum ranging from the least to the greatest amount of force.

Klinger (1995) noted two deficiencies often associated with prior work on nonlethal force. First, previous attempts have failed to examine how various types of force are used within individual encounters. In other words, different types of forceful police actions can take place within single encounters (e.g., grabbing to restrain *and* striking to subdue). Second, such studies have been limited to classifying only force that is physical in nature. However, officers exert force verbally as well as physically, through commands and threats. In Klinger's (1995) analysis of Metro-Dade data, of 241 police-citizen encounters involving disputes he found that officers used some form of physical or verbal coercion 164 times in 97 encounters. Similarly, in Terrill's (2001) analysis POPN data, of the 3,544 police-suspect encounters, he found that officers used some form of physical or verbal coercion 4,179 times in 3,544 encounters. Clearly, multiple forms of force were used within single encounters.

Klinger (1995) and Terrill (2001) also analyzed combinations of force within single encounters. In Klinger's analysis, of the 97 encounters in which some form of force was used, distinct combinations emerged. In 58 of these cases officers only used one form of force (56 commands, 2 firm grip). In 22 cases a command and firm grip was used. Pain compliance, a firm grip, and a command were used in another I I cases. The remaining six cases occurred in numerous combinations. In Terrill's analysis, while a vast array of combinations (n=201) were used over the 2,068 encounters involving force, the top 10 accounted for 77.3 percent (n=1,599) of the 2,068. Of these 1,599 encounters, verbal force was used either used solely or in combination in 73.1 percent (n=1,169). Physical force was used in 774 encounters, but force beyond simple restraint was used in only 83 encounters.

Examining force in these two studies disclose several important findings. First, most of the force applied was verbal. While this type of force has generally been overlooked in the past, it is obviously a behavior that occurs with some frequency. Second, when physical force was used, it generally involved those physical behaviors at the lower end of the force continuum. Unless one distinguishes between types of force, all cases would be grouped together as if the level of force were similar or alike, which is misleading. Third, when higher forms of force were used (e.g., firm hold) within a given encounter, lower forms were also applied (e.g., voice command). For example, of the 97 cases that involved some form of force in the Klinger (1995) analysis, 98 percent involved voice commands.

Garner et al. (1995) also analyzed varying types of force. Like Klinger (1995) and Terrill (2001), they found that most force was at the lower end of the continuum. For instance, of 1,235 cases involving physical force 918 were in the form of restraints. Unlike Klinger (1995), Garner et al. (1995) and Terrill (2001) also incorporated varying levels of citizen resistance into their analysis. In the Garner et al. study, of the 1,585 cases examined, 977 (62 percent) involved no resistance while 608 (38 percent) included varying levels of resistance ranging from psychological to aggressive and firearm use. Terrill found that 3,098 of 3,544 encounters involved no resistance (88 percent), while the remaining 446 (12 percent) included various levels of resistance ranging from passive to active.

The general thrust of the research reviewed above is that verbal police coercion appears to be far more frequent than physical force. However, one study stands in sharp contrast, the large Bureau of Justice Statistics national survey of police-citizen contact. Here researchers found that 65 percent of respondents who reported experiencing some police force experienced physical force only, 13 percent experienced both physical and verbal force, and 23 percent experienced verbal only (Langan et al., 2001:27). We suspect that relying on the respondent's recall of an event that occurred within the last twelve months may overstate the use of physical, compared to verbal, coercion. Police physical force is undoubtedly more memorable than a spoken threat, which may be recalled at a lower rate. This form of bias due to selective recall we regard as a significant limitation in using these data, and we therefore conclude that verbal force is a frequent and important part of the force picture. As the intensity of coercion increases, its frequency decreases. A comprehensive understanding of police coercion, even in its most extreme forms, requires a consideration of the broad range of coercive measures available to police.

Causes of Force

A number of scholars have also investigated what causes officers to use force. Much of this research has examined the role of situational features of the police-citizen encounter. The most consistent finding is that a citizen's violent, rebellious, antagonistic, hostile, or disrespectful behavior toward the police is a strong predictor of whether the police will respond forcefully and at what level of intensity (Chevigny, 1969; Friedrich, 1977; Garner et al., 1995, 1996; Reiss, 1968, 1971; Terrill and Mastrofski, 2002; Toch, 1969; Worden, 1995). Other forms of citizen behavior found to increase the risk of police force are emotional agitation, intoxication, and possession of a weapon (Friedrich, 1977; Garner et al., 1995, 1996; Terrill and Mastrofski, 2001; Worden, 1995). When police possess certain information or beliefs about the citizen, this too increases the risk of police force: suspected of a felony or violent offense, gang involvement, or having a reputation for resisting police (Friedrich, 1977; Garner et al., 1995, 1996).

The characteristics of citizens have proven to be less consistent predictors of police use of force. Lower class suspects have shown a significantly greater risk of police force in some studies (Friedrich, 1977; Reiss, 1968, 1971; Terrill and Mastrofski, 2002; Worden, 1995). Male suspects have also shown a greater risk of police force in some studies (Garner et al., 1995, 1996; Terrill and Mastrofski, 2002; Worden, 1995). Race has been a less reliable predictor of police force, although some studies have shown that black suspects were more likely to experience an increased likelihood of force (Terrill and Mastrofski, 2002; Worden, 1995).

A few studies have considered police behavior during or immediately preceding the encounter with the public as a situational determinant of the subsequent use of force in that encounter. Researchers hypothesize that tactics employed early in the process tend to set in motion a chain of events that affect the likelihood that officers will subsequently resort to more or less coercion. Sykes and Brent (1980, 1983) examined different forms of police "control" in a way that is relevant to the study of police coercion. They proposed that officers are trained to "take charge," and conceptualized three means of control used to do so: definitional (questioning), imperative (commands), and coercive (the threat or actual use of physical coercion). Analyzing police-citizen encounters drawn from field observations in a middle-sized city, they found that officers usually handled situations through definitional and imperative control. Higher-level coercive tactics were relatively rare, usually following the failure of lesser forms of nonphysical tactics to secure compliance.

Examining traffic stops and disturbances, Bayley (1986) found that when officers began encounters with tactics such as listening, questioning, or seeking information, this usually led to a less coercive outcome such as a verbal warning or offering advice. Conversely, taking a more coercive approach at the start (e.g., verbal or physical restraint) had a greater likelihood of leading to a more coercive outcome. Fyfe (1988, 1989) using data from the aforementioned Metro-Dade study, examined actions taken by patrol officers to deal with potentially violent situations (PVs). He found that actions taken before involvement in potentially violent situations (e.g., knowledge of the patrol beat, places, people) may reduce the potential for police force (or subsequent use of police force during the encounter). He also found that some officers in certain situations may not have been aggressive enough in handling potentially violent encounters. That is, they failed to take charge when doing so would have been beneficial to maintaining good order.

Similar to Sykes and Brent (1980, 1983) and Bayley (1986), Terrill (2001) also looked at the transactional nature of the police-citizen encounter. In encounters involving resistant suspects, Terrill found that officers were less likely to apply subsequent forms of more severe force in cases where the officer initially used force (verbal or physical). However, in encounters involving nonresistant suspects, officers who began encounters with a verbal (but not physical) form of coercion were *more* likely to use subsequent forms of more severe force (Terrill, 2001:193).

Officer traits, experiences, and attitudes have demonstrated even less consistency in their capacity to predict police use of force. With the exception of Cohen and Chaiken's analysis (1972), most researchers have not found officer race to be a predictor of force (see Croft, 1985; Friedrich, 1977; Garner et al., 1995, 1996; Terrill and Mastrofski, 2002; Worden, 1995). Nonetheless, Friedrich (1977) did conclude that black officers patrol more aggressively and make more arrests, regardless of citizen race. Worden (1995) and Terrill and Mastrofski (2002) found no gender effects, but Garner et al. (1995, 1996) found males were more likely to use force on male arrestees. Not surprisingly, information regarding race and gender is relatively sparse. Until the past decade, police departments were primarily made up of white males. As a result, making valid comparisons has not been possible in many studies.

While research has shown that less experienced officers are more active (e.g., make more officer-initiated stops) (Worden, 1989) and patrol more aggressively (Friedrich, 1977) than their more experienced counterparts, the effect of officer experience on use of force has received mixed support. Although Terrill and Mastrofski (2002) found that more experienced officers were significantly less likely to use force, Worden (1995) found that officer length of service had no effect on either the use of reasonable or excessive force behavior, while Garner et al. (1995, 1996) found that officer experience was an "inconsistent" predictor of force.[4] Further, although the amount and type of training officers receive has been hypothesized to have an impact on use of force decisions (Fyfe, 1988), this has been largely unexplored. One reason this may be absent in most studies is the difficulty of obtaining training information that can be linked to individual officers.

There has been even less research concerning officer attitudes and beliefs. Worden (1995) tested several officer attitudes (e.g., toward the police role, discretion, and the citizenry) and their relationship to force. He found that officers with negative views toward the citizenry (e.g., believed citizens were unappreciative) were more likely to use both reasonable and improper force. Officers with more favorable views toward force (e.g., believed discretion should be at the officer level) were also significantly more likely to use improper force. However, officer perception of the police role did not have an effect on forceful behavior. Similar to Worden, Terrill and Mastrofski (2002) also tested several officer attitudinal measures, failing to find a significant effect. Others have also constructed typologies of officers based on various dimensions to explain the use of force (Brown, 1981; Muir, 1977; White, 1972), but there is little systematic evidence to document the impact of officer belief systems in relation to force. In short, most explorations regarding the links between attitudes and police behavior have been impressionistic at best.

A number of scholars have also looked at the role of organizations on police use of force. However, the extant research testing organizational hypotheses are limited to a few studies. Friedrich (1977), using a typology developed by Wilson (1968) that classified departments according to the formal structure of the organization and the political environment within which it operated, found little support for a net organizational effect. Others have looked at the impact of the informal structure (police culture) rather than the formal structure (Brown, 1981). Brown's (198 1) study of three Los-Angeles area departments found that individual, not departmental, styles of policing emerged within each of the three departments. Similarly, Maiming (1989) concluded that while first-line supervisors may have some influence on officer behavior, the formal aspects of a police organization have little impact on officer behavior.

Finally, Worden (1995) examined three organizational characteristics: degree of bureaucratization, emphasis placed on crime-fighting activities by the chief, and a measure for informal culture. Of these, only the degree of bureaucratization was significantly related to the use of "reasonable" force. The more bureaucratized the department, the greater the likelihood reasonable force was used.

Issues in Force Research

While we have learned a great deal about how, how often, and why the police resort to force, three issues arise from this body of research. First, prior works have often examined the application of police force in the form of what has been termed excessive force, focusing on extreme police violence such as brutality. Second, studies have tended to conceptualize police force dichotomously: excessive force/nonexcessive force or physical force/nonphysical force thus, obliterating differences in degree. That is, they fail to capture important subtleties in how police use coercion. Third, prior inquiries most often examine or view the application of police force in the context of a static rather than a dynamic process. The following describes these limitations in depth and what must be done to overcome them.

Excessive Police Force: The Need to Capture
Normative Standards of Performance

"Excessive" force is not easily defined. Many scholars have struggled with a variety of terms to describe police violence. These include: excessive use of force, use of excessive force, brutality, unauthorized force, wrongful force, unjustified force, misuse of force, and unnecessary force. While these phrases are interchangeable to some, others note fine distinctions. For example, use of excessive force can be defined as more force than needed to gain compliance in any given incident, while excessive use of force may be defined as using force in too many incidents (Adams, 1995). Fyfe (1986) makes the distinction between brutality (a willful and knowingly wrongful use of force) and unnecessary force (force used by well-meaning officers illequipped to handle various incidents). Worden (1995) also distinguishes between different types of force. He defines excessive force as that which is more than required to subdue a citizen, and unnecessary force as that which precedes a citizen's resistance or continues after citizen resistance has ceased.

Klockars (1995) and Bittner (198 3) note that two very different standards may be used to judge whether force was excessive: legal criteria (from statutes, case law, and departmental rules) and professional criteria (based on what a highly skilled officer would do). Neither standard is easy to apply reliably. Laws governing police use of force, especially less-than-lethal force, are vague, and legal experts do not necessarily agree on what the law permits and requires (see Gould and Mastrofski, 2001). Professional standards are even harder to pin down, are rarely codified, and undoubtedly vary between and within police agencies at any given time.[6] At best, efforts to specify professional standards are frustrated by the recognition that situations vary in ways so complex as to frustrate any effort to be specific beyond listing a set of decision "factors" that the officer should take into account (Kelling, 1999). Indeed, much of the craft of policing rests on a foundation of an officer being able to "read" a situation correctly—what Muir (1977:153ff) calls "judgment." The classic problem, often depicted in film, is the sharp rookie who may know all that the academy could teach her about when to apply what level of coercion, but until she is able to produce a correct diagnosis of the situation (which requires a great deal of knowledge of the people, places and customs on her beat), such professional knowledge is of little utility.

The challenge of determining legal and professional standards for use of force are not insurmountable, but a great deal must be done before either can serve as a reliable standard for evaluating officer use of force. The first step is establishing principles that are readily applied in the field by officers and are observable by evaluators, and the second is to determine that a sufficient degree of consensus exists on those principles among legal or professional experts to make them meaningful. Using panels of legal and professional experts to develop and clarify such principles is important. Legal standards have the advantage of being legitimate by definition. That is, the officer's only task is to avoid violating them; the police presumably have no role to play in deciding whether and when to adhere to the law.

The challenge will be greater for establishing professional standards, since their legitimacy is ostensibly based on the expectation that they "work." Unless we are merely to accept professional standards because "professionals" issue them, we require some independent validation. Yet there has been little scientific validation of the effectiveness of different field tactics in securing citizen compliance (Bayley and Bittner, 1984). That which has been done is relatively crude, but nonetheless instructive. For example, when police display disrespect toward citizens, the citizens are less likely to comply, and thereby more likely to elicit higher levels of police coercion (Mastrofski, Snipes, and Supina, 1996; McCluskey, Mastrofski, Parks, 1999; Tyler, 2001a; 2001b). And when police act in ways to make the fairness of their actions transparent to the citizens involved (that is, explain their justification), those actions are more likely to be accepted by those present as legitimate (Tyler, 2001a; 2001b). These principles are, of course, insufficient to guide professional policing, but they constitute a start. And, inasmuch as police are in the business of coercion, a comprehensive set of professional standards will include affirmative principles about the circumstances under which certain levels of coercion constitute highly skilled police work, recognizing that in most circumstances, "the skill of policing consists in finding ways to avoid its use" (Bittner, 1974:40). Until the challenges of operationalizing normative standards for the use of force are met, researchers will have relatively little to contribute to improvements in the practice of coercion—or avoiding its use.

Capturing the Craft of Coercive Policing

Police ethnographers suggest that competent officers take pride in mastery of the subtle distinctions of the coercive aspects of their craft (Brown, 198 1; Muir, 1977; Rubinstein, 1973). Two dimensions of coercion appear frequently in street-level accounts of the craft: the severity of the coercion and the certainty that the officer can and will deliver it. We have already discussed at some length how the severity of the coercion may vary, but the certainty of its delivery remains virtually unexplored in all but a few ethnographic studies (see especially Muir, 1977). Earlier we noted that most police coercion is verbal—an explicit or implied promise of greater or lesser specificity that the officer will punish or harm the target in some way. The essential element in the efficacy of such a "promise" is the citizen's expectation that it will be fulfilled if the officer's conditions are not satisfied. The higher the level of certainty conveyed by verbal coercion, presumably the greater its coercive capacity. Manipulating certainty of coercion, or at least the appearance of certainty, must then figure as an important tool of the police trade. Factors driving the probability of coercion include the value the officer places on the citizen compliance at issue, the officer's willingness to accept the costs of the contemplated coercion (e.g., physical injury, time expended, exposure to review by superiors and courts), and the availability of resources (personal capabilities and reputation, other officers, equipment, information, connections to people and organizations of consequence to the citizen). Regardless of the officer's actual willingness and ability to fulfill a coercive promise in a given situation, expert practice of the craft requires showing sufficient signals to convince the citizen. This may include references to or displays of will, power, and access to resources. What researchers have left mostly unexplored (except again for Muir) is the interplay of certainty and severity of coercion. Do officers with a limited capacity to signal high levels of certainty tend to rely more heavily on higher levels of severity?

Capturing the Dynamics of Police-Citizen Interaction

A final limitation regarding most prior work on police use of force is the failure to characterize the "history" of police- citizen interaction. One major impediment to identifying the causes or predictors of coercion is that many studies "...do not address the transactional, or stepby-step unfolding, of police-public encounters. Was suspect resistance the result of police use of force, or did police use force after experiencing suspect resistance?" (National Institute of Justice, 1999:ix). Researchers lacking the capacity to distinguish the temporal ordering of citizen and officer behaviors during the encounter are unable to distinguish cause from effect in their analyses. With the exception of a few studies (Bayley, 1986; Sykes and Brent, 1980, 1983; Terrill, 2001) researchers have not embedded their research in an analytic structure that incorporates the transactional dynamics occurring within the police-citizen encounter. As stated by Fridell and Binder, the police-citizen encounter must be "seen to encompass a pattern of interaction between an officer and an opponent and multiple decisions by both" (1992:386). Studies that seek to explain or predict use of force decisions too often look at the police-citizen encounter as if it were a single discrete transaction. The highest level of police force is noted without characterizing all that transpired between police and citizen before and after hitting this peak. If a police officer strikes a citizen, surely our characterization of the event is made more useful by knowing whether this force was preceded by several attempts to subdue the citizen using less force, or whether the officer's first act was the most violent one. We can imagine that each instance of police force during the encounter requires an accounting of the police actions that preceded it. Alternatively, we can imagine characterizing different patterns over the entire encounter in the application of force. A simple distinction is one that charts escalation, de-escalation, stasis, and highly variable patterns.

Inasmuch as we know police actions to be highly reactive to how *citizens* behave and present themselves (Black, 1980; Reiss, 1971; Worden, 1989), we understand a great deal more when we know how *citizens* behaved prior to each instance of police force during the encounter. There is an immense difference between police violence that is provoked by a citizen who respectfully declines to follow a police command and one who responds to the command by assaulting the officer. Indeed, a careful delineation of what the citizen did is essential to making judgments discussed earlier about whether force was justified or not, the best choice or not.

The Force Continuum: A Useful Beginning

Dealing successfully with the above issues will require considerable time and effort, but such an effort has already begun. Researchers have begun to take advantage of a policy framework used in many police departments that is explicitly norm-based, that attempts to capture some of the subtleties of using coercion, and that acknowledges that coercion in the police-citizen encounter is a dynamic process. Known as a "force continuum," this policy constitutes a simple standard against which police practice may be measured, modeled, and evaluated (Alpert and Dunham, 1997; Connor, 1991; Desmedt, 1984; Garner et al., 1995; McLaughlin, 1992; Terrill, 2001). As such it offers a useful example of how to develop more useful measurement and analysis of police use of force.

Force continuum guidelines are built upon Bittner's (1970) now familiar assertion that police coercion is and must be "situationally justified." Situations confronting officers may vary infinitely, but workable standards to be used on the street cannot mirror that level of complexity. They must be based on a limited number of principles and categories. Force continuum policies therefore focus on the degree of threat and resistance exhibited by a citizen, establish a limited number of categories to characterize the level of threat/resistance, and then specify what level of police force is encouraged (but not mandated) in response. A citizen's polite refusal to obey an officer's command is a much smaller threat than a citizen's assault with a firearm on an officer. Both constitute resistance that would justify police coercion, albeit at markedly different levels. So one tactical principle that animates the force continuum is *proportionality*. The police are not to use a cannon to subdue a mouse. The force continuum further anticipates the possibility that a 7 given level of police force may not produce the desired result, so it specifies how to proceed.[7]

Incrementalism is the second tactical principle of the force continuum. Should a given level of police coercion fail to bring the citizen to compliance, officers may escalate the level of force, but they should do so in small increments. Doing this makes it possible for officers to accomplish their objectives with the least force necessary. Such incrementalism runs counter to the claim, popular among some practitioners, that when force is applied it should be well in excess of what is needed to secure compliance (Bayley and Bittner, 1984)—the equivalent of "over- engineering" bridges to withstand much more stress than they are likely to experience. The latter tactic is designed to keep citizens from testing police resolve and continuing resistance, but incrementalism seeks a finely calibrated response and requires a measure of patience.

Table 1 offers a simple version of a force continuum. In the upper part of the table, the first column indicates the citizen presenting resistance/threat at any given point in the face-to-face interaction with the officer. The second column lists the appropriate level of police force to deal with that level of threat/resistance. Department continuum guidelines typically indicate that if a citizen fails to comply in response to the indicated level of coercion, the officer may then escalate to the next level. The columns in the lower half of the table show what evaluative category each police response would be for a given level of citizen threat/resistance.

Table 1:
Force Continuum Analytic Scheme

Levels of Citizen Threat/Resistance	Levels of Police Force
1 -No Resistance	1 -No Force
2-Passive	2-Command
3- Verbal	3-Threat
4-Defensive	4-Restraint and Control
5-Active	5-Pain Compliance/Takedown
	6-Impact

Citizen Threat/Resistance	Less Force	Equivalent Force	More Force
1	---	1,2	3,4,5,6
2	1	2,3	4,5,6
3	1,2	3,4	5,6
4	1,2,3	4,5	6
5	1,2,3,4	5,6	---

If researchers have data on what transpired between citizens and officers in face-to-face encounters—such as that displayed in Table 1— then they can apply the force continuum to evaluate adherence to the guidelines- and thus to the tactical principles of proportionality and incrementalism. [8] Specifically, they can determine the frequency that officers adhere to the continuum, apply less force than the continuum specifies, or use more force than it specifies. Using observational data from the POPN, Terrill (2001) offered a preliminary look at how one might use the concept of force continuum analysis to examine how officers move about the continuum and what factors are associated with those instances when officers follow (or fail to follow) the continuum. He found that most police-citizen encounters appear to involve a simple pattern of adherence or under/over use of force according to force continuum policies. Some, however, involved multiple police-citizen exchanges that do not fit easily into these patterns.

The force continuum is by no means the only standard by which police use of force should be measured, but attempting to use even this overly-simple set of rules offers a cautionary tale for those who seek to make systematic judgments about the use of police force. Legitimate exceptions may well occur with sufficient frequency as to reduce substantially the capacity of the force continuum policy to guide practice in the field. In particular, what are the circumstances when officers should be encouraged to exert more restraint than the continuum justifies? Under what circumstances should officers accelerate the use of force by "jumping" levels? Proper diagnosis of these exceptional circumstances may well distinguish the mediocre from the skilled police officer that Klockars (1995) holds up as the appropriate standard for judging police use of force. A detailed analysis of these exceptional cases should enable policy makers to further refine departmental policies that ultimately produce better officer practice in the use of force.

Conclusion

We have asserted that the growing body of research on police use of force has produced several insights, but that most of this research has limitations in how police coercion is measured and modeled. We have argued that advancing knowledge of police coercion and our capacity to evaluate its practice require that researchers deal with three important issues: establishing a usable set of standards for evaluation, capturing a fuller range of the subtleties by which police practice coercion, and building analytic frameworks that model the dynamics of that practice. We have suggested that police department force continuum policies offer a useful example of one way to address these issues.

Endnotes

[1] Bayley and Garofalo defined "potentially violent mobilizations" as those that involved disputes, intervention by the police to apply the law against specific individuals, and attempts to question suspicious persons.

[2] Fyfe defined "potentially violent situations" as those that involving routine traffic stops, high-risk traffic stops, crimes in progress, and disputes.

[3] Croft reports that the increase from her earlier study is most likely a result of better reporting procedures and officer compliance filling out forms.

[4] Garner and colleagues tested numerous predictors, including officer experience, on three different measures of force: physical force, a continuum of force, and maximum force. They classified each predictor as falling into one of three categories: consistent predictors, inconsistent predictors, or non-predictors.

[5] The Garner et al. (1996) study did examine the number of years since the officers' last "arrest" training, and Terrill and Mastrofski (2002) looked at the amount of verbal mediation training officers received. However, both studies showed no effect on training.

[6] Muir (1977:192) notes that officers in professional departments face a bewildering array of contradictory aphorisms about what to do, such as "Be firm; don't lose face" versus "The first thing ... you're nice."

[7] Police departments that use the force continuum treat it as a guideline, not a hard-and-fast rule. Officers may deviate from it and are expected to do so if there is justification (e.g., the citizen's pattern of behavior in previous encounters with the police). Deviations may be in both directions—less or more force than indicated by the continuum. But it nonetheless establishes a standard against which officer practice may be measured and judged.

References

Adams, K. 1995. "Measuring the Prevalence of Police Abuse of Force."
Pp. 61-97 in *An Justice for All: Understanding and Controlling Police
Abuse of Force*, edited by W.A. Geller and H. Toch. Washington, D.C.:
Police Executive Research Forum.

Alpert, G.P. and R.G. Dunham. 1997. *The Force Factor: Measuring Police Use
of Force Relative to Suspect Resistance*. Washington, DC: Police Executive
Research Forum.

Bayley, D.H. 1986. "The Tactical Choices of Police Patrol Officers."
Journal of Criminal Justice 14:329-348.

Bayley, D.H. and E. Bittner. 1984. "Learning the Skills of Policing."
Law and Contemporary Problems 47:35-59.

Bayley, D.H. and J. Garofalo. 1989. "The Management of Violence by
Police Patrol Officers." *Criminology* 27:1-27.

Bayley, D.H. and H. Mendelsohn. 1969. *Minorities and the Police:
Confrontation in America*. New York: Free Press.

Binder, A. and L. Fridell. 1984. "Lethal force as a police response."
Criminal Justice Abstracts 16:250-280.

Bittner, E. 1970. *The Functions of Police in Modern Society*. Washington, D.C.:
U.S. Government Printing Office.

Bittner, E. 1974. "Florence Nightingale in Pursuit of Willie Sutton: A Theory of
the Police." Pp. 11-44 in *The Potential for Reform of the Criminal Justice
System, Vol 3*, edited by H. Jacob. Beverly Hills, CA: Sage Publications.

Bittner. E. 1983. "Legality and Workmanship: Introduction to Control in the
Police Organization." Pp. 1-11 in *Control in the Police Organization*,
edited by M. Punch. Cambridge, MA: MIT Press.

Black, D. 1980. *Manners and Customs of the Police*. New York: Academic Press.

Brown, M.K. 1981. *Working the Street: Police Discretion and the Dilemmas
of Reform*. New York: Russell Sage Foundation.

Campbell, A. and H. Schuman. 1968. "Racial Attitudes in Fifteen American
Cities." Supplemental Studies for the *National Advisory Commission on
Civil Disorders*. New York: Praeger.

Chevigny, P. 1969. *Police Power: Police Abuses in New York City*. New York: Pantheon Books.

Cohen, B. and J.M. Chaiken. 1972. *Police Background Characteristics and Performance*. New York: Rand.

Connor, G. 1991. "Use of Force Continuum: Phase II." *Law and Order* March:30-32.

Croft, E.B. 1985. "Police Use of Force: An Empirical Analysis." *Unpublished Ph.D. Dissertation*. University of Michigan.

Croft, E.B. and J. Austin. 1987. Police Use of Force in Rochester and Syracuse, New York 1984 and 1985. *Report to the New York State Commission on Criminal Justice and the Use of Force* (Vol Ell, May: 1 128). Albany, NY: New York State Commission on Criminal Justice and the Use of Force.

Desmedt, J.C. 1984. "Use of Force Paradigm for Law Enforcement." *Journal of Criminal Justice* 12:170-176.

Dugan, J.R. and DR. Breda. 1991. "Complaints About Police Officers: A Comparison Among Types and Agencies." *Journal of Criminal Justice* 19(2):165-171.

Fridell, L.A. and A. Binder 1992. "Police Officer DecisionMaking in Potentially \Violent Confrontations." *Journal of Criminal Justice* 20:385-399.

Friedrich, R.J. 1977. "The Impact of Organizational, Individual, and Situational Factors on Police Behavior." *Unpublished Ph.D. Dissertation*. University of Michigan.

Friedrich, R.J. 1980. "Police Use of Force: Individuals, Situations, and Organizations." *The Annals of the American Academy of Political and Social Science* November: 82-97.

Fyfe, J.J. 1979. "Administrative Interventions on Police Shooting Discretion: An Empirical Examination." *Journal of Criminal Justice* 7:303-323.

Fyfe, J.J. 1980. "Geographic Correlates of Police Shootings: A Microanalysis." *Journal of Research in Crime and Delinquency* 17:101-113.

Fyfe, J.J. 1988. *The Metro-Dade Police-Citizen Violence Reduction Project, Final Report, Executive Summary*. Washington, DC: Police Foundation.

Fyfe, J.J. 1989. "Police-Citizen Violence Reduction Project."
    FBI Law Enforcement Bulletin 58 May: 18-25.

Fyfe, J.J. 1986. The split-second syndrome and other determinants of police
    violence. Pp. 207-225 *in Violent transactions*, edited by A.T. Campbell &
    J.J. Gibbs. Oxford: Basil Blackwell.

Gallagher, C., E.R. Maguire, S.D. Mastrofski, and M.D. Reisig. 2001.
    The Public Image of the Police, Final Report to the International
    Association of Chiefs of Police. Manassas, VA: George Mason University.

Gallup, G. 1991. "Americans Say Police Brutality Frequent But Most Have
    Favorable Opinion of Their Local Police." *The Gallup Poll Monthly*,
    March: 53-56.

Garner, J.H., T. Schade, J. Hepburn, and J. Buchanan. 1995. "Measuring the
    Continuum of Force Used By and Against the Police." *Criminal Justice
    Review* 20:146-168.

Garner, J.H., J. Buchanan, T. Schade, and J. Hepburn. 1996. "Understanding
    the Use of Force By and Against the Police." Washington, DC:
    National Institute of Justice.

Geller, W.A. 1982. "Deadly Force: What We Know." *Journal of Police
    Science and Administration* 10: 151-177.

Gould, J.B. and S.D. Mastrofski. 2001. *"Suspect Searches: Using Constitutional
    Standards to Assess Police Behavior."* Unpublished manuscript.
    Manassas, VA: George Mason University.

Kelling, G. 1999. "'Broken Windows' and Police Discretion."
    National Institute of Justice Research Report Series. Washington, DC:
    National Institute of Justice.

Klinger, D.A. 1995. "The Micro-Structure of Nonlethal Force: Baseline Data
    from and Observational Study." *Criminal Justice Review* 20:169-186.

Klockars, C.B. 1995. "A Theory of Excessive force and its Control." Pp. 11-29
    in *An Justice for All: Understanding and Controlling Police Abuse of
    Force*, edited by W.A. Geller and H. Toch. Washington, DC: Police
    Executive Research Forum.

Langan, P.A., L.A. Greenfeld, S.K. Smith, M.R. Durose, and D.J. Levin. 2001. *Contacts between Police and the Public*. Washington, DC: Bureau of Justice Statistics.

Lundstrom, R. and C. Mullan. 1987. "The Use of Force: One Department's Experience." *FBI Law Enforcement Bulletin*: 6-9.

Mastrofski, S.D., J.B. Snipes, and A.E. Supina. 1996. "Compliance on Demand: The Public's Response to Specific Police Requests." *Journal of Research in Crime in Delinquency* 33:269-305.

Manning, P.K. 1989. "The Police Occupational Culture in Anglo-American Societies." Pp. 28-42 in *Encyclopedia of Police Science*, edited by W.G. Bailey. Dallas: Garland.

McCluskey, J.D, S.D. Mastrofski, and R.B. Parks. 1999. "To Acquiesce of Rebel: Predicting Citizen Compliance with Police Requests." *Police Quarterly* 2:389-416.

McLaughlin, V. 1992. *Police and the Use of Force: The Savannah Study*. Westport, CT: Praeger.

Muir, W.K., Jr. 1977. *Police: Streetcorner Politicians*. Chicago: University of Chicago Press.

National Commission on Law Observance and Enforcement. 1931. *Report on Lawlessness in Law Enforcement*. Washington DC: U.S. Government Printing Office.

National Institute of Justice Research Report. 1999. *Use of Force By Police: Overview of National and Local Data*. U.S. Department of Justice, Office of Justice Programs.

Pate, A. and L. Fridell. 1993. *Police Use of Force: Official Reports, Citizen Complaints, and Legal Consequences Vol. 1*. Washington D.C.: Police Foundation.

Reiss, A.J., Jr. 1968. "Police Brutality—Answers to Key Questions." *Trans-action* 5:10-19.

Reiss, A.J., Jr. 1971. *The Police and the Public*. New Haven, CT: Yale University Press.

Rubinstein, J. 1973. *City Police*. New York: Straus and Giroux.

Sykes, R.E. and E.E. Brent. 1980. "The Regulation of Interaction by Police: A Systems View of Taking Charge." *Criminology* 18:182-197.

Sykes, R.E. and E.E. Brent. 1983. *Policing: A Social Behaviorist Perspective.* New Brunswick, NJ: Rutgers University Press.

Terrill, W. 2001. *Police coercion: Application of the force continuum.* New York: LBF Publishing, LLC.

Terrill, W. and S.D. Mastrofski. 2002. "Situational and Officer Based Determinants of Police Coercion." *Justice Quarterly* 19(2), forthcoming.

Toch, H. 1969. *Violent Men: An Inquiry into the Psychology of Violence.* Chicago: Aldine.

Tyler, T. 2001a. *"Public Trust and Confidence in Legal Authorities: What Do Majority and Minority Group Members Want from Law and Legal Institutions? "Behavioral Sciences and the Law* 19:215-235.

Tyler, T. 2001b. *"Trust and Law Abidingness: a Proactive Model of Social Regulation."* Boston University Law Review 81:361-406.

Weisburd, D., R. Greenspan, E.E. Hamilton, K.A. Bryant, and H. Williams. 2001. *The Abuse of Police Authority: A National Study of Police Officers' Attitudes.* Washington, DC: Police Foundation.

Westley, W.A. 1953. "Violence and the Police." *American Journal of Sociology* 59:34-4 1.

White, S.O. 1972. "A Perspective on Police Professionalization." *Law and Society Review* 7:61-85.

Wilson, J.Q. 1968. *Varieties of Police Behavior: The Management of Law and Order in Eight Communities.* Cambridge, MA: Harvard University Press.

Worden, R.E. 1989. "Situational and Attitudinal Explanations of Police Behavior: A Theoretical Reappraisal and Empirical Assessment." *Law and Society Review* 23:667-711.

Worden, R.E. 1995. "The 'Causes' of Police Brutality: Theory and Evidence On Police Use of Force." Pp. 31-60 in *An Justice for All: Understanding and Controlling Police Abuse of Force,* edited by W.A. Geller and H. Toch. Washington, D.C.: Police Executive Research Forum.

9

Third Party Policing: Considering the Ethical Challenges

By Lorraine Mazerolle Griffith University
and Tim Prenzler Griffith University*

Introduction

In 1998, Buerger and Mazerolle coined the term "third party policing" to describe police efforts to persuade or coerce non-offending persons, such as property owners, parents, and business owners, to take some responsibility for preventing crime or reducing crime problems (1998: 301). In third party policing, the police *create* or *enhance* crime control guardians in locations or situations where crime control guardianship was previously absent or ineffective. Sometimes the police use cooperative consultation with community members to encourage and convince third parties to take more crime control or prevention responsibility. At other times, the police use coercive threats, with the backing of a range of regulatory laws, to engage third parties in taking some crime control responsibility.

Third party policing exists in many forms. For example, the police might use coercion or persuasion of third parties to solve ongoing problems within the context of problem-oriented policing programs. Third party policing sometimes exists as an especially designed, stand-alone-policing program. The Beat Health Program in Oakland, California (see Green, 1996; Mazerolle, Price and Roehl, 2000) is an example of a stand-alone thirdparty policing program that targets property owners in a systematic way to control drug and disorder problems in their tenancies.

In most police agencies, however, the police implement third party policing in very unconscious, episodic ways during routine patrol work. This category of third party policing activities, that occur outside of any programmatic intervention, includes coercive and ad hoc conversations with bar owners, parents, property owners, local government regulatory officers and other persons that the police at least believe to have some responsibility for creating or controlling the conditions that encourage lawless behavior. These ad hoc third party policing activities occur frequently and without any systematic consideration of the ethical challenges. It is this ad hoc, episodic category of third party policing that we focus the majority of our attention in this paper.

Our paper begins with an analysis of third party policing. We describe the dimensions of third party policing and provide examples of how third party policing is utilized by the police in both ethical and potentially unethical ways. In the second section of our paper we examine potential ethical challenges of third party policing. For example, some critics argue that third party policing is overly coercive, and has the potential to create indirect harms (see White, 1998). Third party policing may expose third parties to reprisal by offenders or may exacerbate family conflict. The facilitation role adopted by police might also be seen as partial toward some crime victims, or potential victims, over others. Other unforeseen negative consequences may result, such as evictions of disadvantaged persons who become homeless. In response to these issues, our paper concludes by presenting a set of ethical guidelines for a best practice approach to third party policing.

Dimensions of Third Party Policing

Third party policing is an insidious approach to crime control and crime prevention. On the one hand, numerous examples of third party policing reveal that it is a highly effective approach to solving crime problems and creating more positive social environments (see Mazerolle, Price and Roehl, 2000, Mazerolle and Roehl, 1998). On the other hand, very little academic discourse has challenged the ethical basis of third party policing practices (for exceptions see Cheh, 1998; White, 1998). In this section, we identify numerous dimensions and issues with third party policing (see also Mazerolle and Roehl, 1998) and we discuss these dimensions within the context of concrete third party policing examples.

Purpose of Action

We identify two primary purposes of third party policing activities: crime prevention or crime control. In crime prevention, the police seek to anticipate crime problems and reduce the probability of an escalation of the underlying conditions that may cause crime problems to develop. Third party policing that has crime prevention as its purpose of action operates to control those underlying criminogenic influences that may (or may not) lead to future crime problems. By contrast, third party policing that seeks to control existing crime problems explicitly aims to alter the routine behaviors of those parties that the police believe might have some influence over the crime problem. The apparent influence of "involved parties" might be conscious or unconscious, it might be explicit or implicit, and it might be planned or unplanned.

An example of third party policing with a crime prevention purpose includes property owner-training programs. These types of programs are delivered to property owners who manage high-risk apartment blocks and rental properties that are situated in hot spot neighborhoods. Property owner training programs are designed to teach property owners how to screen potential tenants, how to be alert to patterns of drug sale, and how to initiate eviction proceedings when a problem with a tenant emerges (see Smith and Davis, 1998).

An example of third party policing with a crime control purpose is when the police partner with various government departments (such as those responsible for health, sidewalks, water supply, buildings) to initiate inspections of properties where environmental factors either wittingly or unwittingly facilitate crime problems (see for example, Green 1996). In these cases, the police are reacting to an existing crime problem and they have generally utilized a number of traditional police resources already in their attempts to dissipate the crime problem. When the problem gets to the point of being intractable (or seemingly so), the police use every means possible to pressure the property owners to take responsibility for dispersing the crime problem that is occurring on their door step. One third-party approach is using local government resources (such as a building services department) to inspect and enforce regulatory laws (such as building regulations) with an implicit (and sometimes explicit) understanding that the "real problem" to be addressed by the property owner is the crime problem occurring on the premises.

Initiators of Third Party Policing

In our paper we focus on the police as the initiators of third party policing. There are, however, a variety of collectivities and individuals that have (or could) initiate third party policing activities. Police, prosecutors, individual citizens, community groups and law enforcement agents in regulatory agencies are, in fact, all potential initiators of third party policing. Art Lurigio and his colleagues (1998), for example, have conducted numerous evaluations of the Cook County Narcotics Nuisance Abatement Unit. The community-based narcotics nuisance abatement program that is operated by the Cook County (Chicago) State's Attorney Office is similar to others in a number of cities in the U.S. The program in Cook County relies on citizens and police to identify properties involving narcotics sales. Prosecutors then use three primary strategies—voluntary abatement, prosecutorial abatement, and community outreach—to abate such problems.

Other cities have initiated programs or encouraged citizens and community organizations to implement third party policing actions to prevent and resolve neighborhood crime and disorder problems. Some of the community-based programs operate quite separately from either the police or prosecutors whilst others operate in concert with law enforcement, prosecutors, and other governmental agencies. Jan Roehl (1998) conducted a national survey of community organizations to look at the role of organizations and citizens, the types and prevalence of the civil remedies they use, and the obstacles and outcomes they have encountered. Roehl (1998) suggests that the central roles of citizens' groups remain rather traditional, focused on serving as "eyes and ears" for the police and other enforcement agencies and pressuring government agencies to take action. In some cases, however, community groups have taken a more proactive role in third party policing. For example Roehl (1998) reports that one community group worked to increase alcohol tax revenues and then have a larger proportion returned to their community. In another example, the community worked to turn an abandoned property into needed housing for low- income families.

Focal Point

The focal point of third party policing can be people, places or situations (see Mazerolle and Roehl, 1998; Smith, 1998). Sometimes third party policing efforts are directed specifically at categories of people such as young people, gang members or drug dealers. To address some types of crime problems, the focal point of third party policing efforts might be directed against specific places, more often than not places that have been defined by the police as hot spots of crime. Drug dealing corners, parks where young people hang-out, and public malls are typically the focal point of third party policing activities that address specific places as opposed to certain categories of people. We note, however, that when places are the focal point of third party policing efforts, then categories of people (most likely delinquent young people and drug dealers) are the ultimate target of the third party policing efforts.

The third focal point of third-party policing activities include situations that gives rise to criminogenic activity. Examples of criminogenic situations include bus stop placements that facilitate strong-arm robberies, late opening hours of bars that lead to bar room brawls, and the general availability of spray paint in hardware stores operating in high-risk communities. In third party policing, the police utilize the principles of situational crime prevention (see Clarke 1992) to work with government agencies to change the situations that create crime opportunities. But, third party policing is both defined and differentiated from situational crime prevention by the sources and targets of coercion (see Buerger and Mazerolle, 1998). In third party policing, the police convince, coerce, manipulate and draw upon civil remedies to engage a third party to take on a crime control or crime prevention responsibility. Some third party policing activities might overlap with situational crime prevention and aim to alter the situational contributors to a crime problem. Situational crime prevention is replete with examples (and typologies) or situational crime prevention practices (see for example, Clarke, 1992; Clarke 1997), many of which draw on third party policing processes. Situational crime prevention theory, however, is silent on the sources and targets of coercion and abstains from identifying the processes for achieving situational controls. Our evolving theory of third party policing fills this void and illuminates the various dimensions and processes for engaging third parties to prevent or control crime.

Types of Problems

Third party policing can, in theory, be directed against a broad range of crime and quality of life problems (see Finn and Hylton, 1994; The National Crime Prevention Council, 1996). However, most examples and evaluations of third party policing comprise police efforts to control drug problems (see Eck and Wartell, 1998; Green, 1996; Mazerolle, Kadleck and Roehl, 1998) and disorderly behavior (see Mazerolle, Price and Roehl, 2000). There are several reasons why third party policing tends to proliferate in efforts to control low-level, street types of crime activity: first, third party policing practices tend most to occur at the grassroots of policing and in episodic, ad hoc ways. The ad hoc nature of third party policing means that the police are largely unconscious in their implementation of third party policing, linkages are not made between various third-party policing practices, and best practices are not openly discussed, developed and distributed. Second, third party policing is not an articulated or developed doctrine (but see Buerger and Mazerolle, 1998; Roach Anleu, Mazerolle and Presser, 2000). As such, very little discourse surrounds third party policing activities and there exists very little systematic assessment of third party policing practices (for an exception see Mazerolle and Roehl, 1998). Third, the marginalized, young, and disadvantaged targets of third party policing activities are least likely to challenge the basis of third party policing practices (see White, 1998). Finally, while the principles of third party policing could be easily applied to non-street crimes such as high level drug marketing, white collar offending, and fraud, we suspect that third party policing is likely to continue to be relegated to occupy the street level territory of policing. Buerger and Mazerolle (1998) identify the clear-cut distinction between civil forfeiture laws and civil regulatory laws. "Forfeiture penalizes property owners for active or passive participation in criminal activity, and deprives them of the fruits of their crimes. Civil regulatory laws, by contrast, impose duties on property owners [and third parties] in order to control the behavior of other persons" (1998: 323). We expect that the tradition of direct civil penalties for higher level criminal actors will not be superseded by the types of regulations that facilitate third party policing in the manner that we have espoused here and elsewhere (see Buerger and Mazerolle, 1998). As such, we suspect that the coercive, informal nature of third party policing would come under much more stringent scrutiny and offer far less of a lever to deter or control deviant behavior if applied to more sophisticated categories of offending.

Ultimate Targets

The ultimate targets of third party policing efforts are people involved in deviant behavior. In theory, the ultimate targets of third party policing could include those persons engaged in any type of criminal behavior including domestic violence, white-collar offenders, street criminals and drug dealers. In practice, however, the ultimate targets of third party policing are typically those offenders that are vulnerable, disadvantaged and/or marginalized. Young people (see White, 1998), gang members, drug dealers (Green, 1996), vandals, and petty criminals typically feature as the ultimate targets of third party policing.

The classic example of third party policing is using property owners as the "proximate targets" to control the behavior of drug-dealing tenants or customers (ie the ((ultimate targets"). Police use city inspectors and every means possible to convince and coerce property owners to assume some crime control responsibility. Oftentimes, the property improvements they are compelled to do are costly, both in terms of financial outlay as well as losses in income.

Another example of third party policing that seeks to indirectly control the activities of young people is the initiation of anti-cruising legislation. Anti-cruising legislation is an example of "delegated legislation" (or subordinate legislation) whereby municipal councils, medical associations, and other such regulatory bodies are authorized to legislate to regulate the activities of people within certain geographical areas (e.g. local council regulations) or for particular populations of people (e.g. members of a professional group) (see Heilbronn, Kovacs, Latimer, Nielson and Pagone, 1996). Delegated legislative authority is a prime lever for third party policing. For example, in controlling cruising problems, the impetus for the anti-cruising legislation is driven by the police and the local council is lobbied to enact the legislation. The legislative framework is usually developed by the police in consultation with the local government, business owners, and community members. The legislation is limiting in that anti-cruising laws generally target certain streets at certain times of days and days of the week. The police put forth the case that the quality of life of business owners and community groups are impacted by the cruising activities. Enactment of the legislation allows the police to move cruisers along, fine the violators, confiscate their vehicles or, in some cases, arrest the violators. While technically speaking anti-cruising legislation covers all persons engaged in the anti-social behavior in particular places, the actual *ultimate* targets of the legislation are the young people who frequent the designated area.

Proximate Targets, Burden Bearers and Third Parties

A key defining feature of third party policing is the presence of some type of third person (or third collectivity) that is utilized by the police in an effort to prevent or control crime. The list of potential third parties is extensive and can include property owners, parents, bar owners, shop owners, local and state governments, insurance companies, business owners, inspectors, and private security guards. Indeed, any person or entity that is engaged by the police to take on some type of role in controlling or preventing crime could potentially be identified as a third party or what Buerger and Mazerolle (1998) refer to as "proximate targets" and what Mazerolle and Roehl (1998) have also referred to as "burden-bearers." These are the people or entities that actually carry the burden for initiating some type of action that is expected to alter the conditions that allow crime activity to grow or exist.

Proximate targets of third party policing are often stakeholders or regulators that are identified by the police as useful levers in controlling a crime problem. Indeed, the roles in third party policing can change rapidly, they are varied depending on the situation, sometimes reciprocal in nature and idiosyncratic to the problem at hand. Indeed, the proximate targets of a third party policing activity in one context may become the ultimate targets of third party policing in another context. Moreover, cooperative police partners in one context might become hostile "partners" in another context. For example, in one city a building services department (or authority) might enthusiastically partner with the police to target property owners (proximate targets) in their efforts to evict drug involved tenants (ultimate targets) and thus reduce drug dealing problems. In another example, the police may partner with the local prosecutor's office to coerce drug dealers (proximate targets) to provide information about corrupt building practices by the building services agency (ultimate target). We suggest that the dynamic nature of third party policing reflects the fluidity and chaotic nature of crime prevention and crime control more generally.

Statutory Basis

One important way that third party policing is defined and distinguished from problem-oriented policing, community policing, situational crime prevention, and crime prevention through environmental design is through the sources of its coercive power (see Buerger and Mazerolle, 1998). A key defining feature of third party policing is that there must be some sort of legal basis that shapes police coercive efforts to engage a third party to take on a crime prevention or crime control role. The most common basis of third party policing includes local, state, and federal statutes including municipal ordinances, town by laws and other forms of delegated legislation such as health and safety codes, uniform building standards, and drug nuisance abatement laws, and liquor licensing. We point out that the statutory basis does not necessarily need to be directly related to crime prevention or crime control. Indeed, most third party policing practices utilize laws and regulations that were not designed with crime control or crime prevention in mind (e.g. Health and Safety codes, Uniform Building Standards). For the vast majority of third party policing activities, the statutory basis that provides the coercive power for police to gain the "cooperation" of third parties derives from obscure, non-criminal sources.

For example, the application of Uniform Building Standards to law enforcement is an obscure application of the law and its original intent. In Oakland, California, the police hijacked the local building codes to gain some coercive power over property owners whose properties were being used by drug users and dealers (see Green, 1996). If property owners did not cooperate with police efforts to reduce drug problems on their properties, the building code laws were used to pressure the property owner to cooperate.

The police also might utilize specific non-statutory laws to engage entities in third party policing. For example, the police often pressure local governments to change the underlying conditions of a crime problem. Oftentimes the local governments work cooperatively with the police. At other times, however, the police may threaten the local government agency with their potential liability for negligence suits arising from adverse consequences of the local government agency's failure to cooperate with the police. Cases that involve the use of coercive power to engage third parties in crime control or crime prevention pose the greatest opportunity to abuse and ethical dilemmas.

Types of Sanctions and Penalties

Regulatory sanctions utilized in third party policing vary greatly and include: court- ordered repairs of properties, fines, forfeiture of property or forced sales to meet fines and penalties, eviction, padlocking or temporary closure (typically up to a year) of a rented residential or commercial property, license restrictions and/or suspensions, movement restrictions, lost income from restricted hours and ultimately arrest and incarceration (see Mazerolle and Roehl, 1998). Oftentimes, several civil sanctions may be initiated simultaneously to solve one problem. To solve a drug problem, for example, a suspected offender might be evicted and the property owner cited for building code violations and asked to attend a property owner training seminar.

Tools and Techniques

Dozens of examples can be provided to illustrate the processes by which third parties are recruited and used by the police. Against the backdrop of a legal foundation to force a third party to cooperate, the police operate on a continuum to engage third parties in their crime prevention or crime control activities. At the more benign end of the spectrum, the police can approach third parties and politely ask them to cooperate. The police might consult with members of the community as well as local property owners and ask them about ways that they see fit to control an existing crime problem or help them to alter underlying conditions that the police believe might lead to future crime problems. At this low-key, benign end of the spectrum, the ultimate sanctions that might be unleashed on third parties most likely go unnoticed. The police may, themselves consciously utilize their persuasive powers, yet be unconscious about the alternative methods of coercion that they may resort to if the third party target proves to be an unwilling participant. At the more sinister end of the spectrum the police coerce third parties to participate in their crime control activities by threatening or actually initiating actions that compel the third party to cooperate. We point out that there are several stages in the forcible initiation of third parties in taking a crime control role: the first stage may involve a building services agency issuing citations to a property owner following building inspections of their property (see Green, 1996). The latter stage of this most coercive practice involves the initiation of court action to force the third party to comply with the citation. In Green's (1996) analysis of Oakland's Beat Health program, she found that less that three percent of cases ended up in court. That is to say that the vast majority (97 percent) of the property owners that failed to cooperate in the early, subtle stage of police efforts to engage the third party to take some crime control responsibility ended up complying with the police wishes after being issued citations but before the case went to court.

Types of Implementation

There are many different ways that the police implement third party policing practices. The most common manifestation of third party policing is the ad hoc utilization of third party principles initiated in an unconscious manner by patrol officers who are simply trying to find a way to solve a problem. These police are simply "flying by the seats of their pants." There is no script for them to follow, no police department policy that they are working within, and generally very little accountability for their actions. The police are working within the law, but using the law for their gain with little regard to the possible negative side-effects. It is this ad hoc category of third party policing implementation that most interests us in this paper.

Another way that the police implement third party policing is within the context of problem-oriented policing or a situational crime prevention program. Problem-oriented policing provides the management infrastructure (see Goldstein, 1990) and step-wise approach to solving a crime problem (Eck and Spelman, 1988) and situational crime prevention offers the police some ideas for reducing crime opportunities (Clarke, 1992; 1997). Third party policing provides the procedural and strategic foundation for how opportunities might get blocked and problems solved.

Beyond being part of a problem-oriented policing or situational crime prevention initiative, third party policing has been implemented in the past as a stand-alone program. The Beat Health Program, operating under the auspices of the Beat Health Unit in the Oakland Police Department since 1987, is a classic example of how a stand-alone program can operate within a police agency that, at the same time, is working to implement community policing.

Effectiveness

One of the central questions of third party policing is: does it work? Subsidiary questions include: does it reduce crime problems? Does it lead to a displacement or escalation of the problem? What other negative side-effects might the approach lead to? Does the approach lead to any type of diffusion of benefits? Is it a cost-effective approach? The short answer to these questions is that we don't really know. Limited evaluations of third party policing initiatives exist in the research literature and very little systematic effort has been expended to explore the possible negative side-effects of third party policing. As such, we provide a synopsis of the research literature as it now stands with the caveat that the dearth of information surrounding third party policing makes it difficult to provide definitive answers to our questions.

In answer to the first question—does it reduce crime problems?—we know that third party policing seems to be quite effective at reducing low-level drug problems. Reporting the results from an evaluation of a third party drug reduction program, Green (1996) shows that the SMART program had a positive and significant effect in alleviating the level of drug nuisance problems at targeted sites. The study demonstrates that a thirdparty drug-control strategy that aims to clean up the physical conditions of drug nuisance places can significantly reduce the amount of drug- related activity (Green, 1996). Similarly, Mazerolle and her colleagues (2000) demonstrate under experimental field trial conditions that the places targeted using a third party policing strategy improved relative to the control sites. The experiment also found some improvement in catchment areas surrounding experimental residential sites, but a possible displacement of drug problems in and around commercial experimental and control sites. Similarly, Eck and Wartell (1998) show that third party policing efforts that sought to improve the place management of rental properties with drug dealing problems led to a sizable reduction in reported crime within six months of the intervention.

Answering the questions pertaining to the side-effects of third party policing is somewhat more difficult. Green (1996) and Mazerolle and her colleagues (2000) found some evidence of spatial displacement of crime but concluded that the spatial net crime reduction benefits of third party policing outweighed the negative displacement consequences of the intervention (see also Green, 1994). In a study of public housing evictions, however, Justin Ready and his colleagues (1998) found that administrative complaints by public housing officers were used as a civil remedy tool to evict troublesome tenants from public housing. The negative implications of evicted public housing residents were, as the authors note, potentially devastating (see Ready et al., 1998).

The cost effectiveness of the third party policing approach is even more difficult to quantify. In possibly the first attempt to shed some light on the cost-effectiveness question of third party policing, Jon Caulkins (1998) provides a conceptual framework for understanding the cost effectiveness of civil remedies that are used within a third party policing context to reduce drug problems. Caulkins (1998) identifies many factors that need to be taken into account when assessing the cost effectiveness of third party policing. He concludes that at its best, third party policing can make negligent organizations more responsive to the needs of the citizenry and at worst, third party policing can lead individual police officers to hijack the resources of public organizations for private and not necessarily public benefit.

In this section we have discussed the primary dimensions of third party policing and provided a short summary of the effectiveness literature pertaining to third party policing. In the following section we explore the potential ethical challenges with third party policing and provide a best practice approach for implementing third party policing initiatives.

Ethical Challenges in Third Party Policing: Issues of Impact and Process

Policing is considered an occupation characterized by diverse ethical dilemmas, with an extremely high level of risk for misconduct (Cohen and Feldberg, 1991; Kleinig, 1996). Police face numerous opportunities for misconduct and corruption, primarily in the form of offers of payment for not enforcing the law. Nonetheless, even when officers are determined to reject corruption, ethical dilemmas still arise from competing choices about where to prioritize resources and how to maximize efficiency. Perhaps the best known of these dilemmas, and one that has particular relevance to third party policing, is the "Dirty Harry syndrome" or "noble cause corruption". This occurs when police are tempted to use illegal or ethically questionable means to obtain justice—for example to pressure a suspect to confess or misrepresent their powers to coerce people into compliance (Pollock, 1989).

Consistent with the growth of academic research on police ethics, police organizations have refined and extended their professional codes of conduct (Kleinig, 1996). There is now a strong consensus at the official level in most democracies about core principles that should constrain and direct police decision making. Perhaps the best expression of this consensus is the *Law Enforcement Code of Conduct* developed by the International Association of Chiefs of Police (IACP, 2001). The code addresses specific classic dilemmas, enjoining such positions as protection of confidential information, rejection of bribes and gratuities, and co-operation with lawful agencies. The code also sets out general principles of ethical policing. The most significant and encompassing of these is the requirement to enforce the law and assist the public equitably, without discrimination. In the words of the IACP code:

> A police officer shall perform an duties impartially, without favor or affection or in will and without regard to status, sex, race, religion, political belief or aspiration. All citizens will be treated equally with courtesy, consideration and dignity (2001: 1).

Despite the extensive development of police ethics as a field of study, the established literature has not caught up with the relatively new phenomenon of third party policing. In this section of our paper, we integrate existing critiques of third party policing within the more traditional framework of police ethics. We argue that ethical issues in third party policing need to be analyzed systematically, with a view to identifying the core ethical challenges and ways of managing these within established principles of police integrity. The goal should be to maximize the crime reduction and order maintenance benefits of third party policing while minimizing negative effects and ethical conflicts.

Misdirected Interventions at the Macro Level

Left-wing objections to strategies concerned with place management, environmental design and enhanced law enforcement allege that state resources are misdirected from the root social causes of crime "downstream" to crime situations (Rock 1997; see also White, 1998). A flawed process at the macro social level then leads to undesirable impacts. The later the state intervenes in the causal process of crime the less likely it is to succeed and the more likely it is to waste scarce public resources. In this view, third party policing is simply a novel extension of a misconceived system of reactive policing that allows the state to extend control and surveillance practices and technologies to public and semi-public spaces. This then becomes an exercise in asserting power through crime control—as opposed to egalitarian social prevention. It also has a net widening effect in engaging proximate targets and making civil actors part of the policing and state control process.

This Leftist critique, by implication, all but dismisses third party policing methods as inevitably reductionist, repressive and discriminatory (O'Malley 1994, Rock 1997, White and Sutton 1995; see also Clarke 1992: 27-30).

There are two significant problems with this element of the Leftist critique. The first is the assumption that all crime is caused by inequality. The second is that principled crime prevention requires that policing and situational prevention should be largely abandoned in favor of radical social restructuring. Given what is known about the antecedents of crime in low social capital and disadvantaged communities (see Sherman et al, 1997), we acknowledge that the Leftist thesis has a strong basis. However, inequality does not explain all crime, or even the bulk of crime in modern prosperous welfare states. Studies in rational choice theory and situational crime prevention demonstrate how opportunity is often a critical element of the crime equation in creating temptation (Cornish and Clarke, 1986). This is perhaps most pronounced in white-collar crime, where persons who are relatively well off will take advantage of opportunities to commit crime; but it also applies to many "street crime" scenarios. Cohen and Felson's (1979) study of crime rates trends demonstrated, for example, how increases in crime in the 1960s and '70s related more to prosperity—the proliferation of things to steal and more mobile lifestyles reducing guardianship—than to poverty.

The reverse side of the egalitarian critique of situational prevention is a utopian expectation that fundamental social change will stop crime and that policing stands in the way of this revolution. This second problematic aspect fails to appreciate the essential service provided by police in modern societies—whatever the root causes of crime and whatever the political reasons for the failure to put adequate resources into primary prevention. While measures designed to address the social structural causes of crime should be championed, the fact remains that police services are engaged in one of the most egalitarian and direct forms of democracy by responding to calls for assistance regardless of the status of the caller (see Bayley, 1998). From that perspective, Buerger (1998) makes a pertinent argument concerning the variability of police legitimacy. He draws on the social contract theory of police legitimacy (Cohen and Feldberg, 1991; Kleinig, 1996), by way of an early formulation made by Reiss (1971), restated cogently in the context of third party policing:

> Police authority is weakest when officers act on their own initiative, and strongest when they act on behalf of citizens requesting assistance. As the individual call legitimates police intrusion into a private residence, police demands upon managerial practices are justified by the collective weight of calls for assistance, articulated through either crime analysis of call records or communal voices in open meetings or neighborhood surveys (Buerger, 1998: 93).

Hence, third party policing, properly managed, has an ethically justifiable basis in victim protection and public demand.

Inequality of Impacts

In the Left-wing libertarian critique, the more belatedly the state intervenes in the causes of crime the less likely it is to succeed and, most significantly from an ethical perspective, the more likely it is that the intervention will involve repressive and unequally distributed law enforcement. Thus the victims of social injustice who turn to crime as a natural response to their marginalized status are doubly victimized by police attention, criminalization and spatial exclusion. This has a further net widening effect. By engaging civil actors in the policing process the reach of the police is extended to more disadvantaged groups. It "... impacts most negatively on homeless young people, the unemployed, indigenous young people and ethnic minority young people" (White, 1998: 124).

In fact, some studies do highlight the potential of third party policing to compound disadvantage (see for example Ready et al, 1998). This is most evident when third party policing activities result in tenant evictions. In a study of public housing evictions, for example, Justin Ready and his colleagues (1998) found that administrative complaints by public housing officers were used as a civil remedy tool to evict troublesome tenants. The negative implications of evicted public housing residents are, as the authors note, potentially devastating. Displacement is also a potential problem that challenges a basic principle of fairness, especially when displacement occurs from areas with higher economic and social capital to those with less capacity to employ security or other measures against crime (Clarke, 1992).

There might be some grounds, therefore, for a critique that characterize targeted policing and place management initiatives as defensive of middle and ruling class interests, and as serving their paranoia of juvenile delinquency. However, Buerger's analysis of third party policing highlights the responsiveness of police to the concerns of diverse communities. It is not just that police are responsive to community calls for assistance, as argued above, but that police prioritize their services on the basis of need. Third party policing is therefore not entirely reliant on calls for service. Police can act on intelligence about criminal activity without complaints from the public, and without necessarily targeting victimless crimes or acting as agents of social class. Victims may be intimidated into not calling police or feel cynical and disillusioned regarding police inaction experienced in the past. In fact, it is disempowered victims who may have the most to gain from third party policing. Police who rely exclusively on calls for service as measures of crime may be neglecting the fundamentals of egalitarian policing—in the words of the IACP code, to "perform all duties impartially, without favor ... and without regard to status, sex, race, religion, political belief or aspiration".

The Leftist critique understates these dimensions of consultation and responsiveness to community needs. Buerger (1998), on the other hand, relates the origins of third party policing to community policing, and emphasizes how a prime impetus behind third party policing interventions has been neglect of quality of life issues by property owners and managers (bourgeois and state). A core strategy of third party policing is getting place managers to fulfill their responsibilities to tenants and visitors. This neglect, addressed by police, is most pronounced for tenants who are dependent on public housing and lack economic resources to improve their position. The success of third party policing in this domain contradicts the argument that "invariably, the most vulnerable and marginalized sections of the population benefit the least from such strategies and are, in essence, further penalized and ostracized" (White, 1998: 121).

Despite the shortcomings of Leftist libertarian critiques, they serve an important function in highlighting potential unethical practices and unintended consequences of a practice like third party policing. One crucial accountability measure that should assist to relieve the potential for adverse impacts is proper outcome analysis that not only examines the direct effects of third party policing interventions but also the indirect or unintended consequences. Whilst an analysis of the displacement effects of third party policing is a good start, evaluations of third party policing practices need to be designed to look much more broadly than the potential displacement effects.

Unintended Negative Impacts on Third Parties

The importance of an informed awareness of the potential ethical risks of third party policing applies equally to the effects of coercive actions against third parties. Here the Leftist libertarian critique overlaps with, and is extended by, Cheh's (1998) civil libertarian legal analysis. Cheh examines the effects of civil asset forfeiture and injunction laws in the United States. She stresses the attractiveness of these measures to police and other law enforcement authorities. Forfeiture operates on the lower civil standard of evidence of probable culpability, as opposed to the higher "beyond reasonable doubt" criminal standard. When ultimate targets cannot be criminally prosecuted, forfeiture allows for alternative control through third parties. Civil forfeiture laws mean that crime can be stopped by seizing the facilitators or "instruments" of crime—such as cars, boats, planes and houses—without necessarily prosecuting individuals. The impact of crime can also be reduced by seizing assets, thereby returning the proceeds of crime to the public purse or directly to victims.

Despite these manifold advantages in crime control, Cheh also observed a large number of cases of excessive application of forfeiture provisions. Some third party protections have been strengthened, aimed mainly at private dwellings. But the "innocent owner" defense has carried minimal weight in forfeiture proceedings overall. As a result, innocent people, often unaware their property is being misused, can be severely adversely affected by its loss. In some cases, the harm to the third party is out of all proportion to the offense. Cheh includes some nightmare examples:

> In the Calero-Toledo case ... the Court upheld the forfeiture of a yacht because a single marijuana cigarette was recovered on board. The leasor boat company had no knowledge of the drug use (Cheh, 1998: 57).

> In Bennis v. Michigan (1996) ... the Supreme Court permitted the forfei-
> ture of an innocent wife's interest seized from her husband. He had been
> convicted of an indecent act with a prostitute while the two were in the
> vehicle. The wife's interest was sacrificed even though she had no aware-
> ness whatsoever that her husband had behaved or would behave as he
> did (Cheh, 1998: 57).

> A court found a lack of reasonable care where a parent loaned the family
> car to a son who had a minor record. When the son later used the car to
> transport drugs, the care was forfeited (Cheh, 1998: 58).

Cheh emphasizes the urgent need for law reform to protect innocent victims of civil remedies to crime and disorder problems. However, her analysis of case law precedents, and prosecutorial and political attachment to third party measures, is pessimistic of improved legal protections. Consequently, the responsibility falls back on police discretionary decision making for giving much greater consideration to the rights and needs of third parties. Cheh focuses attention on extreme cases and it is difficult to obtain an objective picture of the size of the problem. In addition, it must be kept in mind that third party policing is much broader than forfeiture alone. Nonetheless, this is clearly an area where police ethical decision making could be more systematic. For example, the standard ethical tenet of minimal force can be reconfigured more broadly in terms of minimal harm. When applied specifically to the issue of third party impacts, police actions can be guided by a principal of "distance of influence" or "proximal distance". In other words, the less responsibility a third party has for facilitating crime problems the less should be the adverse impact on them of any police interventions.

Coercive Micro Level Processes

A second important component of Cheh's (1998) critique of third party policing concerns due process issues. As noted, a major attraction of forfeiture mechanisms and civil injunctions is that they operate on a lower standard of proof and can be expedited relatively quickly before a judge or magistrate. The third party or respondent—of protection orders for example—does not even need to be present. This, however, is also a major pitfall for innocent third parties whose rights under criminal law are no longer available. In terms of forfeitures, for example, Cheh notes that:

> Typically the government seizes property without notice to the owner
> and without giving the owner any prior opportunity to object... Once the
> property owner is notified that a seizure has occurred, he or she has a
> stunningly short time (usually 10 to 20 days) within which to file a notice
> indicating a wish to contest the seizure. At a court hearing on the matter,
> the law effectively assumes that the property is subject to forfeiture, and
> the property owner—not the government—must now prove, by a pre-

> ponderance of evidence ... that the property is "innocent"... In addition,
> the property owner must pay all of the costs and expenses associated
> with this legal proceeding (Cheh,1998: 49).

Similar problems apply with injunctions in reversing the onus of proof and in limiting time for objections.

It must be emphasized that duress and abuse of third party rights are potential ethical risks but ones not intrinsic to third party policing. The tendency to bundle all nondevelopmental crime prevention strategies together as "coercive crime prevention" (White 1998) misses the focus on graduated coercion in third party policing. Police have demonstrated a willingness to adopt strong coercive measures in obtaining compliance from proximate targets, but it would seem they tend to prefer persuasion to coercion (Buerger, 1998). Coercion is the avenue of last resort, despite documented cases of excesses in the application of civil remedies. Again, the value of critiques of third party policing is to highlight the risks and in particular the potential for excessive use of coercive measures to obtain compliance. Some police may be tempted to use threats and heavy-handed tactics peremptorily, or to use legal but not necessarily fair or considerate means. Such actions are in fact in breach of code of conduct requirements that "all citizens will be treated equally with courtesy, consideration and dignity"; and that threats and force be used "only after discussion, negotiation and persuasion have been found to be inappropriate or ineffective" (IACP, 2001: 1,2).

Coercion and the Confusion of Ends and Means

Cheh's (1998) focus on police discretion leads to consideration of another ethical issue in third party policing: when police seek third party cooperation by threatening to initiate enforcement of building code and other regulatory laws by government officers. This has the effect of using the threat of enforcement of one law as a means of enforcing another law. Although legal, the approach is ethically questionable and analogous to the Dirty Harry syndrome in confusing ends and means. It makes a mockery of the non-enforcement of the laws being used as leverage, and it exposes public officials to charges of neglect, bias and connivance.

It can be argued, however, that police cannot be blamed for previous non-enforcement of regulatory laws. Violations have come to their attention by virtue of the crime problem they were called to resolve. There is also the argument that police action leads to a "diffusion of benefits" (Clarke 1992) in that both the crime problem and the regulatory problem can be resolved. Nonetheless, the main mitigation of this criticism resides in the focus on graduated coercion—on threat and force as actions of last resort. Police can defer referral of regulatory violations while attempting to first use voluntary compliance mechanisms. In some cases, unsuccessful efforts at persuasion can be followed by making training programs available. Smith and Davis (1998), for example, describe property owner training in how to manage crime problems. At a further step along the law enforcement/threat continuum, training programs can be mandated. Threats to bring in government officials to enforce code violations might then be justified as a last resort—the end justifies the means—subject to consideration of the seriousness of the problem (Pollock, 1989: 174-92).

Guiding Principles for Third Party Policing

The main conclusion of the preceding analysis is that third party policing carries significant diverse ethical challenges. These need to be managed within a coherent framework that blends established norms of police integrity with lessons from the critiques of third party policing. For example, White's critique at times allows some conditional legitimacy to situational prevention. He concedes that "opportunity reduction and situational crime prevention programs ... [may have some merit by] ... engaging people in disadvantaged areas in discussions of how best to adapt specific crime prevention technologies and techniques to their own needs" (1998: 121). Development of this approach provides for a powerful counter to his previously highly negative criticisms. Elsewhere, White, Murray and Robins (1996) have taken an even more positive approach in proposing guidelines for a socially inclusive approach to crime prevention by local government, town planners and other groups. The guidelines address process issues by emphasizing how planners need to consult with different stakeholder groups, including young people, when developing anti-crime initiatives. They address impact issues by emphasizing assessment of the full range of possible consequences of crime reduction measures, especially on those who are pushed into reliance on public facilities by poverty, unemployment, homelessness or family conflicts. Negative social impacts need to be listed as an item for consideration when implementing third party policing.

Cheh's critique draws attention to the fact that police and other law enforcement officers "are left with enormous discretion to employ civil remedies expansively and creatively" (1998: 63). Given the resistance of the courts and law-makers to enlarging procedural rights and protections for potential innocent victims of civil measures against crimes, it is incumbent on the initial decision makers to take this issue much more seriously. In Cheh's words,

> The allure of civil remedies presents a challenge. As the use of this tool proliferates, particularly forfeiture and injunctive decrees, legislators and enforcement officials must maintain principles of fairness and sensitivity. Practices that are constitutional are not necessarily wise. Indeed they may be "intensely undesirable" (Cheh, 1998: 63-64).

This reminder that what is lawful may not always be just is recognized in police codes of conduct. Legal discretion makes a space for police to mediate conflicting principles and interests—despite the risk of under-enforcement, discrimination and corruption. Hence the IACP code also recognizes that what is lawful is not always best in a given situation. Under the heading of "discretion", the code enjoins the following guidance:

A police officer will use responsibly the discretion vested in his position and exercise it within the law. The principle of reasonableness will guide the officer's determinations, and the officer will consider all surrounding circumstances in determining whether any legal action should be taken. Consistent and wise use of discretion, based on professional policing competence, will do much to preserve good relationships and retain the confidence of the public (IACP, 2001: 2).

What is particularly important is that these discretionary decisions be made within a proper accountability system, with formal community input and openness to scrutiny through public complaints mechanisms involving internal affairs departments and civilian review bodies (Kleinig, 1996).

Of particular value in the guidelines developed by White et al (1996) is the idea of prioritizing consideration of win/win alternatives to prosecution and exclusion, especially with reference to multi-agency responses. They provide a number of examples drawing on case studies from shopping mall and other development projects in Australia. For example:

- housing estates or shopping malls experiencing theft or vandalism by young people could experiment with installing recreation facilities such as ping pong tables or basketball courts.
- The same problems could be addressed by employing a youth worker rather than employing a security guard or installing CCTV.
- Idle young people congregating and causing nuisance can be employed collecting trolleys or in other types of low skill work.

These examples can be multiplied. For example, truanting children could be referred to non-traditional schools. Children with nothing to do after school might be referred to after-school care.

A major implication of this perspective for third party policing concerns enlargement of the scope of interactions beyond police and immediate proximate targets. A multi-agency approach needs to be taken that includes government and private welfare agencies. If troublesome tenants are to be evicted and are unable to relocate independently then they need to be referred to emergency accommodation services. If family conflict is causing problems, referral to family support agencies and counseling services might be the best initial response, with resort to noise abatement or nuisance regulations as a last resort.

In sum, third party policing initiatives need to include consideration of ethical issues from the beginning of the planning process. The best way to ensure a comprehensive inclusion of all possible ethical issues is by way of a formal list. This has been developed for policing via a number of mechanisms. Cohen and Feldberg, for example, propose a five point checklist for ethical policing covering "fair access, public trust, safety and security, teamwork and objectivity" (1991: 43). Pollock (1989) reviews a number of ethical decision making frameworks organized around sets of questions. As with checklists, when dealt with systematically, questions oblige the decision maker—whether an individual police officer, a patrol team, a supervising officer or a policy making body—to think through the diverse implications and alternatives associated with the issue they face. Some core questions supported by Pollock (1989: 338-42) are grouped and paraphrased as follow:. Do I understand the nature and causes of the problem? Have I explored all alternatives to threats, deception, manipulation and coercion? What are the possible consequences of my actions for all parties concerned? What harm might result? Is the possible harm justified by the severity of the harm that I am trying to stop? What are my intentions? Am I acting fairly and without prejudice or favoritism? Am I using anyone as a means to an end? Have I discussed the issue with all interested parties?

The following set of questions integrates established policing principles and ethical tests with elements of the Left- wing and civil liberty critiques in a third party policing context.

1. Is the planning process inclusive of all groups who may have a stake in the crime problem or may be affected by interventions? In other words, has consultation been biased or exclusive? White et al. suggest that this be avoided using a "space, people, use and power audit" with a comprehensive list of possible areas, interests and groups to be considered (1998: 20-23). The inclusion in their list of groups such as young people, the elderly and people with disabilities ensures that consideration is given to the least powerful groups who may have the most to lose.

2. Is the program prioritizing negotiation and persuasion over threats and use of force? What alternatives are there to threats or force? Is it possible to find win/win solutions before resorting to law enforcement, prosecution and exclusion? Is there potential for informal or formal conflict resolution or mediation?

3. What will be the impacts of the initiatives? In particular, what negative impacts might be foreseen, such as homelessness, increased family conflict, retaliatory actions, loss of essential property or loss of reputation by innocent third parties? Is it likely that crime will be displaced onto other areas and persons?

4. Are mechanisms in place for assessing the full range of possible impacts of interventions, including displacement of crime? Are social science techniques being used to control variables and properly evaluate the impact of interventions, especially in terms of possible adverse effects?

5. Are all the impacts of the proposed remedy proportionate to the harm it is supposed to be stopping? For example, are people in danger of losing houses or vehicles over a minor drug infraction? Are third parties being put through intimidating legal processes over what may be a relatively minor problem, such as noise, that might be solved by other means such as mediation? Are police using evictions, forfeitures, injunctions and other civil actions as a means of punishing proximate and ultimate targets rather than achieving substantive justice or real reductions in crime and harm? Has a principle of "proximal distance" been applied in insuring that the less responsibility third parties have for facilitating a crime problem the less adverse will be the impacts they experience?

6. Is recognition being given to the fact that offenders have numerous needs and may themselves be victims of abuse? For example, if drug addicted people are causing a problem, have they been referred to drug assistance agencies? If young people are "hanging out" in public and causing a nuisance they may be victims of domestic violence who are too afraid to return home.

7. *Are any third parties that might be affected afforded notice and an opportunity to explain or propose alternatives responses?* People don't like to be surprised by court orders. Police need to consider whether surprise injunctions are necessary or whether fair notice and opportunities for feedback are afforded to third parties. Personal contact and explanation might be less intimidating than the formal serving of a summons.

8. *Are basic principles of fairness and equal access being considered?* Are police showing partiality to one group over another or making unreasonable demands or severely disadvantaging specific groups? This applies to victims, primary and proximate targets, and any other groups. Are police being used for "vigilante justice" by people with a hidden agenda against their neighbors?

9. *Are all groups, including young people, being treated with dignity and respect?* Are police labeling or stereotyping certain groups, using aggressive language and failing to act courteously and professionally? Are police exacerbating the problem by racist or other derogatory language?

10. *If police officers engaged in a third party policing initiative are presented with ethical challenges should they consult with police internal affairs or the civilian oversight agency for advice?* Where police are uncertain about the ethical issues they face or want official confirmation of their interpretation of the guidelines, they should obtain advice from internal affairs or the oversight agency.

11. *Has the development phase of a third party policing program involved any other challenges to the police professional code such as requests for confidential information, offers of gratuities or bribes, or requests for preferential treatment that might risk the integrity and impartiality of the police service? Should any such circumstances be reported to police internal affairs?* Variants of community policing, such as third party policing, are designed to make the police and community work more closely together. However, this carries with it some risk in terms of possible. attempts to unduly influence police, garner preferential treatment through gifts and hospitality or generate corrupt relations. Third parties, for example, may offer police bribes to ignore violations of the law or may request police supply confidential information about tenants or neighbors. The integrity of the third party policing process, especially in the eyes of host communities, needs to be protected by immediate reporting of this type of ethical challenge.

Conclusion

Rather than dismissing third party policing as coercive, repressive and unethical, its significant potential for reducing crime needs to be understood and managed within a conscious framework of ethical risk. Like the new bio-technologies of cloning and fertility enhancement, third party policing is a technology that holds great promise for improving the quality of life for many citizens. At the same time, it carries significant potential for misuse and harm. The potential for both benefit and harm appears to be most heightened for the least powerful, most vulnerable, members of society. It is therefore incumbent on exponents and practitioners of third party policing to develop a more explicit ethical framework within which the benefits of third party policing can be advanced. This position follows logically from one of the basic premises of third party policing: that a deliberative, systematic and conscious approach to engaging third parties in crime prevention will maximize the benefits of an approach that is often taken by police on an ad hoc basis without evaluation. A further and essential dimension of that approach is to integrate ethical criteria into strategic planning and assessment of third party policing.

Our paper has provided a description of the key dimensions of third party policing, identified some of the primary ethical challenges to third party policing, and suggested an approach to implementing third party policing that we believe would minimize the potentially negative procedural and outcome effects of third party policing. Many models exist for implementing third party policing that might consider the eleven questions presented above. Minimalistically, we would expect police officers to at least consider these questions during their ad hoc utilization of third party policing practices. Alternatively, police departments might consider integrating these eleven questions into procedures that guide the use of third party policing.

References

Bayley, David. (1998). Policing in America: Assessment and Prospects. *Ideas in American Policing*, Police Foundation, February 1998.

Buerger, Michael E. and Lorraine Green Mazerolle. 1998. Third Party Policing: A Theoretical Analysis of an Emerging Trend. *Justice Quarterly*.15 (Number 2) pp 301-328.

Buerger, M. (1998). The Politics of third party policing. *Civil Remedies and Crime Prevention: Crime Prevention Studies*, Vol 9, pp89-116.

Caulkins, Jon. (1998). The Cost Effectiveness of Civil Remedies: The Case of Drug Control Interventions. In Lorraine Green Mazerolle and Jan Roehl (eds), *Civil Remedies and Crime Prevention: Crime Prevention Studies*. Vol 9. Mousey, NY: Criminal Justice Press. pp 219-240.

Cheh, M. (1998). Civil Remedies to Control Crime: Legal Issues and Constitutional Challenges. *Civil Remedies and Crime Prevention: Crime Prevention Studies,* Vol 9, pp45-66.

Cheh, M.M.(1991). Constitutional Limits on Using Civil Remedies to Achieve Criminal Law Objectives: Understanding and Transcending the Criminal-Civil Law Distinction." *The Hastings Law Journal,* 42:1325-1413.

Clarke, R.V. (1992). *Situational Crime Prevention: Successful Case Studies.* Albany, NY: Harrow and Heston.

Clarke, R. V. (1995). Situational Crime Prevention. In Michael Tonry and David P. Farrington (eds), *Building a Safer Society: Strategic Approaches to Crime* Prevention. Crime and Justice. Vol 19. Chicago, IL: University of Chicago Press.

Cohen, L.E. and M. Felson. (1979). Social change and crime rate trends: A routine activity approach. *American Sociological Review*, 44,588-608.

Cohen, S. and Feldberg, M. (1991) *Power and Restraint: The Moral Dimension of Police Work*. New York: Praeger.

Cornish, D. and Clarke, R.V., Eds. (1986). *The Reasoning Criminal. Rational Choice Perspectives on Offending*. New York, NY: Springer-Verlag.

Eck, J.E. and Spelman, W. (1987). *Solving Problems: Problem-oriented Policing in Newport News*. Washington, DC: Police Executive Research Forum.

Eck J. E. and J. Wartell (1998). Improving the Management of Rental Properties with Drug Problems. In Lorraine Green Mazerolle and Jan Roehl (eds), *Civil Remedies and Crime Prevention: Crime Prevention Studies*. Vol 9. Mousey, NY: Criminal Justice Press. pp 161-183.

Finn, P. and Hylton, M.O. (1994). *Using Civil Remedies for Criminal Behavior: Rationale, Case Studies, and Constitutional Issues*. Washington, DC: National Institute of Justice, U.S. Department of Justice.

Goldstein, H. (1990). *Problem-oriented Policing*. New York: McGraw Hill.

Green, Lorraine. (1995). Cleaning Up Drug Hotspots in Oakland, California: The Displacement and Diffusion Effects. *Justice Quarterly* 12 (Number 4), pp. 737-754.

Green, L. (1996). *Policing Places with Drug Problems*. Thousand Oaks, CA: Sage Publications.

Heilbronn, G., D. Kovacs, P. Latimer, J. Nielson, T. Pagone. (1996). *Introducing the Law*. 5th Edition. CCH Australia. Sydney.

IACP (2001). "Law Enforcement Code of Conduct". *International Association of Chiefs of Police*. http://www.theiacp.org/. Accessed 6 March 2002.

Kleinig, J. (1996). *The Ethics of Policing*. New York: Cambridge University Press.

Lurigio, A., R. Davis, T. Regulus, V. Gwiasda, S. Popkin, M. Dantzker, B. Smith, and L. Ovellett. (1998). More Effective Place Management: An Evaluation of Cook County's Narcotics Nuisance Abatement Unit. In Lorraine Green Mazerolle and Jan Roehl (eds), *Civil Remedies and Crime Prevention: Crime Prevention Studies*. Vol 9. Monsey, NY: Criminal Justice Press. pp 187-218.

Mazerolle, Lorraine Green, James F. Price, and Jan Roehl. (2000). "Civil Remedies and Drug Control: A Randomized Field Trial in Oakland, CA." *Evaluation Review*. Vol 24, No 2 pp 211-239.

Mazerolle, L. Green and J. Roehl (1998). Civil Remedies and Crime Prevention: An Introduction. In Lorraine Green Mazerolle and Jan Roehl (eds), *Civil Remedies and Crime Prevention: Crime Prevention Studies*. Vol 9. Monsey, NY: Criminal Justice Press. Pp 1-20.

Mazerolle, L. Green, C. Kadleck and J. Roehl. (1998). Controlling drug and disorder problems: the role of place managers. *Criminology* 36:371-404.

Mazerolle, L. Green, J. Roehl, and C. Kadleck. (1998). Controlling Social Disorder Using Civil Remedies: Results from a Randomized Field Experiment in Oakland, California. In Lorraine Green Mazerolle and Jan Roehl (eds), *Civil Remedies and Crime Prevention: Crime Prevention Studies*. Vol 9. Mousey, NY: Criminal Justice Press. Pp 141-160.

National Crime Prevention Council (1996). *New Ways of Working with Local Laws to Prevent Crime*. Washington, DC: National Crime Prevention Council.

O'Malley, P. (1994) "Neo-Liberal crime control: Political agendas and the future of crime prevention in Australia". In D. Chappell & P. Wilson (Eds.) *The Australian Criminal Justice System: The Mid-1990s*. Sydney: Butterworths.

Pollock, J. (1989). *Ethics in Crime and Justice: Dilemmas and Decisions*. Belmont, CA: West/Wadsworth.

Ready, Justin, Lorraine Green Mazerolle and Elyse Revere. 1998. "Getting Evicted: Social Factors Influencing Public Housing Evictions." In Lorraine Green Mazerolle and Jan Roehl, (Eds) *Civil Remedies and Crime Prevention: Crime Prevention Studies*. Vol 9 pp 307-328 Monsey, NY: Criminal Justice Press.

Reiss, A.J. (1971). *The Police and the Public*. New Haven, CT: Yale University Press.

Rock, P. (1997) "Sociological Theories of Crime". In M. Maguire, R. Morgan & R. Reiner (Eds.), *The Oxford Handbook of Criminology*. Oxford: Clarendon Press.

Roach Anleu, Sharyn, Lorraine Green Mazerolle and Lois Presser. 2000. "Crime Prevention and Social Regulation: An Analysis of Insurance as a Form of Third Party Policing." *Law and Policy*. Vol. 22, No. I pp 67-87.

Roehl, J, (1998). Civil Remedies for Controlling Crime: The Role of Community Organizations. In Lorraine Green Mazerolle and Jan Roehl (eds), *Civil Remedies and Crime Prevention: Crime Prevention Studies*. Vol 9. Mousey, NY: Criminal Justice Press. Pp 241-260.

Sherman, L.W. (1990). "Police Crackdowns: Initial and Residual Deterrence". In M. Tonry & N. Morris (Eds.), *Crime and Justice: A Review of Research*, Volume 12: 1-48. Chicago: University of Chicago Press.

Sherman, L., D. Gottfredson, D. MacKenzie, John Eck, P. Reuter, S. Bushway. (1997). *Preventing Crime: What Works, What Doesn't, What's Promising?*. Washington: National Institute of Justice.

Smith, M. (1998). Regulating Opportunities: Multiple Roles for Civil Remedies in Situational Crime Prevention. In Lorraine Green Mazerolle and Jan Roehl (eds), *Civil Remedies and Crime Prevention: Crime Prevention Studies*. Vol 9. Monsey, NY: Criminal Justice Press. Pp 67-88.

Smith, B. and R. Davis. (1998). What do landlords think about drug abatement laws? In Lorraine Green Mazerolle and Jan Roehl (eds), *Civil Remedies and Crime Prevention: Crime Prevention Studies*. Vol 9. Mousey, NY: Criminal Justice Press. Pp 291-306.

White, R. & Sutton, A. (1995). Crime prevention, urban space and social exclusion. *Australian and New Zealand Journal of Sociology*, 3: 82-99.

White, R. (1998). "Curtailing Youth: A Critique of Coercive Crime Prevention". *Crime Prevention Studies*, Vol 9, ppl 17-140.

White, R., Murray, G. and Robbins, N. (1996). *Negotiating Youth-Specific Public Space: A Guide for Youth and Community Workers, Town Planners and Local Councils*. Sydney: Youth Programs Unit, Department of Training and Education Co-ordination.

Part IV
Community Factors

Public confidence in the police is ultimately shaped by perceptions of police honesty, fairness, equity, and service to justice. When the police are seen as self-serving, brutal in the use of force, racist, sexist or ageist and uneven in the application of the law, individual officer actions and the broader police institution loose public legitimacy. Conversely, when the police are seen as lawful, public willingness is likely to increase in support of individual police actions and the broader goals of police agencies. The history of policing to date suggests that such public acceptance is a necessary ingredient to safer communities.

The monitoring of police agencies by those external to them has grown in importance as a tool to oversee police agency actions. Often, these actions arise in response to a consent decree that identifies a police failing and seeks redress in part by monitoring the department to assure that efforts to rectify the problem are indeed occurring. External monitors have been part of several consent decrees where police agencies agree to external oversight on selected issues for some period of time. In a few instances, such monitoring has become a more permanent aspect of agency performance measurement.

Community feedback relative to the quality of police service received and community assessment of police ethical behavior is also becoming a part of the process to assure integrity among the police. The community is, after all, both the client and subject of police interventions. How communities, variegated by age, race, gender, income, and lifestyle perceive the ethical character of their police is an important barometer of police legitimacy.

The final chapters of this volume address these important aspects of police integrity. In *Public Perceptions of Police Misconduct and Reform*, Weitzer reviews the literature on correlates of public attitudes toward the police with a particular eye toward the effects of controversial media incidents as well as city and neighborhood contexts. Weitzer also discusses available material on public attitudes toward reforms or solutions to police misconduct, including racial diversification, community policing, and leadership change. Throughout, Weitzer identifies several directions for future research.

In *Turning Necessity into Virtue*, Davis, Ortiz, Henderson, and Miller discuss lessons learned from the City of Pittsburgh's experience with a Federal consent decree that required several changes in oversight, training, and supervision of officers in the Pittsburgh Bureau of Police. Davis and his colleagues assess the extent to which various city officials believe departmental change occurred, community beliefs and attitudes regarding the consent decree and changes in policing, and objective indicators of police performance. A variety of methods were used, including in-depth interviews with police staff, city officials, union officials, and others, a survey of 400 residents, and police performance indicators (police data concerning use of sick days, separations, Part I and 11 crimes and clearance rates, traffic citations, and disciplinary action). These data helped to generate a rich description of the Pittsburgh experience, highlighting some of the improvements that have taken place as a result of the decree as well as some of the pitfalls and remaining work to be done.

10

Public Perceptions of Police Misconduct and Reform

Ronald Weitzer, George Washington University

Police misconduct can severely damage the image and integrity of a police department. While public opinion of the police is shaped by a variety of factors, real and perceived misconduct has a powerful influence on attitudes, especially when the action attracts media coverage.

The literature on police-citizen relations is deficient in at least three respects. First, most surveys focus on the attitudes of whites and blacks, neglecting Hispanics and Asians. Second, most analyses are conducted at the individual level, ignoring possible contextual-level influences on attitudes. And third, surprisingly little research has investigated citizens' views of possible solutions to policing problems. Survey questions about police misconduct are seldom followed up with questions about the kinds of corrective measures that would help to remedy these problems and improve the overall quality of policing.

This chapter begins with a review of some of the main determinants of citizen perceptions of the police and assessments of police misconduct, and then explores popular assessments of some reforms that might reduce police misconduct and improve police practices.

Predictors of Citizen Attitudes Toward the Police
Race
Race is one of the strongest predictors of citizen attitudes and experiences with the police. Blacks are consistently more likely than whites to believe that the police mistreat people, are racially biased, and lack accountability for misconduct. Very little attention has been given to Hispanic and Asian assessments of the police, but the limited literature available indicates that Hispanics are less critical than blacks but more critical than whites. Data on Hispanic residents of Los Angeles document their intermediate position between blacks and whites in their rating of the police department's overall job performance, belief that police brutality is common in the city, perception that the police are "tougher" on minorities than on whites, and belief that "racist feelings" are common among Los Angeles officers (Tuch and Weitzer 1997).

Like blacks, many Hispanics desire more police protection and a greater police presence in their areas. In New York City, 61 percent of Hispanics and 72 percent of blacks report that police protection in their respective neighborhoods is worse than in white neighborhoods (*New York Times* poll, June 1994). In Los Angeles, the majority of Hispanics (60 percent) and blacks (74 percent) say that too few police officers work in their neighborhoods; only 1 percent of each group said there are too many officers in their neighborhood (*Los Angeles Times* poll, March 1988). And in Texas, 59 percent of Hispanics desire more police patrols and investigative work in their communities; most of the respondents who had reported a problem to the police felt that the problem would not be solved or that the police would not even file a report (Carter 1985).

Almost no research has been done on variations within the Hispanic population, along the lines of national origin, immigrant vs. native-born status, or social class. One study found significant differences between English-speaking and Spanish-speaking Hispanics in two Texas towns. The Spanish-speakers were more likely than the English speakers to cooperate with police officers and to endorse the idea that the police department should be racially representative of the city population, but the two Hispanic groups did not differ in their belief that the police use excessive force in their neighborhoods (Cheurprakobkit and Bartsch 1999). More research is needed on differences within racial and ethnic groups, including social class differences, as discussed in the following section.

Social Class

In addition to race, social class may affect a person's experiences with and opinions of the police. A small body of research examines intraracial class effects. Some studies detect no significant class differences in whites' or blacks' attitudes toward the police; some find more favorable attitudes among middle-class blacks than among lowerclass blacks; and others find that middle-class blacks are more critical than disadvantaged blacks. These mixed findings may be a function of the kinds of policing issues examined in various surveys. It is possible that race is the most important determinant of attitudes on certain issues, while class significantly affects views on other issues. If so, the key question is not whether race or class is generally a more powerful predictor, but instead the *under what conditions* race or class predominates in shaping citizens' attitudes and experiences.

Class makes a difference in perceptions of police practices at the neighborhood level. Residents of disadvantaged neighborhoods are more likely to negatively evaluate police services to their neighborhood (e.g., response time, crime prevention, treatment of crime victims) than residents of middle-class communities, which is roughly consistent with differences in police practices across these neighborhoods (Klinger 1997). Regarding police misconduct, if disadvantaged blacks experience, observe, or hear about police abuse of residents of their neighborhoods, they may be prone to believe that police routinely engage in such abuse of blacks both within their neighborhoods and throughout the nation; members of middle-class black communities may be less likely to hold this belief, insofar as their neighborhoods are subjected to less of this abuse (Weitzer 1999). However, on global issues—such as the extent of police brutality, corruption, or racial profiling in America—middle-class blacks hold more critical views. Hagan and Albonetti (1982) found that blacks in professional and managerial occupations were more likely than blacks in lower occupational strata to believe that police treat affluent and poor people differently. Similarly, middle-class blacks are more likely than disadvantaged blacks to think that the criminal justice system treats African Americans more harshly than whites and that police racism is widespread (Weitzer and Tuch 1999), and more likely to disapprove of racial profiling, to view it as a pervasive practice, and to say that they have personally experienced it (Weitzer and Tuch 2002).

Why would middle-class blacks hold more critical views on these issues? One explanation is greater exposure to the media, including news coverage of instances of police misconduct (Newman et al. 1992). Such exposure may affect their perception of the scope of such problems and their disapproval of these practices, to a greater degree than for less educated, disadvantaged blacks, as a Toronto study found (Wortley et al. 1997). It is also possible that middle-class African Americans expect their status to translate into proper treatment by police and other public officials, as it does for whites, whereas disadvantaged blacks may be more fatalistic about their treatment by the authorities. For middle-class blacks, the clash between class-based expectations and their experiences with the police may amplify their belief that certain police practices are objectionable and widespread (Feagin and Sikes 1994). Middle-class blacks are also more likely to perceive racial bias in other institutional arenas, such as employment and housing (Hochschild 1995; Schuman et al. 1997).

More attention should be devoted to identifying the specific policing issues on which class predominates over race in shaping citizens' opinions, and those issues on which race overshadows class. The next step is to explain these patterns. Why are disadvantaged blacks more critical of the police on certain issues, while middle-class blacks are more critical on other issues? And does class shape Hispanics' attitudes in similar ways?

Personal Experience

African Americans are more likely than whites to report that they have been verbally abused, subjected to excessive force, and unjustifiably stopped by police. The gap between the reported experiences of blacks and whites varies from modest to substantial, depending on the type of experience, as shown in Table 1. About twice as many blacks as whites report that an officer has used insulting language or treated them disrespectfully, while eight times as many blacks as whites report that they have been stopped by the police because of their race. These self-reports on stops appear to be corroborated in some research on racial profiling along the nation's highways, where blacks are stopped disproportionately to their numbers as motorists (Harris 2002), and in studies of stops in certain cities (Fagan and Davies 2000; Smith 1986).

Table 1:
Personal Experience with Police

	Blacks %	Whites %
Police ever showed disrespect or used insulting language toward you[1]	28	16
Police ever "roughed up" you or someone you know, in your neighborhood[2]	26	10
Police ever physically mistreated someone in your household[3]	18	7
Police ever treated you unfairly because of your race[4]	38	7
Police ever stopped you because of your race[5]	40	5

Personal experience with police officers may influence an individual's general attitudes toward the police. Unpleasant contacts tend to lower opinions of the police, whereas positive contacts do not necessarily produce positive views of the police (Leiber et al. 1998; Scaglion and Condon 1980; Smith and Hawkins 1973; Walker et al. 1972). Negative contacts with officers tend to affect African Americans' attitudes more strongly than whites' (Bordua and Tifft 1971; Dean 1980; Walker et al. 1972), though a race effect is not always found. The feeling that one has personally experienced racial profiling, for example, is a strong predictor of attitudes toward the police irrespective of citizens' race. Both blacks and whites who feel that they have been stopped solely because of their race (**Table 1**) are more likely than those who do not have this belief to express dissatisfaction with the police and to view profiling as a widespread practice (Weitzer and Tuch 2002).

Personal experience is not a necessary condition for evaluating the police, and experiences themselves may be colored by pre-existing opinions of the police (Brandl et al. 1994). Some persons who have had no contact with officers still view police negatively. For example, more people believe that police frequently use abusive language or excessive force against citizens than the number who report a personal experience with these actions. Similarly, positive contacts with officers do not necessarily translate into favorable attitudes. A segment of those who have had a good interaction with the police hold very critical views of the police. In sum, personal experience influences the attitudes of many people, but perceptions are also shaped by other factors. One such factor is a person's knowledge of friends' and family members' encounters with the police, which is more prevalent among minority groups than among whites. When asked in one poll whether they knew of anyone who had ever been physically mistreated by the police, 40 percent of blacks and 17 percent of whites answered affirmatively, and a similar disparity (18 vs. 7 percent) was found for physical abuse of one's family members (Gallup 1991:79). In addition to personal experience and vicarious experience (via family members and friends), witnessing police misconduct toward others can significantly affect a person's perceptions of the police. People who observe even minor police wrongdoing are more likely to rate police negatively (Smith and Hawkins 1973:141).

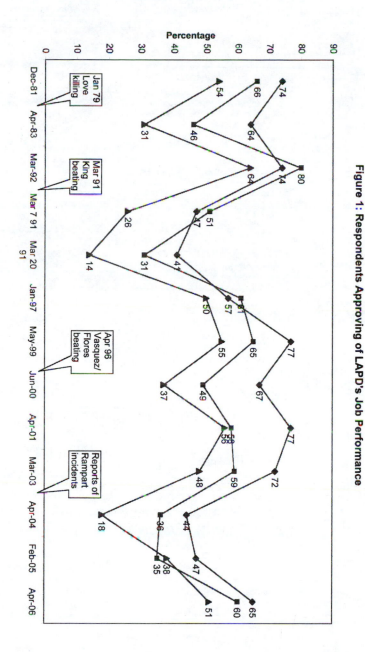

Figure 1: Respondents Approving of LAPD's Job Performance

Percentage

White ◆   Hispanic ■   Black ▲

Dec-81   Apr-83   Mar-92   Mar 7 91   Mar 20 91   Jan-97   May-99   Jun-00   Apr-01   Mar-03   Apr-04   Feb-05   Apr-06

Jan 79 Love killing

Mar 91 King beating

Apr 96 Vasquez/ Flores beating

Reports of Rampart incidents

74   66   54

64   46   31

80   74   64   26   14

51   47   31   41

57   50

81   65   55   77

49   37   67

56   59   48   72   58

18   36   44   59   72

38   35   47   60   65   51

Controversial Incidents

Highly publicized incidents of police misconduct appear to influence perceptions of the police, at least for a period of time. Actions that attract media coverage can dramatically shake citizens' confidence in the police, and even a single high-profile, incident can damage the image of a police department (Kaminski and Jefferis 1998; Lasley 1994; Sigelman et al. 1997). hi addition to discrete incidents, public trust in the police may be affected by problems that receive protracted, adverse media coverage, such as an unfolding scandal. A case in point is the Mollen Commission's investigation of police corruption in New York City. A series of Commission hearings in 1993 and 1994, covered by the media, aired allegations of serious police abuses in certain precincts, including police brutality, drug selling, stealing money and drugs from suspects, and other crimes. At the height of the scandal, in June 1994, a survey of New Yorkers reported that 58 percent of blacks and 32 percent of whites thought corruption was "widespread" in the NYPD (*New York Times*/WCBS poll, June 1994).

Weitzer (2002) tracked trends in opinion of the police before and after several incidents in Los Angeles (the 1979 killing of a black woman, the 1991 beating of Rodney King, a 1996 videotaped beating, and the recent scandal involving the LAPD's Rampart Division), and in New York City (the 1997 beating of Abner Louima, the 1999 killing of Amadou Diallo, and the 2000 killing of Patrick Dorismond). Each incident was followed by a spike in unfavorable ratings of the police department, and the magnitude of the change was usually greatest for the racial group associated with the victim. In New York, for instance, the percentage of blacks who said the police were doing a "poor job" (the lowest rating out of four options) increased from 14 percent in March 1997 (prior to the Louima beating) to 52 percent in April 2000—after the Louima, Diallo, and Dorismond incidents. The "poor" rating increased from 13 to 36 percent among Hispanics and from 6 to 11 percent among whites. Opinion in Los Angeles can be tracked over a longer time period. Figure I shows just how dramatically attitudes can change after a publicized incident.

Citizen confidence in the police eventually rebounded to pre-incident levels in Los Angeles, though the attitudes of the minority groups took longer to recover than did white opinion (Weitzer 2002). And even when minority views of the police improve after an incident, some long-term, diffuse damage to public confidence may persist. The most disturbing incidents are not easily forgotten, and can become deeply rooted in the collective memory of minority communities. The cases involving Rodney King, Abner Louima, and Amadou Diallo are now part of the cultural repertoire with which African Americans view the police. As a result, they may become more predisposed to accept allegations of police misconduct, even when officers act properly.

It goes without saying that media coverage of controversial police actions is not the sole predictor of post-incident changes in public opinion of the police; other factors shape citizen perceptions as well. However, the often dramatic increases in unfavorable opinion in the wake of highly publicized events suggest that such incidents do indeed have a significant effect on public opinion.

City and Neighborhood Contexts

Most surveys on perceptions of the police are either national or involve a single site, rather than multi-site comparisons. Little is known about the amount of variation in satisfaction with the police from one locale to another. Surprisingly little research has been done on *cities* as a locus of police-citizen relations, though there are good reasons to expect that city context makes a difference: Cities vary along a number of dimensions that may influence citizens' evaluations of the police—e.g., the city's socioeconomic and racial profile, police practices, local media reporting on the police, and the police department's racial composition. A 1968 study of 14 cities (Decker and Smith 1980) and a 1975 study of 13 cities (Skogan 1979) found that black residents of cities with greater black representation on the police force were somewhat more likely to hold positive views of the local police department than black residents of cities with lower black representation on the police force. These studies were conducted at a time when the number of black officers in these cities was far below a majority of the force; today, several large cities have majority-black or majority-Hispanic police departments, which may influence overall police-citizen relations in those cities. Two other studies examine popular attitudes across a number of cities. Skogan (1979) found variation among 13 cities in satisfaction with the police and in the black-white gap in satisfaction, and a survey of 12 cities found little variation in whites' satisfaction with the police, but greater variation among blacks—satisfaction ranged from 63 percent in Knoxville to 91 percent in Tucson (BJS 1999). Unfortunately, in neither study were the cities selected purposively according to any theoretically important variables, and the policing question was limited to the job performance of the city's police (Skogan 1979) or satisfaction with the officers who serve the respondents' neighborhood (BJS 1999).

Almost all contextual-level analyses focus on neighborhoods rather than cities, and almost all of the studies that include a neighborhood variable find differences in citizen attitudes by neighborhood (Brown and Benedict 2002). Neighborhoods may differ in residents' perceptions of police by virtue of variations in demographic composition, economic conditions, crime rates, and patterns of policing. With respect to neighborhood variations in police practices, police tend to be both less responsive to the needs of residents of poor, high-crime communities (Klinger 1997) and harsher in their treatment of people in such areas (Smith 1986)—a combination of underpolicing and aggressive policing. If police practices differ across neighborhoods, we should expect parallel differences in residents' relations with the police.

Citizen attitudes toward police also appear to be influenced by the racial composition and class position of their residential neighborhoods. One study found that residents of largely black, low-income communities were most dissatisfied with the police, while residents of largely white, upper-income areas were most satisfied—regardless of individual race and class position (Schuman and Gruenberg 1972). Thus, a black resident of a predominantly white neighborhood would tend to share the attitudes of his or her white neighbors, and similarly for a white resident of a predominantly black community. Some studies find that neighborhood socioeconomic status is a stronger predictor of residents' attitudes than neighborhood racial composition. Residents of disadvantaged neighborhoods hold more negative views of police services to the neighborhood and of police treatment of residents. Such neighborhoods are typically the least able to secure needed police protection and services, as indicated in residents' complaints and in data on police practices. In a Chicago study, after controlling for neighborhood racial composition and violent crime, residents of impoverished areas were significantly more likely than residents of other areas to report that officers performed poorly in preventing crime and maintaining order on the streets, responded poorly to crime victims, and were not responsive to "local issues" (Sampson and Bartusch 1998). Dissatisfaction with police services in poor neighborhoods is similarly reported for other cities (Reisig and Parks 2000). In Rochester, St. Louis, and Tampa, an average difference of 18 percentage points separated low and extremely disadvantaged communities in terms of residents' satisfaction with the quality of police services to the neighborhood; likewise, there was a 14-percentage point difference on the question of whether police provide the kind of services desired by community members (Velez 2001). Findings from studies using objective neighborhood conditions are mirrored in studies using residents' perceptions of neighborhood conditions. Residents who perceive their community as disorderly (Cao et al. 1996) or who believe their community is afflicted by gangs, drug dealing, and graffiti (Jesilow, Meyer, and Namazzi 1995) are more likely than residents of other areas to hold negative views of the police.

People living in disadvantaged areas are critical not only of poor service but also of mistreatment by officers. In Washington, DC, residents of a low-income black community were much more likely than residents of a middle-class black community to report that police misconduct occurred in their neighborhood. People in the disadvantaged black neighborhood were more likely to say that the police engaged in verbal abuse, excessive force, and unwarranted stops of people in their neighborhood. Regarding the police in Washington as a whole, they were more likely to express overall dissatisfaction with the police, to perceive police corruption as very common, to believe that officers who violate the law "usually get away with it, and to say that police community relations were worse in the city's black neighborhoods than in white neighborhoods. The middle-class black community was attitudinally similar to a middleclass white neighborhood included in the study, both of which registered rather positive views of the police (Weitzer 1999, 2000a).

These studies suggest that a neighborhood's social class position, rather than its racial composition or the race and class of individual residents, is the strongest predictor of opinions of the police, but much more research is needed to corroborate this finding.

Perceptions of Reforms

The overwhelming majority of blacks and whites in America believe that the criminal justice system should operate in a race-neutral fashion and favor federal government intervention to ensure that minorities and whites receive equal treatment by the police and courts—even if it would mean paying higher taxes to achieve this: 74 percent of whites and 89 percent of blacks subscribe to this view (*Washington Post* poll, July-September 1995). We should expect similarly broad support for other principles of good policing (responsive, respectful, noncorrupt, etc.) since it is easy to endorse police integrity and professionalism in the abstract. But what specific kinds of reforms receive the greatest public support? Though this question has seldom been investigated, some data exist with respect to the following remedies.

Civilian Oversight

Police accountability has long been a contentious issue in the United States. Minorities have less confidence than whites in the capacity of internal, police department mechanisms to effectively control officers. A majority of the public believes that police officers would be "too lenient" in investigating complaints against fellow officers—the opinion of 62 percent of whites, 70 percent of blacks, and 58 percent of Hispanics (Harris poll, October 1992). One change favored by the majority of Americans is the creation of civilian review boards to handle complaints regarding police misconduct. A national survey found that 58 percent of whites and 75 percent of blacks believe that authorities external to the police are needed to investigate and discipline officers accused of brutality against citizens (*New York Times*/CBS News poll, April 1991). In Los Angeles, 75 percent of whites, 88 percent of blacks, and 78 percent of Hispanics favor the creation of a civilian review board (*Los Angeles Times* poll, March 199 1), and in Boston, 5 9 percent of whites and 82 percent of blacks favor such a board (*Boston Globe*, September 2, 1991).

This does not necessarily mean that citizens will be satisfied with a civilian review board once it is in operation. Such boards may have greater public credibility than an oversight system internal to a police department, but a board with low substantiation rates (the norm) is likely to raise public concerns (Goldsmith and Lewis 2000). Moreover, persons with firsthand experience of such boards are often dissatisfied with both the process and the outcome. In New York City, for instance, two-thirds of those who had filed complaints with the city's civilian review board were dissatisfied with their experience, and 84 percent of those whose complaints had been fully investigated were dissatisfied (Sviridoff and McElroy 1989).

Still, the very existence of a civilian review board may have at least some symbolic value, indicating that the police are not wholly free of external oversight, even if the board substantiates a modest number of complaints. Virtually no studies have examined whether a civilian review board helps to improve public evaluations of police accountability or general assessments of policing in a city (Walker 2001). A Detroit study that asked citizens their impression of the Board of Police Commissioners (a citizens' body that sets police department policies and supervises the investigation of complaints against officers) found that 94 percent of blacks and 77 percent of whites considered the Board important in helping to reduce police brutality (Littlejohn et al. 1984).

The Los Angeles Police Commission seems to inspire less public confidence. The Commission sets policy and has oversight authority over the LAPD, but civil rights leaders have long criticized the Commission for its inability or unwillingness to hold the LAPD accountable. Most city residents, when asked whether the Commission or an "independent body" should conduct an investigation into the Rampart allegations favored the latter: 75 percent of Whites, 88 percent of Blacks, and 74 percent of Hispanics (*Los Angeles Times* poll, April 2000). The commission is evidently viewed as either too weak or as insufficiently independent of the LAPD to investigate the department in a satisfactory manner. A consent decree between the Los Angeles City Council and the Justice Department in 2000 resulted in the appointment of an independent federal monitor to oversee reforms. In 2001, 52 percent of whites, 58 percent of blacks, and 61 percent of Hispanics thought that such a monitor was needed to ensure that "a Rampart-like scandal will not happen again and will ensure that much-needed changes will be made within the department"(*Los Angeles Times* poll, February 2001). A minority of whites (33 percent), blacks (28 percent), and Hispanics (15 percent) took the opposing view that a monitor would "lower police officer morale and hamper their ability to do their job as they see fit."

Racial Diversification

The principle of proportional representation, or matching the racial composition of a police department to that of the city, is now widely accepted in national political and law enforcement circles (Walker 1985; Weitzer 2000b). The U.S. Department of Justice (200 1), for instance, proclaims, "A diverse law enforcement agency can better develop relationships with the community it serves, promote trust in the fairness of law enforcement, and facilitate effective policing by encouraging citizen support and cooperation. Law enforcement agencies should seek to hire a diverse workforce." There is considerable popular support for giving minorities preference in hiring to render police departments racially representative of their city's population: 48 percent of whites and 69 percent of blacks endorse this practice (*Newsweek* poll, March 1995). Most police departments remain unrepresentative of their city's minority populations, though seven large majority-black cities now have majority-black police departments and two large majority-Hispanic cities have majority-Hispanic police departments.

The notion that a police department's image and/or operations will be improved by greater racial diversity is an assumption that rarely has been tested.

If many citizens endorse the principle of racial diversity, the population is divided on whether police officers of different racial backgrounds behave differently toward citizens. A Milwaukee survey found black residents to be almost evenly split on the question of whether black officers treat blacks more fairly than white officers (Dresner 1981). Unfortunately, research on (1) public perceptions of the police in cities with varying degrees of racial diversity (which finds only slightly higher ratings of police in cities with higher percentages of black officers [Decker and Smith 1980]) and (2) the behavior of black and white officers (which finds that they tend to behave similarly toward citizens [Riksheirn and Chermak 1993]) is confined to cities where, or a time period when, the black proportion of the police department is small. Do police officers behave differently and are they perceived differently by the public in cities where blacks or Hispanics comprise the majority of the department? Sherman (1983:22 1) writes, "The fact that, as individuals, black and white officers show little difference does not exclude the possibility that a department with more black officers behaves differently from a department with fewer black officers. As blacks comprise a larger portion [or the majority] of a police department, they may become less isolated and more influential in shaping the values and culture of the entire police department," with potentially positive consequences for police behavior and citizen confidence in the police. This proposition has yet to be systematically tested, but a study of Washington, DC—where blacks comprise 69 percent of the police department—found diverse views among African Americans on the question of whether black officers act differently than white officers. Some saw no difference in the behavior of black and white officers, some believed that black officers treated civilians with more respect, and some believed that black officers behaved more harshly toward citizens. At the same time, a large number of blacks indicated that they preferred to see racially mixed teams of officers in their neighborhoods, rather than exclusively black officers, for both practical and symbolic reasons (Weitzer 2000b). Mixed teams were valued because they were seen as moderating or balancing each officer's behavior, as preventing citizens from concluding that questionable police actions were racially motivated, and as symbolizing racial integration and harmony in the police department.

Community Policing

Although community policing is gaining increasing favor throughout the United States, very few studies have explored (1) citizen attitudes toward various types of community policing or (2) whether an existing community policing program helps to improve residents' views of the police. If citizen relations with the police are shaped in part by neighborhood-level interactions, it is possible that community policing might help to improve those relations.

The evidence suggests that community policing can, but does not necessarily, improve citizen evaluations of the police. An evaluation of community policing programs in eight cities, based on focus groups with residents, found that few people knew about community policing in their neighborhoods, and few wanted to be involved in these projects, partly because police made little effort to involve them and partly because of fear of retaliation from local offenders if residents associated with the police (Grinc 1994). Williams' (1997) study of Athens, Georgia, again using focus groups, revealed that African Americans saw community officers as insensitive to residents' needs and did not show respect toward residents. Other research, however, indicates that community policing can improve residents' attitudes toward the police (CCPEC 2000:124; Skogan and Hartnett 1997; Trojanowicz 1983), and perhaps reduce citizen complaints against officers (Greene 1999). One study of fourteen community policing programs in six cities found that residents' views of the police improved in nine of the project areas (Skogan 1994).

The limited attitudinal data available indicates public support for most types of community policing, but even greater support for traditional crime-fighting approaches. Insofar as community policing is directed at conditions that appear somewhat removed from immediate criminal activity, public support may be muted. In Omaha, Nebraska, for example, residents rated eleven police practices on a five-point scale: The greatest public approval was given to the traditional police practices of anti-gang activities (4.71) and drug sweeps (4.43), while community policing received more modest support: meetings with neighborhood groups (3.83), after-school youth programs (3.77), bike patrols (3.62), and meetings with business owners (2.93) (Webb and Katz 1998). A survey of 12 cities found that half of the residents thought the police practiced community policing in their neighborhoods, defined as "officers working with the community to address the causes of crime" (BJS 1999:28-30). Of those who said community policing did not exist in their neighborhoods, 86 percent favored the introduction of community policing in their area, 25 percent of whom wanted officers to "work with the community," 13 percent wanted officers to "work with kids," and 7 percent wanted the same officers assigned to their neighborhood over time. Some other major options, such as foot patrol and community meetings, were not included in this question.

While there appears to be considerable public support for community policing, we do not have sufficient data at this time to determine if existing community policing programs live up to their promise of improving police-community relations.

Leadership Change

A change in police leadership can help to increase public confidence in a police department. For instance, the appointment of Willie Williams to replace Daryl Gates as chief of the LAPD was seen as a positive change by Los Angeles residents. A majority thought that Gates should receive "most" or "a good amount" of the blame for the Rodney King incident—50 percent of whites, 67 percent of Hispanics, 70 percent of blacks (*Los Angeles Times* poll, March 1991). And a substantial majority credited Gates' successor, Williams, for helping to improve the LAPD-58 percent of whites, 70 percent of Hispanics, and 80 percent of blacks (*Los Angeles Times* poll, January-February 1997). Replacement of a widely disliked and reform-resistant police chief may help improve police practices and/or police-community relations in other cities as well.

A related remedy pertains to a city's political leadership. After a series of publicized police abuses in New York City in the 1990s, a growing percentage of the population believed that the policies of Mayor Rudolph Giuliani's administration had "caused police brutality to increase" in the city. The number of blacks who took this view increased from 49 percent in October 1997 to 82 percent in April 2000 after three highly publicized brutality incidents, and the same trend was found among whites (18 and 38 percent, respectively) and Hispanics (33 and 69 percent, respectively) (*New York Times* polls, October 1997, April 2000). In March 1999, many New Yorkers believed that Giuliani's public statements about the Amadou Diallo incident had "made the situation worse": this was the opinion of 47 percent of whites, 61 percent of Hispanics, and 79 percent of blacks. After the Dorismond killing, the Mayor attempted to discredit Dorismond by releasing his arrest record to the media, claiming that he was not an "innocent" victim. New Yorkers roundly criticized this action: 67 percent of whites, 83 percent of Hispanics, and 94 percent of blacks thought that Guiliani's action was "unjustified" (*New York Times* poll, April 2000). And, once again, the mayor's statements had made the situation worse, according to 64 percent of whites, 77 percent of Hispanics, and 92 percent of blacks. It is possible that the election of a mayor who is less of a cheerleader for the police may help to reduce residents' impressions that city leaders condone police abuse of citizens. Mayors of some other cities have been less prone to defend the police in the aftermath of serious allegations of misconduct.

Other Reforms

Popular support for more sensitivity training of officers can be inferred from research showing that citizens want officers to maintain a proper demeanor in their contacts with people—including listening to people, being police and respectful, and explaining their actions, such as the reason for a stop. People who have been treated in these ways during a stop are much more positive about the police than those who have not been treated well (Skogan and Hartnett 1997:217) and much more likely to cooperate with officers (Wiley and Hudik 1974). Intensive sensitivity training for both new recruits and more seasoned officers might help to improve police treatment of citizens. In two precincts in the Bronx, New York, where residents' had frequently complained about officers, complaints dropped substantially after precinct commanders retrained officers in respectful treatment of civilians and instituted more robust monitoring of officers who receive multiple complaints, backed up with meaningful sanctions for recidivists (Davis and Mateu-Gelabert 1999). A concerted effort to improve police treatment of residents and bolster police accountability resulted in significant improvement in policecommunity relations.

Information is lacking on citizen impressions of several other types of changes, such as hiring more female officers, installing video cameras in police cars to monitor police conduct, requiring officers to record the race of persons they stop, requiring officers in Spanish-speaking areas to learn Spanish, and so forth. It is expected that these changes would register substantial public support and, if implemented, might help to improve police practices and the overall integrity of a police department.

References

BJS [Bureau of Justice Statistics]. 1999. *Criminal Victimization and Perceptions of Community Safety in 12 Cities, 1998.* Washington, DC: U.S. Department of Justice.

Bordua, David, and Larry Tifft. 1971. "Citizen Interviews, Organizational Feedback, and Police-Community Relations Decisions," *Law and Society Review* 6:155-182.

Brandl, Steven, James Frank, Robert Worden, and Timothy Bynum. 1994. "Global and Specific Attitudes toward the Police," *Justice Quarterly* 11: 119-134.

Brown, Ben, and William Reed Benedict. 2002. "Perceptions of the Police," *Policing* 25:543-580.

Cao, Liqun, James Frank, and Francis Cullen. 1996. "Race, Community Context, and Confidence in Police," *American Journal of Police* 15:3-22.

Carter, David. 1985. "Hispanic Perception of Police Performance," *Journal of Criminal Justice* 13: 487-500.

CCPEC [Chicago Community Policing Evaluation Consortium]. 2000. *Community Policing in Chicago: Year Seven.* Chicago: Illinois Criminal Justice Information Authority.

Cheurprakobkit, Sutham, and Robert Bartsch. 1999. "Police Work and the Police Profession: Assessing the Attitudes of City Officials, Spanish-Speaking Hispanics, and Their English-Speaking Counterparts," *Journal of Criminal Justice* 27:87-100.

Davis, Robert, and Pedro Mateu-Gelabert. 1999. *Respectful and Effective Policing: Two Examples in the South Bronx.* New York: Vera Institute of Justice.

Dean, Deby. 1980. "Citizen Ratings of the Police: The Difference Contact Makes," *Law and Policy Quarterly* 2:445- 47 1.

Decker, Scott, and Russell Smith. 1980. "Police Minority Recruitment," *Journal of Criminal Justice* 8:387-393.

Dresner, Morris, Tortorello, and Sykes Research. 198 1. The State of Police-Community Relations. *Report to the Milwaukee Fire and Police Commission.* Milwaukee, Wisconsin.

Fagan, Jeffrey, and Garth Davies. 2000. "Street Stops and Broken Windows: Terry, Race, and Disorder in New York City," *Fordham Urban Law Journal* 28:457-504.

Feagin, Joe, and Melvin Sikes. 1994. *Living with Racism: The Black Middle Class Experience.* Boston: Beacon.

Gallup. 1991. *The Gallup Poll: Public Opinion 1991.* Gallup Organization.

Goldsmith, Andrew, and Colleen Lewis (eds.). 2000. *Civilian Oversight of Policing.* Portland: Hart.

Greene, Judith. 1999. "Zero Tolerance: A Case Study of Police Policies and Practices in New York City," *Crime and Delinquency* 45:171-187.

Grinc, Randolph. 1994. "Angels in Marble: Problems in Stimulating Community Involvement in Community Policing," *Crime and Delinquency* 40:437-468.

Hagan, John, and Celesta Albonetti. 1982. "Race, Class, and the Perception of Criminal Injustice in America," *American Journal of Sociology* 88:329-355.

Harris, David. 2002. *Profiles in Injustice: Why Racial Profiling Cannot Work.* New York: New Press.

Hochschild, Jennifer. 1995. *Facing Up to the American Dream: Race, Class, and the Souls of the Nation.* Princeton: Princeton University Press.

Jesilow, Paul, J'ona Meyer, and Nazi Namazzi. 1995. "Public Attitudes toward the Police," *American Journal of Police* 14:67-88.

Kaminski, Robert, and Eric Jefferis. 1998. "The Effect of a Violent Televised Arrest on Public Perceptions of the Police," *Policing* 21:683-706.

Klinger, David. 1997. "Negotiating Order in Police Work: An Ecological Theory of Police Response to Deviance," *Criminology* 35:277-306.

Lasley, J. 1994. "The Impact of the Rodney King Incident on Citizen Attitudes toward the Police," *Policing and Society* 3:245-5 5.

Leiber, Michael, Mahesh Nalla, and Margaret Farnworth. 1998. "Explaining Juveniles' Attitudes toward the Police," *Justice Quarterly* 15:151-173.

Littlejohn, Edward, Geneva Smitherman, and Alida Quick. 1984. "Deadly Force and its Effects on Police-Community Relations," *Howard Law Journal* 27:1131-1184.

Newman, W. Russell, Marion Just, and Ann Crigler. 1992. *Common Knowledge: News and the Construction of Political Meaning.* Chicago: University of Chicago Press.

Reisig, Michael, and Roger Parks. 2000. "Experience, Quality of Life, and Neighborhood Context," *Justice Quarterly* 17:607-629.

Riksheim, Eric, and Steven Chermak. 1993. "Causes of Police Behavior Reconsidered," *Journal of Criminal Justice* 21:353-382.

Sampson, Robert, and Dawn Bartusch. 1998. "Legal Cynicism and (Subcultural?) Tolerance of Deviance," *Law and Society Review* 32:777-804.

Scaglion, Richard, and Richard Condon. 1980. "Determinants of Attitudes toward City Police," *Criminology* 17:485- 484.

Schuman, Howard, and Barry Greenberg. 1972. "Dissatisfaction with City Services," in Harlan Hahn (ed.) *People and Politics in Urban Society.* Beverly Hills: Sage.

Schuman, Howard, Charlotte Steeh, Lawrence Bobo, and Maria Krysan. 1997. *Racial Attitudes in America.* Cambridge: Harvard University Press.

Sigelman, Lee, Susan Welch, Bledsoe, T., and Combs, M. 1997. "Police Brutality and Public Perceptions of Racial Discrimination," *Political Research Quarterly* 5 0, 777-9 1.

Sherman, Lawrence. 1983. "After the Riots: Police and Minorities in the United States, 1970-1980," in N. Glazer and K. Young (eds.) *Ethnic Pluralism and Public Policy*, Toronto: Lexington.

Skogan, Wesley. 1994. "The Impact of Community Policing on Neighborhood Residents," in Dennis Rosenbaum (ed.) *The Challenge of Community Policing.* Thousand Oaks: Sage.

Skogan, Wesley. 1979. "Citizen Satisfaction with Police Services," in R. Baker and F. Meyer (eds.) *Evaluating Alternative Law-Enforcement Policies.* Lexington: Lexington Books.

Skogan, Wesley, and Susan Hartnett. 1997. *Community Policing, Chicago Style*. New York: Oxford University Press.

Smith, Douglas. 1986. "The Neighborhood Context of Police Behavior," in Albert Reiss and Michael Tonry (eds.) *Crime and Justice*, Vol. 8. Chicago: University of Chicago Press.

Smith, Paul, and Richard Hawkins. 1973. "Victimization, Types of Citizen-Police Contacts, and Attitudes toward the Police," *Law and Society Review* 8:135-152.

Sviridoff, Michele, and Jerome McElroy. 1989. *The Processing of Complaints against the Police in New York City*. New York: Vera Institute of Justice.

Trojanowicz, Robert. 1983. "An Evaluation of a Neighborhood Foot Patrol Program," *Journal of Police Science and Administration* 11:410-419.

Tuch, Steven, and Ronald Weitzer. 1997. "Racial Differences in Attitudes toward the Police," *Public Opinion Quarterly* 61:642-663.

U.S. Department of Justice. 200 1. *Principles for Promoting Police Integrity*. Washington, DC: U.S. Department of Justice.

Velez, Maria. 2001. "The Role of Public Social Control in Urban Neighborhoods," *Criminology* 39:837-863.

Walker, Darlene, Richard Richardson, Oliver Williams, Thomas Denyer, and Skip McGaughey. 1972. "Contact and Support: An Empirical Assessment of Public Attitudes toward the Police and the Courts," *North Carolina Law Review* 51:43-79.

Walker, Samuel. 1985. "Racial Minority and Female Employment in Policing," *Crime and Delinquency* 31:555-572.

- - - - - 2001. *Police Accountability: The Role of Citizen Oversight*. Belmont, CA: Wadsworth.

Webb, Vincent, and Charles Katz. 1998. "Citizen Ratings of the Importance of Community Policing Activities," in Geoffrey Alpert and Alex Piquero (eds.), *Community Policing: Contemporary Readings*. Prospect Heights, IL: Waveland.

Weitzer, Ronald. 1999. "Citizens' Perceptions of Police Misconduct: Race and Neighborhood Context," *Justice Quarterly* 16:819-846.

- - - - - 2000a. "Racialized Policing: Residents' Perceptions in Three Neighborhoods," *Law and Society Review* 3 4:129- 15 5.

- - - - - 2000b. "White, Black, or Blue Cops? Race and Citizen Assessments of Police Officers," *Journal of Criminal Justice* 28:313-324.

- - - - - 2002. "Incidents of Police Misconduct and Public Opinion," *Journal of Criminal Justice* 30:397-408.

Weitzer, Ronald, and Steven Tuch. 1999. "Race, Class, and Perceptions of Discrimination by the Police," *Crime and Delinquency* 45:494-507.

- - - - - 2002. "Perceptions of Racial Profiling: Race, Class, and Personal Experience," *Criminology* 40:435-456.

Wiley, Mary, and Terry Hudik. 1974. "Police-Citizen Encounters: A Field Test of Exchange Theory," *Social Problems* 22:119-127.

Williams, Brian N. 1997. *Citizen Perspectives on Community Policing*. Albany: State University of New York Press.

Wortley, Scot, John Hagan, and Ross Macmillan. 1997. "Just Deserts? The Racial Polarization of Perceptions of Criminal Injustice," *Law and Society Review* 31:637-676.

11

Turning Necessity into Virtue
Pittsburgh's Experience with a Federal Consent Decree

Robert C. Davis Christopher W. Ortiz Nicole J. Henderson Joel Miller
Vera Institute for Justice

Introduction

The last few years have seen the emergence of a new figure in American policing: the external police monitor. Monitors are responsible for auditing the performance of law enforcement agencies which have entered into an agreement to implement reforms. Some police departments, such as the Los Angeles County Sheriff s Department, have installed their own monitors voluntarily in the wake of local scandals or following the recommendations of commissions. Others, such as the Pittsburgh Police Bureau, have agreed to monitoring as a part of a consent decree, settling civil rights litigation brought by the U.S. Department of Justice or private parties. There are now more than a half dozen such external police monitors in place across the country.

As the number of monitors grows, so does the need for a systematic body of knowledge about how police departments work under their watch. What are the real dangers, and what are the real opportunities for improvement? How have successful monitors forged constructive partnerships with law enforcement agencies and helped them achieve significant reform?

The growth in the number of monitors is largely due to a change in federal law made as part of the Violent Crime Control and Law Enforcement Act of 1994. With that law, Congress gave the Attorney General power to sue state and local governments over patterns or practices of policing that violated the Constitution or laws of the United States. In the first four lawsuits that reached settlement, the settlement included the appointment of a federal monitor or auditor to oversee compliance with the decree. The monitors both measure police performance and assist in the development of more effective police management. Today there are monitors, auditors, or independent consultants in place as the result of Justice Department or other investigations in Pittsburgh; Steubenville, Ohio; Los Angeles; Walkill, NY; the State of New Jersey; Riverside, CA.; Montgomery County, Maryland; Philadelphia; Washington, D.C.; and Cincinnati.

In this chapter, we discuss lessons drawn from the monitoring experience in Pittsburgh. The Pittsburgh Bureau of Police now has more experience with federal court monitoring than any other urban department. Moreover, the Pittsburgh experience is widely recognized as having brought about significant reforms through a cooperative relationship between the monitor and law enforcement administrators.

The Consent Decree is Born

In April 1996, Justice Department investigators came to Pittsburgh to conduct an inquiry into police misconduct and failure to discipline officers against whom citizen complaints had been substantiated. Armed with the new provisions of the Violent Crime Control and Law Enforcement Act of 1994, the department began one of its first formal "pattern or practice" investigations. In a letter to the city solicitor in January 1997, Justice Department lawyers charged use of excessive force, false arrests, improper searches and seizures, failure to discipline officers adequately, and failure to supervise officers.

City officials were skeptical that the Justice Department could successfully make its case and initially decided to fight the allegations. But by the time the city received formal notification that the Justice Department intended to sue, the city solicitor recommended that Pittsburgh seek a settlement with the federal government, and the city gave up its fight. There were three main factors in the city's decision. The first involved the arrival of a new, reform-minded police chief who wanted to make changes similar to those proposed by the Justice Department, and city officials saw a consent agreement as a more desirable alternative than the possible loss of control over policing to the federal government. Second, city officials realized that police record keeping was so bad that they couldn't adequately defend against Justice Department charges. Finally, the changes the Justice Department was demanding would include a new database system that would, among other benefits, allow the city to produce statistics on misconduct and racial bias that could refute future critics.

A consent decree was filed on April 16 in the United States District Court, Western Pennsylvania District. The settlement instrument outlined specific policy and practice changes that the city had to comply with. It instructed the Bureau of Police to make comprehensive changes in oversight, training, and supervision of officers. Among the key elements was a requirement that the Bureau develop a computerized early-warning system to track individual officers' behavior; document uses of force, traffic stops, and searches; and provide annual training in cultural diversity, integrity and ethics. The decree also required changes in the processing of citizen complaints, including liberalized filing procedures and more thorough investigations. The reforms were to be overseen by a monitor who would report quarterly on the city's compliance to the federal judge who issued the decree.

Purposes and Organization of the Research Project

We used a variety of methods to abstract lessons from the Pittsburgh experience. Our primary means of gathering information was through in-depth interviews.

We interviewed the police chief, members of his command staff, and other city officials to find out how the city had responded to the consent decree. We asked how had they organized themselves? What reforms had been implemented? What was the nature of the relationship between city officials and the monitor? We spoke to union officials, supervisors, and rank and file officers to find out how the decree had affected the way in which officers approached their jobs. Had accountability increased? Were officers more circumspect in their dealings with citizens? Were officers slower to get involved in discretionary situations? We also interviewed community leaders and human rights activists to gain their perspectives on changes brought about by the decree. Did they believe that police accountability had increased? Did they believe that the reforms would be long-lasting?

We surveyed 400 residents of one police zone to find out the public's reaction to the decree. To what extent was the public aware of the consent decree? Did the community perceive changes in policing since the decree was signed? Were the reactions similar between black and white residents?

Finally we examined trends in police performance indicators to verify information gained through interviews. Had there been changes in indicators of officer morale, public safety, or racial bias by officers? Were there changes in the filing of citizen complaints, or dispositions of citizen complaints since the decree was signed?

The City Responds to the Decree

Upon signing the consent decree, the city brought together a team that consisted of a broad range of representatives from city agencies-agencies that would serve an important ancillary role in the implementation of the decree as well as those directly affected by the decree. In all, 13 people sat on the committee that was charged with spearheading the implementation of the decree provisions. This team included the police chief and two of his command staff, the deputy mayor, the city solicitor, the public safety director, the manager of the Office of Municipal Investigations (the city agency that handles citizen complaints), the director of personnel, a representative from the budget office, the director of city information systems, and two consultants. Conspicuously absent from the list was a representative from the police union, the Fraternal Order of Police (FOP). There was discussion among committee members about inviting the FOP to participate, but in the end, participation of the union was considered too risky given that it expressed strong opposition to the decree.

The work of the committee included developing specifications for the early warning system, allocating funds for police training, and planning reforms to the Office of Municipal Investigation (OMI). The large allocation (eventually $1,000,000) needed for an early warning system was immediately recognized, but the city did not foresee the sizable allocation necessary for additional investigators for OMI.

The Monitor

The role of the monitor was defined within the consent decree as monitoring the city's compliance with the provisions of the decree. He was to do this by examining official documents, analyzing information from Police Bureau and OMI databases, and interviewing staff of the two agencies. The monitor was also directed to create quarterly reports outlining compliance by the city. Selection of the monitor was a joint process between city and DOJ officials. Both parties screened and interviewed applicants, with the successful candidate approved by the judge who issued the decree. In our interviews with city officials, it was clear that they appreciated their involvement in choosing the successful candidate. Allowing the city to play the primary role in making the selection likely increased the confidence of city officials in the monitor and facilitated his work.

The monitor initially played an active role, going beyond the requirements of the decree and assisting the city with its implementation rather than simply evaluating its performance. When requested, the monitor aided the implementation committee, which was facing the decree one deadline at a time without developing a master plan. "He gave us the framework for compliance," stated one committee member. The monitor produced a compliance manual, which broke down the provisions of the decree into manageable steps. He outlined the things he was going to look for at each stage.

The monitor played a significant role as well in implementing the legal requirements in the consent decree. (For example, he operationalized "substantial compliance" in the decree as 95 %.) His willingness to act as intermediary between the city and DOJ helped avoid disputes over interpretation of the decree.

In his first year, the monitor made an effort to meet with community leaders and interested parties. He attended several community meetings at which the consent decree was discussed. Some community leaders were disappointed when he failed to continue these appearances or to provide regular feedback to community organizations, but these issues were never officially part of his duties.

Bureau of Police

The chief of the Bureau of Police played the most important role in implementing the consent decree. In his job for only a year when the decree was signed, the chief had been committed to pushing forward a reform agenda. The consent decree negotiated between Justice Department lawyers and the city incorporated many of the initiatives that the police chief had intended to implement. In fact, in some ways, the consent decree was a godsend to the police chief. It circumvented the political battles that he would have had to fight with the union to implement reforms. It also ensured the City Council's commitment to provide funds for the reforms. Agreeing to the decree, the city had no choice but to come up with the necessary dollars.

An important part of the implementation process involved gaining the trust of officers who were hurt and angry over the implication that they were bad cops and suspicious that the early warning system would be used against them. Each officer was given a copy of the consent decree and told to read it. If they had any questions, they were directed to go to their commanding officer for an explanation. But officers remained afraid that they would be automatically disciplined if they were "indicated" by the newly-developed early warning system. According to union officials, the rank and file remained suspicious of the decree and the changes that were occurring in the Bureau. The FOP had vehemently opposed the decree, and the chief s support of it damaged further an already strained relationship between him and the union.

The Bureau made other changes that promoted the philosophy embodied in the consent decree. The chief directed the controversial narcotics Impact Squad to deemphasize high profile drug "sweeps." Instead, he ordered them to conduct surveillance operations in order to establish cause for their actions so that searches and seizures would be based on observations rather than suspicions. All police officers were trained in a new approach to policing that characterized citizens as customers. Officers were asked to put themselves in the public's shoes and deal with citizens respectfully. Through its community policing unit, the Bureau began problem-solving initiatives in which community police officers worked with citizens to identify problems and then worked with city agencies to solve them. Community police officers also increased their outreach efforts to the community and became more involved in promoting block watch, property serial number marking, and other citizen anti-crime efforts.

The Office of Municipal Investigations

OMI is the complaint investigation body in Pittsburgh. It investigates citizen complaints concerning all city employees, but complaints about police officers and police practices form the majority of OMI's workload. OMI is an amalgam of a civilian review body and an internal affairs office. The office employs both civilians and sworn police personnel as investigators. Even though OMI has sworn police investigators, the office remains independent of the Bureau of Police within the city organization, falling under the authority of city attorney.

The consent decree made it much easier to file complaints against police officers, and by 1998 the average number of complaints per year had reached 800 compared to just 300 complaints prior to the decree. The decree also required that the investigative process become far more thorough and required more extensive reporting as investigators documented each step in the process. However, the resulting need for a substantial increase in OMI's investigation staff was not immediately realized. The city initially did not allocate funds for additional investigative positions nor did the city solicitor request that additional police officers be assigned as investigators. In fact, OMI actually lost staff due to a provision in the decree that limits the amount of time a police officer can serve as an OMI investigator to three years. Some of the Bureau of Police investigators had as many as six years with OMI. They left, and OMI operated with a staff of just four investigators for most of 1997.

The early inaction forced the city to play "catch up" in an effort to bring OMI within the levels of compliance demanded by the consent decree. Between 1997 and 2000, OMI's budget grew substantially from $173,000 to $353,000.[1]

OMI hired several new investigators, most of them attorneys, and made improvements in the way the agency is managed. According to OMI officials, the new staff were put through a lengthy training program, including enrollment in the police training academy, but many soon left for more lucrative law jobs. Other new staff members were added, bringing the caseloads; to a manageable 20 cases per investigator. By this time, however, there was a backlog of 500 unresolved cases that proved difficult to whittle down.

Policy Change
Bureau of Police

Use of Force: The consent decree requires the Pittsburgh Bureau of Police to "develop and implement a use of force policy that is in compliance with applicable law and current professional standards." The policy on the circumstances in which officers could use deadly force was already quite conservative and well within professional standards. Where the Bureau made changes was in the reporting of lethal and less-than-lethal force, and the process by which the use of lethal and less-than-lethal force is reviewed by supervisors.

With the introduction of the consent decree, the Bureau policy changed to mandate reporting of less-than-lethal force by police officers. This was accomplished through the creation of the Subject Resistance Report, which is to be completed each time a Bureau officer uses force, be it lethal or less-than-lethal. Prior to this policy, the use of less- than-lethal force was explained within the narratives of other Bureau reports such as arrest reports. The new Subject Resistance Report had the objective of capturing both the use of force by police officers and the level of resistance on the part of the subject in one document, completed each time an officer uses force in an incident.

As part of the reporting system required by the Department of Justice, supervisors are mandated to review each force incident. Each Subject Resistance Report is reviewed by the shift sergeant and then by the shift lieutenant. It is then forwarded to the zone commander for final review. Aggregate statistics are compiled and present a picture of the overall use of force by the Bureau officers.

Search and Seizure: The second policy that the consent decree slated for revision is the Bureau of Police policy pertaining to strip searches. As with the use of force policy, the consent decree states that the new policy must conform to any applicable state laws and to current professional standards. Unlike the use of force recommendation, the strip search mandate goes into great detail defining the provisions of the policy. According to the consent decree, strip searches are to be performed only with the authorization of a supervisor. They are to be carried out by specially trained personnel in a room specifically designed for these searches. Only the fewest number of personnel necessary are allowed in the room and they must be of the same sex as the subject.

As a result of the decree, the Pittsburgh Bureau of Police created the Field Contact/Search/Seizure Report. This report goes beyond the requirements of the consent decree in some respects. In addition to capturing information about all searches (strip searches, warrantless searches, consent searches, etc.), it captures information regarding the seizure of any property resulting from a search and field interviews of persons stopped by the police.

The form contains a space for the officer to articulate the justification for the search and a "consent to search" statement that is signed by subjects who are waiving their Fourth Amendment rights. The fact that consent is obtained in writing on an official police form goes beyond the requirements of the consent decree and distinguishes Pittsburgh from prevailing police practice. As is the case with other reports, this report is reviewed by the shift supervisor and forwarded to the zone commander for final review. These reports are examined individually and in the aggregate.

Traffic Stops: The consent decree required the Bureau of Police to revise its traffic stop policy. In response, the Bureau created the Traffic Stop Report and trained its officers in the use of Verbal Judo, a strategy widely used by police departments nationally to provide officers with an effective method of handling interactions with citizens during traffic stops and other routine encounters. The Traffic Stop Report documents pertinent demographic information concerning the drivers and passengers of vehicles stopped by officers as well as the results of any searches. The policy directive also contains provisions for internal checks on officer reporting. At the time of a traffic stop, officers are required to radio dispatch and relay information concerning the reason for the stop, the location, the license plate number of the stopped vehicle, and the race/gender of everyone in the car.

Training: In response to the consent decree, the Bureau now trains new recruits in cultural diversity, verbal de-escalation, and the citizen complaint investigation process. Current officers are instructed in these skills once a year as part of their in-service training. All supervisors receive annual training in supervisory and leadership skills, including instruction in accountability, integrity, and cultural diversity.

Rotation: The consent decree states that, "The city shall develop and implement a rotation schedule that ensures that officers regularly are supervised by and work with different officers." The Bureau decided to comply with the requirement by transferring 25% of supervisors and 20% of officers annually. This has been one of the most unpopular policy changes with the union, which argues that the transfers reduce officers' knowledge of the area they are patrolling and discourage bonds between officers and community residents.

Office of Municipal Investigations

The consent decree touches on all aspects of OMI's operation, from its physical location to the definition of its dispositions to initiation of civilian complaints to complaint investigation.

OMI Offices and Procedures: One of the first provisions within the consent decree for OMI deals with the physical location of the office. Prior to the decree, the agency was located in the Public Safety Building along with Bureau of Police headquarters. In response to the consent decree, the city moved the OMI office to a downtown location in a private office building.

Training of OMI Investigators: The consent decree set minimum requirements for the training of all OMI investigators. According to these guidelines, OMI investigators must be trained as police officers on certain issues, falling just short of certification. Specifically, it requires that they attend police academy training in policies related to use of force, searches and seizures, pursuits, transporting individuals in custody, restraints, arrests, traffic stops, racial bias, report writing, cultural sensitivity, ethics, integrity, professionalism, and investigative and interview techniques. OMI investigators also have attended relevant seminars given by outside agencies. Examples of these include a search and seizure seminar given by the local bar association, seminars in interviewing techniques, and use of force seminars.

Complaint Intake: OMI's complaint intake policy was completely revamped as a result of the consent decree. Prior to the decree, OMI only accepted complaints filed in person by the victim within 90 days of the alleged incident. The consent decree mandated that complaints could be filed by telephone, mail, or fax, in addition to in person. The consent decree also mandated that OMI accept and investigate anonymous and third party complaints.[2]

Complaint Investigation: The consent decree mandated many changes to the complaint investigation policies of OMI. Prior to the consent decree, OMI operated under an internal policy directive that put a limit on the amount of time it had to investigate a complaint. This policy (it is unclear whether it was a written policy or just an understood directive) mandated that all complaint investigations be completed within 60 days of the filing of the complaint.

Under the decree, OMI changed its policy to allow 90 days to complete investigations. This was done in an effort to allow investigators increased time to conduct the thorough type of investigation outlined in the decree. Even so, the court-appointed monitor believed a proper investigation sometimes needed more time. OMI again changed its policy, taking into account the monitor's concerns, and increased the investigation limit to 120 days. Policies with regard to uncooperative complainants also changed as a result of the consent decree. In the past, complainants who refused to cooperate with an investigation after initiating a complaint found that their complaint would not progress past filing. As a result of the consent decree, OMI now investigates fully cases with uncooperative complainant.[3] OMI's *Compliance with the Consent Decree.* Over the five years of the consent decree, OMI was in compliance with a large majority its requirements. However, the monitor's reports near the end of the five-year period found an unacceptably large backlog of open cases, which he attributed to understaffing. The monitor also found an unacceptably high proportion of OMI investigations lacking in thoroughness and reports lacking in documentation. These compliance problems continued and even worsened through the fifth year of the decree.

The Early Warning System

The early warning system is the centerpiece of the Police Bureau's reforms in response to the consent decree. Such systems are intended to highlight poor officer performance and provide a system to correct behavior, thus potentially saving a career rather than destroying one. Early warning systems use algorithms to alert supervisors that officers have exceeded a predetermined threshold for significant events such as citizen complaints, traffic stops, use of force, etc. These databases can also be used to monitor aggregate trends for a department or a sub-unit within the department. Monitoring of officers entails three phases: selection, intervention, and post-intervention monitoring.[4] In the selection phase, highlighted officers are brought to the attention of the command staff. Once an officer is selected or "indicated" by the criteria built into an early warning system, supervisors closely review the officer's conduct and circumstances to determine if there is a potential problem. In many cases, no action is warranted. But officers who are found to have problems enter the intervention phase. Corrective action may simply consist of a talk with a first line supervisor, or it may be quite in-depth, involving retraining and psychological counseling. After intervention, officers then enter the monitoring phase. Here, an officer's performance in the field is evaluated and scrutinized. This is usually accomplished through informal random evaluations by a first line supervisor.

The consent decree required that the Pittsburgh early warning system capture office data in nine separate areas: civilian complaints, officer involved shootings, criminal investigations of officers, civil claims against officers, lawsuits against officers, warrantless searches, use of force, traffic stops, and the use of discretionary charges. The decree further stipulates that the system have the ability to report this information categorically by individual officer, squad, zone, shift, or special unit. For most categories of data, the decree does not stipulate what thresholds need to be exceeded to warrant intervention. These decisions were left to the Pittsburgh Bureau of Police. Neither does the decree make specific reference to a particular system. In essence, all of the operational details of the system were to be decided upon by the city.

The system developed by the Police Bureau met all of the requirements listed in the consent decree. But the Performance Assessment and Review System (PARS) surpasses those requirements and other early warning systems in that it collects data on 18 categories of incidents. Moreover, in some of those categories a unique threshold was created. PARS determines acceptable limits in comparison with officer's peer group through the use of a standard deviation calculation. Instead of being compared to fixed numbers, each officer's figures are compared to his or her peers. Figures for traffic stops, arrests, sick time, use of force, and search and seizures fall around a central number, a mathematical mean or average. Some officers will have higher figures and others will have lower figures. Officers whose activity falls one or more standard deviations away from the average for their peers are indicated. Therefore, officers working in Zone 2 on the evening shift will be compared to other officers working that same shift in that same zone. At the time of its creation, this feature was unique to PARS. Since then, the use of peer group comparison has been employed in other systems.[5]

An alert feature lists any officer who has had a critical incident, such as a car accident or a civilian complaint that was recorded in the PARS system since the last time the supervisor logged in. This does not mean that the officer exceeded a threshold and therefore needs intervention; it only alerts the supervisor to the fact that the officer is one step closer to being indicated. For example, if an officer misses a court appearance or is the subject of a civilian complaint, his or her name will appear in the alert list. This allows supervisors to notify the officer about the incident, checking that it is valid and not an error in reporting. And it allows supervisors to counsel the officer informally and discuss other performance issues in a proactive "localized" manner prior to any formal action.

The system also transmits corrective action or notifications from the command staff or senior supervisors to sergeants. A notification may consist of an order to a supervisor to observe an officer's performance or to take additional corrective action. If the first line supervisor does not return a message describing the action taken and the completion date, then the notification is marked "overdue." First line supervisors who fail to take action in a timely manner may be subject to corrective action themselves. This ensures that all notifications are addressed and adds to an atmosphere of accountability within the department.

Unlike many early warning systems, PARS was designed to identify positive behaviors as well as negative. This is made possible by the algorithm PARS uses to target officers, which identifies any exceptional behavior—good as well as bad. Officers identified by PARS often receive positive recognition, a feature which makes PARS highly unusual among early warning systems.

PARS represents a sweeping change in the duties of the lowest level supervisors. In traditional policing, sergeants are associated with field supervision and management. In many police agencies, sergeants perform policing duties alongside their officers, often making arrests, answering calls for service, and performing other law enforcement duties themselves. The Pittsburgh Police Bureau, through the PARS system, has substantially changed to the duties of the first line supervisor. But this change comes at a price. Supervisors are expected to continue performing many of their traditional duties while meeting the required duties associated with PARS and the consent decree. These new duties, such as reviewing all Subject Resistance Reports, Daily Activity Reports, and Search and Seizure Reports, and performing guided field evaluations, have proven to be extremely time consuming and leave less time for sergeants to perform more traditional field supervision and management.

PARS is made an even more potent force for accountability through quarterly COMPSTAR meetings. COMPSTAR is a command level meeting modeled after COMPSTAT, the crime management initiative that began in New York City and quickly spread to departments nationwide. COMPSTAR shares the same philosophy, but the focus is on personnel management rather than crime statistics. The entire command staff discusses officers who have been indicated by the PARS system.

Each commander at the COMPSTAR meeting makes a presentation based on a report submitted to the chief This report details all of the officers indicated within that zone, the reasons behind the indication, and any corrective action taken that may be deemed necessary. The report concludes with a recommendation by the zone commander to intervene or not. The presentations follow the same pattern. First, zone commanders detail the aggregate figures for their zone. Commanders often list the aggregate data for use of force, searches, and complaints, noting any increase or decrease over the last reported quarter. Large increases must be explained and justified.

After the aggregate reporting, the commanders focus on individual officers. Officers who have been indicated are discussed in detail. The first group covered consists of officers who were indicated in the current quarter, usually 20- 30 officers per zone. As he or she discusses an officer, the commander may add pertinent information that may not be clear from the PARS reports, such as assignments and special details or initiatives. For instance, an officer may be taking part in a quality of life campaign in a public housing area that would generate higher numbers of summonses issued than his or her peers. Often commanders advise each other about officers who were once under their command but who have subsequently been transferred out. The ultimate decision to intervene or not lies with the chief, but he follows the recommendations of unit commanders in the vast majority of cases. Few of the indicated officers will have action taken against them. When an action is taken, it is usually to monitor an officer through supervisory field checks. In rare cases, officers are ordered to undergo counseling or retraining.

The second group of officers discussed in the meeting consists of those indicated in a prior quarter and still undergoing intervention and monitoring. Commanders focus on the officers' performance after intervention. They also describe the type of intervention the officer underwent and how he or she responded. Again, the commander concludes with a recommendation either to continue or end the monitoring.

COMPSTAR is also an opportunity for the Bureau to review data that may lead to changes in policies or training. At one COMPSTAR meeting, it was noted that many of the use of force incidents resulted from a lack of communication and de-escalation skills. As a result, the entire department was re-trained in the use of better communication skills. At another meeting, administrators discussed the results of a recent policy advocating the use of pepper spray in certain situations and how information captured on subject resistance reports could be used to tailor training programs at the academy.

Community Views on the Consent Decree and its Impact on Policing

Concerns about policing within segments of the community were a key force leading to the consent decree, and public confidence in policing is, therefore, an important yardstick by which its success should be measured. As well as allowing us to assess some of the decree's successes and limitations, an examination of the community's views also highlights opportunities for understanding and taking into account

Figure 1:
Perceptions of change in police-community relations over last 5 years

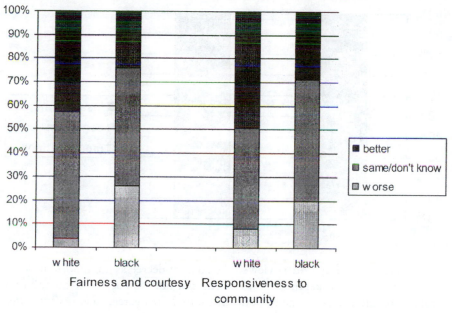

the views of the community in the implementation of future consent decrees.

A number of the leaders we spoke with underscored the notion that for many years the city of Pittsburgh, like many urban areas, has been grappling with a past characterized by racism and segregation. Against this backdrop, the idea of the consent decree drew strong public support. Among community leaders, it was viewed with hope. The survey of Pittsburgh residents in Zone 2 revealed that they were also positive about the decree. About half (47%) had heard of the consent decree. After the decree was described to respondents, all were asked whether they thought it was necessary. The consent decree drew overwhelming support from both whites and blacks, with 84% of people saying it was necessary to improve the quality of policing.

Many of the community leaders we spoke with emphasized that they viewed the leadership within the city and in the Police Bureau as a key factor in the effective implementation of the decree. Several expressed confidence in the police chief, describing him as "progressive," and noting that "he cares about standards and accountability." The federal monitor was given high marks by community leaders for his efforts to implement the decree.

All of the community leaders saw the consent decree as a useful management tool that functioned to increase accountability and improve practice. One leader mentioned that the data collection system was "excellent" and that the decree had given the community greater confidence in the police. Another leader commented that the consent decree got the police "headed in the right direction."

Figure 2:
Perceptions of change in police abuse of force over last 5 years

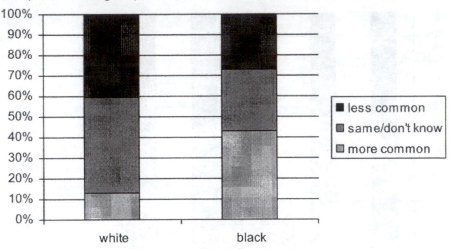

While community leaders viewed the consent decree as an important development, many voiced skepticism as to whether or not the Police Bureau had fully complied on all levels. As one respondent praised the decree, she also expressed concern:

> The consent decree has very lofty management goals. The early
> warning system is a well thought out, very sophisticated monitoring tool.
> However, when you rely on self-reporting, the system is problematic.
> Unless supervisors are out on the prowl, who's to say things are being
> properly reported?

The opinions of residents of Zone 2, as captured on the survey, echoed those of community leaders. Among those who had heard of the decree, 45% felt that policing in Pittsburgh had improved since the decree was signed. However, 41% saw no improvement, and I I% felt that things had gotten worse (3 % had no opinion).

Two questions about change in the relationship between the police and the community revealed substantial racial differences. While more than 43% of white people thought policing had improved in terms of fairness and courtesy, this was true for just 24% of African-Americans. Similar patterns were observed on the question of changes in police responsiveness to the needs of the community: while half of white people thought it had improved, this was true for less than a third of African-Americans (see **Figure 1**).

When asked for their views on the current state of police community relations, respondents were generally positive, with 65% thinking the police were

Table 1:

Experiences of police contacts in the last 2 years

Perceptions of police treatment	All those *who* approached the police %	All those approached *by* the police %
How were they treated, overall…		
very well	36	20
reasonably well	34	32
neither well nor badly	8	24
Somewhat badly	15	16
very badly	5	8
don't know	2	1
	100	100
	(170)	(124)

doing a good job of treating citizens in a fair and courteous manner, and 64% claiming they were doing a good job of responding to the needs of the community. There were, once again, sizeable disparities between the perceptions of whites and African-Americans. For example, 73% of white people compared to 53% of African-Americans thought the police were fair and courteous.

Overall, 34% of survey respondents felt that police used excessive force less often than five years ago. This compares to 29% who felt things had stayed the same, and 27% who thought things had become worse. African-Americans were, once again, more pessimistic than whites as to whether change had taken place: 43% of AfricanAmericans, compared to only 13% of whites, actually thought abuse of force was more common than prior to the decree (see **Figure 2**).

When asked about *current* use of force, 48% of Zone 2 residents still believed use of excessive force was "somewhat" or "very" common, with substantial variation between whites and African-Americans. While 33% of white people believe that excessive force is commonly used by the Police Bureau today, 68% of African-Americans believe excessive force is common.

In the context of enhanced accountability ushered in by the consent decree, community leaders felt that police officers had become discouraged from actively enforcing the law. Many leaders we spoke with suggested that some officers were afraid to enforce the law because of potential citizen complaints. One interviewee worried that police officers tend to use force less now than might be justified because they fear consequences. Others perceived slower response times and a reluctance to get involved, especially in minority communities. As one black police officer stated, "The areas in greatest need do not get police protection."

The survey provided an opportunity to assess whether such perceptions are shared more widely by the public. Two questions addressed the issue. One asked about changes over the last five years in crime-fighting and the other about changes in police visibility. Answers to these questions provide little evidence that police are withdrawing from proactive policing activities, at least in terms of public perception. In terms of crime fighting, 42% felt the police had improved since

Figure 3:
Perceptions of change in the complaints process over Last 5 years

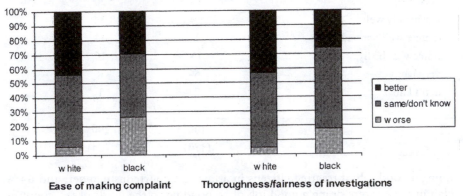

five years ago, and just 10% felt that the police were doing worse. Looking at police visibility, 5 1 % of respondents thought that police could be seen patrolling more often, and just 20% thought that police could be seen patrolling less often than five years ago. Thus, in contrast to the opinions of some police officers and community leaders, survey respondents gave little indication that police are less active or less effective now than they were prior to the decree.

The survey included a series of questions for people who had direct encounters with the police. The survey reveals that within the last two years, nearly 54% of whites and 43% of African-Americans had approached the police for some reason (e.g. to report a crime or to provide information) and 38% overall had been approached or stopped by the police. There were no significant differences in the percentages of whites and AfricanAmericans reporting voluntary or involuntary contacts. Respondents who reported contacts were asked about their satisfaction with encounters they had with the police.

Table 1 indicates that, in a large majority of for both public- and police-initiated contacts, respondents believed that the police had treated them "reasonably" or "very" well. Less than one in four respondents who were approached by the police and one in five of those who approached the police thought they were treated badly.

Community leaders were less positive about reforms in processing citizen complaints, Most of the leaders we spoke with continued to regard the agency with suspicion. One leader said, "I don't know about the thoroughness of OMI; OMI was always viewed as a police cover-up." Another perceived part of OMI's problem to be its connection to the city solicitor's office. The respondent argued that since the agenda of the solicitor's office was to protect the city and reduce liability, OMI's location and affiliation represented a conflict of interest.

Several leaders mentioned a lack of transparency in OMI's operations. As one stated, "They are not good about how they communicate with the public. I wish I knew more about what is required during an investigation." Another expressed the need for a public disclosure law which would mandate publication of the number of officers indicated by the early warning system and the number disciplined. Along with the perception that OMI did not disclose important information to the public, several leaders stressed that there was little publicity or notification about its existence and purpose. As one respondent stated, "People don't believe in the OMI process. They also do not know that it exists. It's a marketing issue."

Community leaders' lack of confidence in the complaint process was also reflected in the views of the general public. Survey respondents were asked about changes in the ease of making complaints and the thoroughness and fairness of investigations. Overall, 37% of people thought it had become easier to make a complaint, and 35% thought the thoroughness of investigations had improved. Responses differed substantially according to race, with African-Americans more pessimistic than whites. In fact, for both citizen complaint indicators, there were more Aftican- Americans who felt that things had gotten worse since the decree was signed than ones who felt that things had improved (see **Figure 3**).

Respondents' views of the *current* complaint process were less than enthusiastic. More than half (52%) of all people felt that making a complaint against a police officer today would be "somewhat" or "very" difficult. On this question there was an extreme separation by race, with three quarters (74%) of Affican-Americans claiming it would be difficult, compared to about a third (32%) of whites. When asked about the thoroughness and fairness of investigations into complaints, views were more positive: 41% of people, overall, felt the authorities would do a good job of investing complaints, with less than one in three (29%) thinking they would do a bad job. Once again, however, there was a large difference by race: whites were twice as likely as African-Americans to believe that complaint investigations today are fair and thorough.

Community leaders acknowledged that the consent decree brought about positive changes, but they were also worried that it may not be sustained. They expressed a building sense of apprehension as they looked towards the expiration of the decree. Most people we spoke with voiced concern over whether the Bureau would return to "business as usual" with low accountability and frequent misconduct. Further, according to some African-American community leaders, the community still has "absolute distrust" of white officers in particular. The message seemed to be that there is still work to be done and that the momentum created by the decree should not fade.

How the Decree Has Affected the Way in which Officers Approach Their Jobs

The 13 police officers and five supervisors we spoke to in Zone 2 had some positive things to say about the decree. Supervisors all felt that one of the good things to come from the decree was more frequent and better training. We heard supervisors say that the concept of an early warning system was an idea that could benefit the Bureau. One supervisor said that the new Subject Resistance Reports are "...a good thing. It makes officers explain their actions in detail." An officer admitted that the consent decree may have helped to "tone down" problem officers. Another acknowledged that "the department was antiquated and out of date. The consent decree made us update our computers and some policies." But, overwhelmingly, the comments of both officers and supervisors about the decree were negative. The reader is cautioned, though, that, in the absence of a formal survey, we do not know whether strong negative opinions were held by a large majority of officers or only by small numbers of vociferous officers.

Several supervisors and officers told us that the decree had a serious negative effect upon officer morale. Many officers took the decree as a slap in the face. Some respondents expressed a belief that policing in Pittsburgh was not in trouble prior to the decree, and resentment that the federal government had intervened. "The stats didn't justify the decree," one officer said. "Other departments were a lot worse off than we were... Why were we investigated?" One officer described officer morale in particularly blunt terms: "We're worn out. We hate our jobs." A supervisor said that "morale is at the lowest point I can remember."

Yet we also picked up the sentiment that the decree's effects upon morale may be waning. One officer stated that the decree was "not talked about much within the zone anymore. It's been so long that it's become a way of life. You don't think about it." Some officers and supervisors suggested that morale had been diminished, but they did not appear vehement in this belief. Other officers, new to the Bureau since the decree, remained silent on the issue of morale.

Supervisors thought the early warning system was a useful concept to alert them to problems with officers. One supervisor said, "When you get a new officer on your shift, you can look him up in PARS." However, several supervisors expressed the thought that "as a supervisor, you already know who the good cops are and who the hotheads are. The system just tells us what we know already." Supervisors also had complaints about the demands that the system made on their time. Their primary complaint was that the system as it is currently constituted has generated an extreme amount of paperwork. One supervisor said, "Everything a police officer does is documented and we have to review it." Another complained that the paperwork is "incredible."

The supervisors we spoke to claimed repeatedly that the paperwork generated by PARS drastically cut back on the time they were able to spend on the street supervising officers and on their responsibilities to respond to homicides, fires, and other serious incidents. One said he was torn between doing mandated paper-

Figure 4. Pittsburgh Bureau of Police Use of Sick Days–1995 through 1999

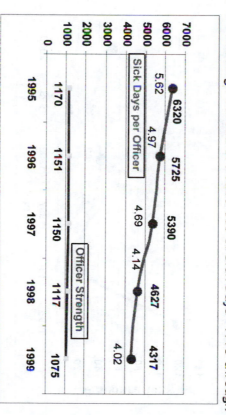

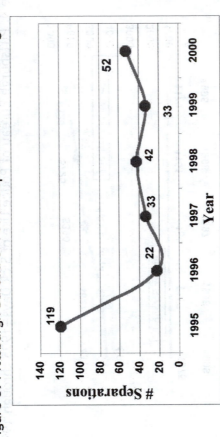

Figure 5. Pittsburgh Bureau of Police Separations—1995 through 2000

work in the stationhouse and conducting field checks mandated for certain situations by Bureau regulations. He believed that, "they [the administration] don't want us on the streets." Another said that the city had been made less safe by virtue of the fact that there were fewer officer and supervisor hours spent on the street.

Some personnel we spoke to objected to the use of PARS as a tool to single out officers for what they perceived as minor infractions. Several of the officers related stories about disciplinary action reports (DARs) they had received as a result of actions or omissions (such as forgetting to turn in a traffic stop report) for which they previously would have had an informal talk with a supervisor. Officers complained that verbal reprimands wind up in written files and remain there indefinitely. Officers told us that "lots more" disciplinary action reports were being given out since PARS had been instituted, and one said that DARs are "free flowing" now. One officer stated that he thought that the administration sought to maximize the number of disciplinary action reports issued in order to impress federal authorities: "They're just waiting for you to screw up. The more you do, the more of a chance that you will screw up."[6]

Both supervisors and officers told us that officers were hesitant to conduct searches and to use force since the consent decree was signed. Of course, care in conducting searches and in the use of force was one of the goals of the decree. But officers and supervisors told us that officers, afraid to use force, were taking extra time to react, putting themselves in danger.

Supervisors told us that arrests and traffic summonses were down since the decree was signed. Officers said that they were afraid to be proactive in their police work. They said that they were less active on the street, making fewer traffic stops and basing stops on observed violations rather than on hunches. Officers said that, as a result of PARS, it was safer not to produce in order to avoid being indicated and kept from overtime work, promotions, or transfers. We were told that "a lot of cops are afraid to do their jobs" and that officers were often unwilling to go above or beyond minimal requirements of their assignments. One officer said that "the harder you work, the more likely it is that you'll be indicated."

We were also told that the fear of bogus citizen complaints kept officers from doing their jobs effectively. Officers said the public was well aware of the consent decree and recognized that they could make false complaints anonymously against officers who were homing in on criminal activity. This was thought by officers to be a tactic of drug dealers, who would make anonymous complaints in an effort to get effective officers transferred to other areas. "There are lots of good officers afraid to do their jobs proactively" because the threat of anonymous complaints strike fear into them, according to one officer. [7]

According to officers with whom we spoke, the consent decree mandated that supervisors be regularly rotated in their assignments. However, they believed that the administration went beyond the terms of the decree in applying the same rule to officers as well. (In actuality, the decree specifies that officers must be supervised by and work with different officers, leaving the specific implementation to the city.) One officer described the mandatory transfers as a "big morale buster." Another said that rotation of officers from one zone to another produced a force of officers who "don't know the streets, neighborhood problems, or local perpetrators." A supervisor said that the frequent rotation was a bad idea because "police officers don't get to learn their zone and the people in it. This goes against the idea of community policing."

Analysis of Trends in Police Performance, Public Safety, Disciplinary Actions, and Citizen Complaints

Interviews with officers and community leaders in Pittsburgh produced contradictory and sometimes disturbing information about how the consent decree had affected police officer morale, police activity, public safety, and disciplinary actions. We obtained data from the Police Bureau on changes over time in performance indicators related to these issues. We would have liked to examine these indicators quarterly over a long enough period to allow us to apply time series analysis to verify apparent increases or decreases over time. However, we were only able to obtain annual data. We also would have liked to examine trends in police use of force and search and seizures, but these data were not collected prior to the signing of the consent decree. Still, the hard data we were able to obtain were useful in confirming or negating claims about negative effects that the consent decree may have had on police performance.

If the decree had had a serious negative effect on police morale, we believed that it ought to be apparent in the number of sick days taken by officers and in the number of separations from the Bureau. **Figure 4** shows trends in annual sick days per officer from 1995 to 1999. The figure shows a steady decline in sick days taken that was not affected by the signing of the consent decree in 1997.

Figure 5 depicts separations from the Bureau between 1995 and 2000. It shows a peak in separations in 1995 that was the result of mass retirements when officers 50 years and over were offered special pension incentives to retire early. The number of separations showed no pronounced upward or downward trend from 1996 to 1999, the years surrounding the signing of the consent decree in 1997.

To examine claims that the consent decree had jeopardized public safety, we looked at trends in Part I and Part 11 crimes reported to the police. **Figure 6** shows similar trends in Part I and Part 11 crimes between 1989 and 2000. The main trend is a substantial and sustained decline over time, particularly pronounced in

Figure 6. Part I & Part II Crimes between 1989 and 2000

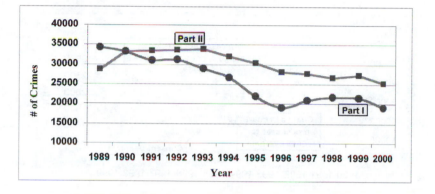

Figure 7. Clearance Rates for Part II Crimes —1990 through 2000

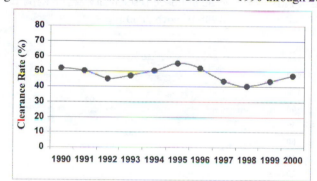

Figure 8. Traffic Citations 1990-1999

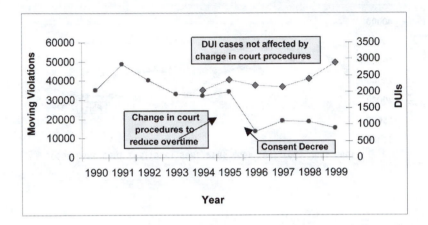

Figure 9: Pittsburgh Bureau of Police Disciplinary Action Reports
1995 through 2000

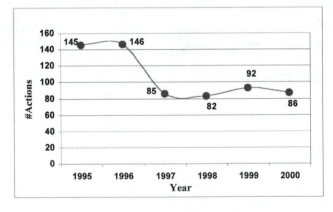

the early 1990s. Part I crimes show a slight bump up in 1997 when the decree was signed, but by 2000, the number of Part I crimes was virtually the same as it was in 1996. Part Il crimes have shown a steady march downward through the years, both before and after the signing of the decree.

Over the period between 1994 and 2000, arrests declined by more than 40% mirroring the drop in crime. One measure of police activity is the ratio of arrests to reported crimes for minor offenses. If police were less aggressive, it would be most likely to be seen in their response to lesser crimes rather than to felony offenses. We therefore looked to see whether the *clearance rate* for Part 11 (misdemeanor) crimes declined following introduction of the consent decree.

We found some evidence of a decline in clearance rates for misdemeanors coinciding with the signing of the decree (see **Figure 7**). The percentage of Part 11 crimes cleared went from the low 50s in the three years prior to the decree to the low 40s for the three years following the decree. However, by 2000, the proportion of misdemeanors cleared had climbed back into the high 40s.

Another place where we might look for a reduction in police activity is in traffic summonses issued. **Figure 8** presents trends in traffic summonses before and after the decree. The figure shows that traffic summonses declined sharply in the middle of the period between 1990 and 1999. However, the decline came not in 1997, the year of the consent decree, but in 1996 when court procedures changed to reduce police overtime. There is no evidence of a further decline after 1996 during the period of the consent decree. Figure 8 also displays trends in DUI violations. DUI cases, not affected by the new court overtime rules in 1996, did not show a decline during the consent decree years (and, in fact, they have increased somewhat). Thus, trends in traffic summonses provide no support to the argument that the decree reduced officer activity.

Figure 9 presents data on disciplinary action reports issued against officers between 1995 and 2000. Surprisingly, the figure shows a large decline in the number of disciplinary action reports in 1997 and subsequent years following the signing of the consent decree. There was a slight uptick in the number of disciplinary action reports in 1999 and 2000, but they remained far below pre-1997 levels.

Synthesis and Lessons Learned

It is irrefutable that the consent decree has led to many positive changes in Pittsburgh policing. The early warning system and COMPSTAR meetings all but ensure that officers heading for trouble will be identified and efforts made to straighten them out. The system also ensures that cases cannot slip through the cracks due to lax supervision. COMPSTAR and the early warning system are a check on supervisors' actions as much as they are a way to identify problem officers. The system is both redundant and timeconsuming: most of the potential problem officers identified by the early warning system may already be known to supervisors. But the advantage of the system is that supervisors are forced to take action (or to justify their inaction). There is no room for playing favorites or for individuals to exercise discretion.

The new policies with respect to capturing information on all use of force incidents, search and seizures, and traffic stops place Pittsburgh police among law enforcement agencies with best practices in this area. The new procedures make it possible to spot officers whose performance differs significantly from their peers. They also make it possible for the Bureau to monitor any department-wide trends in racial bias and excessive use of force and to respond to critics who charge that abuses are occurring in these areas.

Police training in Pittsburgh has been improved, even according to critics of the police administration in the police union and in the community. Officers receive more training on how to avoid use of force and how to apply force appropriately when it is necessary.

The process of filing and investigating citizen complaints also is much improved. OMI still has a battle to fight to win the respect of the community, and it has not yet hit a consistent stride in keeping pace with the increased volume of complaints. But citizens now can file complaints in the modality most convenient for them. If they choose to do so, they can even file anonymously. All complaints— even those filed anonymously and those in which the complainant is unwilling to cooperate or cannot be found—must be investigated. And the investigations must be thorough, including a visit to the scene by the investigator and canvassing for potential witnesses.

We also heard about problems from community leaders and police officers. The community leaders we spoke to agreed that the decree helped make police more accountable, although some were convinced that the early warning system was being circumvented by some officers and supervisors. Some community leaders and police were concerned that officers were less likely to take action when it was warranted in minority communities. Police officers also told us that officers were slower to get involved because of low morale and fear of complaints filed anonymously by criminals eager to get the officers off their backs.

The reservations of both police officers and community leaders deserve to be taken seriously. It is unlikely that anyone can ever measure with any certainty whether officers are slower to enforce the law or avoid certain areas or encounters with citizens of particular demographic characteristics. But the trend data we examined helped to mitigate some of the negative perceptions about public safety, police activity, and police morale. Rates of reported crime did not increase following the decree. Traffic summonses, a barometer one would expect to be affected if police were less active, did not decline as a result of the decree (although the clearance rate for misdemeanors did decline temporarily). And two indicators of officer morale (use of sick time and terminations from the Bureau) did not show negative trends following the decree.

One of the most important measures of change in Pittsburgh is community opinion. Only slightly more than half of Pittsburgh residents had heard of the consent decree. But among persons who had, those who believed policing had improved since the decree outnumbered those who believed that it had gotten worse by a 4-1 margin. We found similarly large margins between those who thought things had improved and those who felt things had worsened in response to questions about fair and courteous treatment of citizens by police officers and thoroughness of investigation of citizen complaints. Whites were much more likely to believe that police use of excessive force had decreased rather than increased since the decree, while more African-Americans believed that use of force had increased than believed that it had decreased.

The success of Pittsburgh's reform efforts can be attributed to several important factors. Initially, the swift and unified response from all of the departments within the city government greatly aided their efforts. Infighting was minimized and the central goal of implementing the decree took precedence. The agenda of the Chief of Police also served to assist the reform effort. The chief embraced many of the provisions of the decree, often mandating greater reforms than that required. Once the decree was signed, the chief made it clear that the Bureau would be in compliance and thereby set the tone for the effective response to the requirements. Pittsburgh also benefited from an involved monitor. Early in the reform effort, the monitor played a vital role by creating an overall plan of action and operationalizing some of the more imprecise standards of the decree. In addition, the creation of the compliance manual gave city officials an exact idea of what milestones he expected them to achieve at each stage of the process. Lastly, two innovative systems allowed the city to make accountability a driving force within the Police Bureau, the PARS early warning system and the quarterly COMPSTAR accountability meetings. PARS quickly became the most robust early warning system of its time, monitoring officer behavior across a wide range of indicators. Much of this analysis was made possible through the use of innovative thresholds, thereby avoiding the denominator problem and making measurements meaningful. COMPSTAR ensures that information produced by PARS is acted upon. Commanders discuss individual officers under them and add insight and depth to the figures.

There were as well areas in which the city could have done better. Many citizens were unaware of the decree and the reforms that occurred, and many black citizens remain unconvinced that police abuses had lessened during the five year period of the decree. There has been too little interaction between city officials and civil rights groups before or after the consent decree was signed and little systematic dissemination of information about the city's progress in complying with the decree. A cooperative relationship between the two camps is essential to bringing the message to Pittsburgh's minority community that significant changes have been achieved.

Bureau officers also were not convinced of the decree's positive value and remain suspicious of the decree and the reforms it engendered. There was clearly an effort by the police and command staff to educate officers and supervisors about the decree and to defuse the notion that it would necessarily be detrimental to officers. But judging by our focus groups, these efforts were not highly successful. Officers remain resentful about the decree and worry about being disciplined for good faith enforcement actions. Our trend data refuted some of the more serious officer claims about reduced morale, officer activity, and public safety. Nonetheless, the fact that these perceptions persist is a continuing challenge for the Bureau.

Lastly, the city should have recognized the demands the new complaint investigation policy would place on OMI. Predictably, the number of complaints rise and the time to investigate cases increased substantially as a result of the decree. Yet there was no immediate move to add staff to cope with the greatly increased workload. The backlog that developed as a result has plagued the agency to this day and is the major reason that it has not been able to stay in compliance with the requirements of the decree.

The judge who issued the consent decree recently lifted it with respect to the Pittsburgh Bureau of Police (although the monitor will continue to track processing of citizen complaints by the Office of Municipal Investigations). The decree has clearly made a significant difference in how policing is conducted in Pittsburgh. The question now will be whether the progress that has been made will be solidified and expanded.

Endnotes

[1] All budgetary information was retrieved from the City of Pittsburgh Public Documents website and staffing figures are as reported by the manager of OMI.

[2] Anonymous complaints also were accepted prior to the decree. However, they were terminated as "unfounded" if no corroborating evidence was found. The same is now true post-decree as a result of an arbitration settlement of a district court case between the city and the police union.

[3] An exception exists for complaints filed more than 90 days after the incident that do not involve allegations of criminal behavior. Such complaints are classified as "unfounded" pursuant to a 1998 arbitration settlement of a district court case between the city and the police union.

[4] Walker, Alpert, Kenney.

[5] As per personal conversation with Karen Arnendola of the Police Foundation.

[6] Data presented in the next section directly refutes the contention that disciplinary actions became more frequent following the consent decree.

[7] We cannot confirm or deny that anonymous complaints affect the behavior of officers. We do know, however, that such complaints are rare. Extrapolating from data presented in the monitor's reports, anonymous complaints make up 1-2% of all complaints lodged against officers with OMI